Donated to
Augustana
University College
by
Augustana's
Students' Union
Capital Development Fund
2001-2004

And On That Farm He Had a Wife

And On That Farm He Had a Wife

Ontario Farm Women and Feminism, 1900–1970

MONDA HALPERN

McGill-Queen's University Press
Montreal & Kingston · London · Ithaca

Legal deposit third quarter 2001
Bibliothèque nationale du Québec

Printed in Canada on acid-free paper

This book has been published with the help of a
grant from the Humanities and Social Sciences
Federation of Canada, using funds provided by the
Social Sciences and Humanities Research Council
of Canada. Funding has also been received from the
Faculty of Social Science, The University of
Western Ontario.

McGill-Queen's University Press acknowledges the
financial support of the Government of Canada
through the Book Publishing Industry Development
Program (BPIDP) for its activities. It also
acknowledges the support of the Canada Council
for the Arts for its publishing program.

**National Library of Canada Cataloguing
in Publication Data**

Halpern, Monda M., 1963–
    And on that farm he had a wife: Ontario farm
women and feminism, 1900–1970
    Includes bibliographical references and index.
    ISBN 0-7735-2184-4
    1. Women in agriculture – Ontario – History –
20th century.   2. Feminism – Ontario – History –
20th century.   3. Rural women – Ontario –
Attitudes.   4. Farmers' spouses – Ontario – Social
conditions.   I. Title.
HQ1459.O57H34 2001   305.43'63'09713
C2001-900125-8

This book was typeset by Dynagram Inc.
in 10/12 Palatino.

Contents

Acknowledgments

This book was written with the help of many people. To all of them I offer my sincere appreciation and thanks. I am especially grateful to Philip Cercone, John Zucchi, Joan McGilvray, Lesley Barry, and Joanne Pisano at McGill-Queen's University Press for their steadfast commitment to this project, and to my advisers at Queen's University, Professors Klaus Hansen and Joy Parr, whose expertise, insights, and unwavering support guided my doctoral work. I am also indebted to University of Western Ontario professors Jean Matthews (Professor Emeritus), Margaret Kellow, Robert Hohner, Jack Hyatt, Roger Hall, George Emery, Tom Sea, Madeline Lennon, Michael Carroll, and Sam Clark for their wisdom and generosity; the staff at all of the libraries, archives, and special collections cited in this book for their assistance and dedication; the many people, including Elaine Bitz, Melanie Clare, Vera May Hood, Jean Lozier, Doug Mitchell, and Helen Wilson, who graciously contributed to this study through their personal collections, interviews, or writings; technology specialists Charles Deschenes and Merran Neville for their invaluable computer knowledge; art historian Sonia Halpern for bringing to my attention with great enthusiasm the image used on this book jacket; and former Western undergraduates Robyn Matlin, Erika Empey, and Joel Porter for their research help and willing spirit.

On a more personal note, I am forever indebted to wonderful friends and family. A loving thank you goes to Andrew Pateman, Craig Marucci, Simon Johnston, Sheila Johnston, Arye Berk, Clarence Seunarine, Jodi Norrison, and all of my treasured Or Shalom and theatre friends for nourishing me with humour, understanding, and kindness. My deepest appreciation is reserved for my parents Clara Halpern and Dr George Halpern whose respect for intellect, education, and tradition have been a gift to me; Barbara, Shelley, Marnie, Lori, Robert, and their families; and for my sister Sonia, who has been so much a part of my life, and has contributed so significantly to my work, that it is impossible – even for a moment – to imagine otherwise. This book is dedicated to her.

And On That Farm He Had a Wife

1 "But on the farm ... feminism means something else": Social and Agrarian Feminism

This book investigates the historical relationship of Ontario farm women and feminism. It argues that many Ontario farm women were indeed feminist, and that this feminism was more progressive than most of us would presume. I have heard it often enough: "a relationship between Ontario farm women and feminism – you mean, there was one?" After all, goes the reasoning, farm women were conservative and deferential, feminism was extremist and militant, and above all urban – how could farm women be feminist? The answer, of course, rests in the fact that neither Ontario farm women nor feminism conformed to such circumscribed labels. Such an alliance, therefore, could – and did – exist.

The subject has been addressed primarily by political scientists and sociologists, but they have focused on the possible feminism of contemporary farm women, and profile early farm women's groups only as background for their more immediate concerns. Initially, they seemed reluctant, although not entirely unwilling, to identify farm women in history as feminist.[1] More recently, emboldened by their shared findings supporting contemporary rural feminism, some scholars have simply assumed its historical origins,[2] while others, impressed by the success of new farm women's groups, have quickly discounted the possibility of rural feminism before 1970.[3]

With little concern for redressing this cursory historical treatment, most historians have either avoided the subject of Ontario farm women and feminism or quickly dismissed the connection.[4] Even those who have examined rural expressions of female identity, agency, activism, and reform, have, by omission or purposefully, resisted designating farm women as feminist.[5] Only historian Linda Ambrose acknowledges Ontario farm women's "surprising degree of sympathy with familiar strains of feminist thinking." Indeed, she goes so far as to proclaim the existence of a "pragmatic rural feminism" but undermines its insurgent possibilities by emphasizing that it was "not a radical political feminism to be sure."[6]

The historian's assumption (both unspoken and expressed) that farm women were not feminist is apparent in several historiographical tendencies: to assume that women who were not self-identified feminists were not feminist at all; to presume that gendered conflict on the farm did not exist; to dismiss farm women's groups as conservative; to equate feminism solely with the organized battle for suffrage; and to use the "separate spheres" paradigm to plot the "progress" of women.

The issue of feminist self-identification is addressed by Elizabeth Adell Cook in her article "Measuring Feminist Consciousness." In it, she defines group consciousness as comprising four elements: "social group identification," which refers to "the psychological attachment and recognition of shared values and interests with a social or political group"; "power discontent," which is "a belief that one's own group has less power than it should"; "system blaming," which is marked by "a belief that structural barriers, not individual failings, keep group members down"; and "collective orientation," which is characterized by a belief that "group members should work together for change rather than working separately as individuals for their own achievements." These four facets of group consciousness, says Cook, "all mesh together."[7]

All of these components of group consciousness were evident among farm women between 1900 and 1970, but it would be misleading to assert that all farm women were united by a shared feminist consciousness, or that they consistently wore their feminism on their sleeve. Political scientist Naomi Black points out, however, that poll data suggest that "even if a majority identification with feminism is unlikely, disavowals are fully compatible with support of women's organized campaigns for policy changes intended to improve the situation of women." In assessing the data, Black concludes that "it seems clear that the majority of women prefer to say 'I am not a feminist but ...' and then support ... any of the wide range of issues that have concerned women activists."[8] While most farm women might not have professed being feminist, they did not seem compelled to disown it either. Nevertheless, historians have used this absence of feminist self-identification to deny farm women their feminist character.

Secondary historical literature has largely offered surveys of farm women's labour, describing their work, not their thoughts, as related to men, and depicting them as "equal partners" with farm men, as paragons of virtue who dutifully deferred to their husbands and farms, or as stolid workhorses who "were simply too busy to complain."[9] The inference has been that farm women neither needed nor wanted feminism because, whether they were equals, altruists, or stoics, gender conflict necessarily could not or would not arise on the farm. Thus, historians have overlooked women's challenge to patriarchy, and have examined instead the ways in which farming communities, governed by fathers, brothers, husbands, and sons, responded to the "real" oppressors of government, big business, and urban life. Farm women, however, "had their own sensibilities and reactions" within the androcentric rural culture.[10] Historians cannot assume that farm women were necessarily satisfied with their status at home, or acted only in the interest of family and farm. Nor can historians impose on these women every concern of their male kin, or render invisible their female-specific grievances. It has been sociologists (and some female farm activists and journalists), exploring issues of family and marital conflict, who have offered in a contemporary context a more realistic depiction of farm life. They seem particularly interested in the gendered aspects of decision-making, power acquisition, generational ties, division of labour, and stress.[11]

Historians have also dismissed the feminist impetus of farm women by judging Canada's leading farm women's organization, the Women's Institutes (wi), as conservative and politically impassive. This impression largely lies in the wi's close ties to the home economics movement, which historians have commonly criticized for creating in working-class women an exploitable labour-pool of servants for bourgeois homes, and for promoting in middle-class women wholesale domesticity, domestic drudgery, limited career choices, and a subordinate place in the oppressive nuclear family.[12] That the wi was in Ontario an arm of the provincial Department of Agriculture has also prompted accusations of the organization's conservatism: the wi was merely a government pawn, devoid of a reformist, independent agenda.[13] The government dictated, after all, that politics, as well as other potentially controversial issues of religion, ethnicity, and class were not to be discussed at Institute meetings. Historians have pointed to the absence of provocative discourse in wi minutes as evidence not only of farm women's parochialism, but of their anti-suffrage, hence anti-feminist sentiment. Armed with additional assumptions about the group's older, female membership, historians, then, have branded the wi as a trite, traditional social club that was politically unaware or apathetic.[14]

The WI, however, was not unlike most turn-of-the-century urban women's groups which have been freely labelled progressive, reformist, and feminist. Like these organizations, the WI believed in upholding some fundamental social, economic, and political conventions, but in no way did it desire to perpetuate the status quo. Although the charges against home economics are not without merit, the WI emphasized this discipline in order to elevate the status of women. Indeed, historian Veronica Strong-Boag asserts that "in critical ways home economics was to have some of the same consciousness raising and research goals of the modern women studies programmes."[15] That WI members avoided discussing "controversial" issues such as religion, furthermore, may be seen as revolutionary rather than regressive, given the general religiosity of farm folk. One 1947 newspaper story on the history of the WI noted that for farm women to join an organization not affiliated with their church "took some courage."[16] And when members did refer to religion at Institute meetings, historical interpretation could rest less on their traditional leanings, and more on their willingness to resist and defy restrictive government policy. Adherence to such policy did not mean, moreover, that members opposed suffrage: many Institute women supported suffrage in the pre-war years,[17] while others did not care to engage in the subject because of their sincere belief that they could better women's lot without the male-conceived vote.

Indeed, another reason why the feminism of Ontario farm women has been denied is that historians have defined feminism in the early twentieth century solely in terms of suffrage. When attempting to locate feminism, they look to turn-of-the-century suffrage organizations – which were characterized by urban, not rural, participation.[18] And when historians want to examine rural feminism, they turn to politics of the West, where rural issues were championed by a proportionately larger agrarian population, and where suffrage agitation by farm women was active and overt.[19] Prairie farm women, unlike Ontario farm women, had vocal suffrage leaders, including Nellie McClung, Irene Parlby, Violet McNaughton, and E. Cora Hind, and were represented by women's groups that were part of a highly organized, highly political, pro-suffrage farm movement.[20] If historians were to extend their search for rural feminism into the post-suffrage era and entertain the possibility that feminism among women did not necessarily coincide with the first- (or second-) wave women's movement of urban centres, they would find leaders who spoke on behalf of Ontario farm women, and who were committed to advancing their cause. The *Farmers' Sun* columnist Emma Griesbach, rural MP Agnes

Macphail, and home economist and journalist Ethel Chapman, for example, were feminist activists who are all deserving of study.

Women's participation in public life, however, is not the only yardstick by which to measure their progress and their commitment to feminist goals. For too long, historical scholarship has presented the move of women from their allegedly private, apolitical sphere into the public, political realm of men as the exclusive signal of their modernity, enlightenment, and coming of age, especially in their pursuit of paid work, professional careers, and a place in party politics.[21] Because most farm women were not active in these ways, and were inextricably tied to the home, they have been cast as possessing no political, and thus no feminist, leanings; however, "the assumption that private = apolitical is clearly open to question."[22] Indeed, the "private world – the world of personal relations and marriage, of friendships and family, of domestic routine and childcare – is, as feminists have persuasively demonstrated time and again, political as well as personal."[23] This recognition that the private sphere is political is undoubtedly valuable, but the distinction between public and private, tenuous in any case, is especially dubious for farm women. For them, home was the site of both public and private life: of production and reproduction, of farm work and housework, of farm owner and husband, of farmhands and boarders, of workers and children, and of livelihood and leisure.

But even the "public" participation of farm women in movements like the WI has also been denied its political, and thus feminist, character. As Jill McCalla Vickers points out, "in customary terms, most social movements are not understood to be political in nature, unless they end up running candidates or forming parties."[24] This point is exemplified in the historical treatment of the farm women's reform group, the United Farm Women of Ontario (UFWO), which was affiliated with the United Farmers of Ontario (UFO), first a farmers' movement in 1914, and then a political party by 1918. The UFWO has been described in political terms to a greater extent than has the WI, despite their many similarities. Vickers declares that "community-based groups and organizations" like the WI were "where a volunteeristic tradition of politics flourished," and asserts that local and provincial Institutes, just like other women's organizations, "provided an arena for political debate and a conduit for political pressure more authentic and meaningful for many women than political parties. In short, women whose circumstances precluded a professional political role nevertheless created organizations adaptable to their life circumstances in which they exercised leadership and engaged in their own form of political discourse informed by domestic community needs and values."[25] For farm women, especially those who belonged to the immensely popular WI, "their own form of political discourse" was the language of social feminism, which was "informed by domestic community needs and values" tied to farm women's profound connection with agrarian life.

My work borrows from feminist theory espoused by political scientists Naomi Black and Louise I. Carbert in their respective works *Social Feminism* and "Agrarian Feminism: The Politicization of Ontario Farm Women."[26] Black's historical and revisionist approach extols social feminism as a women-identified ideology that promoted political and social reform and exhibited a radical potential; Carbert adopts Black's definition of social feminism to construct her interpretation of modern agrarian feminism, stating that it incorporates both social feminism and consideration of household commodity production.[27] She also underscores the limitations to feminism inherent in the patriarchal farm family as the centre of both commodity production and intimate human relations.[28] Black challenges the presumed conservatism of twentieth-century social feminist movements and organizations; Carbert concedes the conservatism of the contemporary farm women whom she studies, partly because she takes into account the inextricable connection between family and farm, and the farm woman's relationship to both.

Social feminism emphasizes the specificity of women by highlighting the experiential differences between women and men. Its most significant feature is its focus on the priorities and values of women, which include "nurturing, cooperation, love and peace."[29] Social feminism is a variant of maternal feminism, which is founded on women's biological capacity to reproduce and the moral superiority which that capability is thought to engender. Social feminism, however, regards women's distinctiveness less as a direct result of biology, which precludes the opportunity for flexibility and change, and more as a product of "what a sexually segregated society has imposed on females in terms of special experience."[30] The two feminisms also differ in that while maternal feminism is supposed to be an expression of influence within the private sphere of the home, social feminism is sceptical about leaving the public sphere exclusively in the hands of men.[31] Social feminists, then, as an offshoot of their domestic role, seek to enter the public sphere in order to infuse it with female values, "as necessary supplements and then as correctives for public life."[32] Thus, at the root of social feminist activism is "the refusal to allow the exclusion from social influence not just of women as individuals but of the values and competencies associated with women."[33]

In contrast to social feminism, equity feminism denotes those feminisms which assert that women deserve equality by virtue of their similarity to men. This division of feminism into two distinct ideologies of sexual similarity (equity feminism) and sexual difference (social feminism) is not new. In the last thirty years, Canadian and American historians have approached the nineteenth and early twentieth-century women's movement in this way. Their studies most often focus on the women's suffrage campaign, and categorize various suffrage groups as premised on either the battle for justice and human rights (equity feminism) or social reform (social feminism). In these studies, historians such as Wayne Roberts and Carol Bacchi, for instance, have generally dismissed Canadian social feminists as conservative and misguided, and have cast their equity feminist sisters as progressive and enlightened.[34]

In recent years, however, there has been a growing appreciation of social feminists, particularly by those scholars interested in the female origins of the welfare state. Theda Skocpol, for example, in her book *Protecting Soldiers and Mothers: The Political Origins of Social Policy in the United States* (1992), demonstrates that unlike other countries that cultivated a paternalist welfare program, the United States forged a "maternalist" one, where women, long before New Deal social policies, and prior to female suffrage, spearheaded progressive public reforms like mothers' pensions and protective labour laws. *Mothers of a New World: Maternalist Politics and the Origins of Welfare States* (1993), a compilation of essays edited by Seth Koven and Sonya Michel, exemplifies the international scope of this maternalist approach with research on American, British, German, French, Australian, and Swedish maternal reform efforts in the cause of women's rights. While my study on the social feminism of Ontario farm women is not chiefly intended as an assertion of their contributions to the origins of the welfare state, their early work within the WI can certainly be contextualized in this way.[35]

As an early advocate of this relatively new scholarly appreciation for maternalist discourse and activism, Naomi Black attacks the prevailing criticisms levelled against social feminists. She denounces the implication that their "conservative" arguments for the vote were motivated by expedience, an assumption which casts the equity or justice feminist platform as more authentic and pure.[36] She notes that justice arguments were also "intended to be persuasive and could be expected to be effective in a political culture based on a theory of equal rights."[37] Nevertheless, many scholars, says Black, help perpetuate the notion that an "'expedient' move away from equal rights feminism was a suffragist decline from the high standards of those who had earlier used arguments based on justice";[38] social feminists had supposedly forsaken enlightened, feminist ideas in order to rally the support of politically influential, conservative men.[39] Indeed, Carol Bacchi insists that the "motivations" of social reformers were in fact governed by their affiliation with this "social elite," as the wives of white, Anglo-Protestant professionals.[40] As Black indicates, however, "all feminists were influenced by the need to seek support from men hostile to everyone except other men like themselves: all politicians and all voters were men, and they alone could decide on suffrage legislation and constitutional amendments."[41]

With regard to the conservatism of social feminist suffragists, Black points out that the demands of equity feminists relied on the rhetoric of equal rights, and "were thereby located squarely within the established [male] tradition of political discourse."[42] That the suffrage victory did little to augment women's participation in public life should be blamed not on the maternal ideology of reform, as Bacchi suggests,[43] but on the intrinsic conservatism of a pre-existing male right. While equity feminists were able to adopt a "familiar set of doctrines that counteracted any impression of female appropriation of non-domestic roles," for social feminists, who espoused a new female-centred discourse, "the use of acceptable, explicitly domestic arguments masked possible radical implications."[44]

Black objects to those scholars who fault social feminists for shattering the insurgent possibilities of American feminism by providing no critique of the locus of women's oppression – the bourgeois family.[45] As Canadian historian Veronica Strong-Boag notes, all suffragists, including social feminists, "called into question the appropriateness of women's subordinate position within the patriarchal family itself." Strong-Boag insists that within a political mandate that called for a variety of women-centred legal and social reforms, "lay a powerful threat to male supremacy."[46] Even Wayne Roberts concedes that maternal feminism "did not preordain women's acceptance of subordination within the family or state."[47]

As evident in its historical treatment, social feminism, unlike equity feminism, has often been denied its political character. This is due, in part, to the opposition that was set up in the late nineteenth century between suffragists labelled either political (equity feminist) or reformist (social feminist).[48] All suffragists were in fact political, not only because they participated in lobbying, and had a vested interest in election outcomes, but also because they addressed matters of power and policy.[49] We must not limit the term "political," therefore, only "to those who use existing public rhetoric,"[50] as this renders inconsequential those feminists, including social feminists, who formulate their own discourse.[51]

Neither equity feminism nor social feminism preceded, or precluded the presence of, the other. In both Canada and the United States, the two sides co-existed within the suffrage movement.[52] Canadian women's historians recognize along with Black that most activist women supported both feminist doctrines, embracing the one that proved more advantageous at any given time, and sensing no contradiction between the two.[53]

It was social feminism, however, that outlived equity feminism and the suffrage victory. As the vote was a right that men already possessed, and the language of equal rights could be, and was, readily absorbed by the discourse of modern male-defined politics, suffrage was seen by contemporaries as synonymous with equal rights, and they saw no need for feminism to persist once this right was achieved through the vote.[54] But social feminist suffragists did not abandon feminism. Stanley Lemons asserts that "social feminism was slowed in the 1920s, but it neither failed nor was destroyed. If … feminism 'failed,' the tombstone will have to bear another date, perhaps the 1930s or 1940s."[55] Yet Eugenia Kaledin's *Mothers and More: American Women in the 1950s* could be used to dispute the claim of social feminism's demise before 1950. Her work demonstrates that although the 1950s might have lacked a structured feminist movement, social feminism was still very much in evidence. Kaledin writes that "when women are discouraged from competing as equals with men they seem to evolve, perhaps to invent and reinvent, a set of values designed to confront or assuage their powerlessness. We find them during the 1950s working in a number of ways to enhance the quality of life so that more of their voices might be heard. What they had to offer, even when they were successful on male terms – as a few women always were – was a way of regarding the world often overlooked or undervalued by men. Their priorities were often different."[56] When dating the eclipse of social feminism, both Lemons and Kaledin focus on an urban (and American) model of social feminism. I will argue that within a rural setting, social feminism thrived in Ontario until 1970.

Perhaps it is the longevity of social feminism, its arguments based on female specificity and domestic virtues, or the presumed elitism and conservatism of its proponents that prevent its radical potential from being considered. Social feminism, however, may be seen as radical for a variety of reasons. First and foremost, within a patriarchal culture, social feminists, unlike equity feminists, emphasized women-identified traits and experiences, and rarely expressed a desire to conform to male standards and behaviours.[57] Accordingly, they argued that the abilities and aptitudes arising from these female traits and experiences were produced by a patriarchal society "often against their will"; that those female traits which patriarchal society had encouraged in women were at the same time denigrated by men as individuals and as a group; and that the standards by which to categorize and measure male experiences were not necessarily useful in assessing women's differing experiences: men's rights sometimes offered no comparable protection for women regarding pregnancy, rape, and wife battering.[58] Out of the recognition of women's distinctive values and experiences emerged women-only clubs, which "developed in women a sisterhood which extended beyond the membership to all women, a respect for women's sphere, and a critique of male values."[59] Annette K. Baxter writes in the preface to *The Clubwoman as Feminist: True Womanhood Redefined, 1868–1914* that whether women's clubs emphasized reform or personal development, they afforded women a more complete, and therefore "a more authentic self expression."[60]

Social feminism may also be deemed radical because it called for women's influence in the male-defined public sphere, and catalyzed women, armed with their domestic values, for action there.[61] Social feminism, then, "made the political personal and used that claim to move into the political," where there developed an unorthodox association between female activists and "malestream" politics. What resulted was the blurring of private and public, and thus a reconceptualization of both spheres.[62] In seeking to use "feminine" traits cultivated in the private sphere to transform the public sphere, "social feminism inverts the political consequences of conservative arguments about separate spheres."[63] At the same time, social feminism allowed women to adopt a public posture without upsetting both their self-concept as domestic caretakers and the similar expectations by watchful men – "this," says Black, "is not an insignificant achievement."[64] Moreover, it ensured that within the context of this relationship, women chose and laboured on behalf of their own causes, "which is the core of the feminist quest for autonomy."[65]

Most importantly, social feminism, unlike equity feminism, sought for women to remake, not simply fit into, patriarchal systems and values, and thus functioned as an expression of opposition to them.[66] Even Roberts acknowledges that social feminism "subverted traditional patriarchal norms."[67] Black maintains that "women's resistance to male domination, logically distant from what men and women share, provides the record of women's assertion of their autonomy."[68] She notes that although social feminists rejected dependency "by implication rather than by any form of theoretical defiance," the essence of feminism is the female repudiation of male control, and this principle is necessarily subversive within a patriarchal culture, however constrained particular feminist dictates.[69]

Social feminism as a conceptual category is not without its critics. They argue that social feminism tries to do both too much and too little, and that both failings are rooted in its vast and uncertain borders.[70] A just criticism of social feminism, defined as it is by an emphasis on female specificity and solidarity, is that it disregards group loyalties outside what could be perceived as the tenuous bonds of womanhood, loyalties which help shape the kind of feminism that individual women assert – that it ignores minority women, for example, who, because of the profound intersection of racism and sexism, and their rejection of or by inimical feminist groups, have articulated their own brand of feminism.[71] Social feminism also neglects to address the leanings of women on the conventional political spectrum, political affiliations that surely bisect their feminism.[72] Social feminism, then, in failing to include in its analytic framework particular group loyalties, masks the significance of what propels certain women to promote or dismiss the reform causes that they do, and the ways in which they go about doing this.[73]

Given these weaknesses of social feminism as a conceptual category, it is clear that social feminism alone cannot adequately represent the surge of feminist expression that Ontario farm women articulated between 1900 and 1970. As historians have most often applied the category to urban, middle-class women who were wives, women's group members, and consumers, it cannot entirely account for the feminism of rural, economically diverse women, who might have been wives and women's group members but who assumed a role within household commodity production. This arrangement dictated to a great extent the course and pattern of their lives. The farm woman, unlike most of her urban sisters, engaged in domestic production for much of the era, and performed both domestic and non-domestic work as part of her husband's enterprise, and in both physical and emotional proximity to her husband and his agricultural labour.

Louise I. Carbert, in her study of contemporary rural women, uses the term agrarian feminism to label the feminism of Ontario farm women, informed as it is by household commodity agricultural production.[74] According to Carbert, agrarian feminism is a variant of social feminism because it is "defined by its central commitment to domestic values," and "family farming represents domestic affairs at their most complex."[75] But social feminism and agrarian feminism differ markedly because agrarian feminism is, in fact, "driven" by household agricultural production.[76] Carbert, along with other scholars of farm women, rightly observes that focusing on petty-bourgeois production highlights the crucial contributions that farm women made to the perpetuity of the enterprise, which was almost always owned by the husband. Given that scholars have ignored until recently the value of this usually unpaid labour, this focus is surely valuable.

Just as important, however, are the social relations of household commodity production which would necessarily shape farm women's feminism.[77] The notion of petty commodity production allows for "causal links to be drawn between agriculture and feminism through marital and family dynamics."[78] Put another way, because the patriarchal farm as livelihood and as household are so inextricably connected, the farm marriage, and the farm family, may be understood as a locus of feminist struggle.[79]

This struggle may play out conservatively, but it is imbued with radical possibilities. Its conservatism likely rests in the fact that "when farm women negotiate their work relations or claims to family assets, the division of the labour and authority throughout the entire household, divided by gender and age, is simultaneously negotiated."[80] Thus, for farm wives, there exists a "latent challenge to one's marriage in almost any demand," and this challenge is a potential threat to the cohesion of the family and, in turn, the continuity of the farm.[81] That farm women may exercise caution in their resistance to male rule, then, should be of little surprise. As early twentieth-century women had almost no financial or legal protection within the patriarchal farm family, it was in their best interest to promote the mutuality of family relations and of work relations.[82] By the same token, because the farm woman potentially risked her marriage and family in censuring the conditions of either her domestic or agricultural work (and potentially jeopardized her financial security in censuring the state of her marriage), any challenge that she presented to the authority of her husband must be regarded as no less than profound. Carbert insists that "the radical potential of farm women lurks between the lines of recent research [about them]."[83] She also echoes scholars who contend that "farm women might produce a more decisive and radical challenge to patriarchy than where class and gender domination are separated into public and private spheres."[84]

Arguably, the indispensable domestic and non-domestic labour of farm women (in addition to their dwindling numbers in rural Ontario) should have empowered women within the system of household commodity production – certainly, they should have enjoyed more influence than urban, middle-class wives who were relatively detached from their husbands' workplace and livelihood – but the farm woman was too readily vulnerable to issues of law and rural social convention, which ensured that men claimed almost indisputable rights to the family farm. Under the Married Women's Property Act (1872, 1884, 1897), a farm wife (like all wives) who made no direct monetary contribution to the purchase or maintenance of marital property, regardless of her indispensable work contributions, was not legally entitled to a share of that property in the event of divorce.[85] In the case of the husband's death, a wife could legally claim only one-third of the estate if her husband did not sufficiently provide for her in his will (that is, if he left her less than one-third).[86] The act did confer property rights to those rare wives who held claim to separate assets, but "it had done nothing to address the fundamental imbalance of economic power within most marriages or to deconstruct the social belief in marital unity, male authority, and wifely obedience."[87] Indeed, according to one outraged observer, few wives contested the will of refractory farmers, who commonly bequeathed farmland to sons, and consigned widows to a small cash allowance.[88] Rural social convention privileged sons as profoundly as property law did husbands. Farm inheritance was based on the "patrilinear tradition" which dictated that fathers regularly passed their land down to sons, all but excluding wives and daughters from ever owning property.[89] The farm woman was further vulnerable to her husband-mediated community standing, to her intense desire to keep farm and family intact, and to her limited low-wage job options should farm or marriage collapse.

In the end, the farm woman had no choice but to depend on the uncertain benevolence of her capital-owning husband. The crucial contributions of farm women, therefore, seemed to invite more exploitation than adulation by farm men, who, backed by a patriarchal culture, and despite their necessary reliance on their wives (or, resentfully, because of it), could get away with minimizing women's status on the farm.[90] Clearly, the term "family farm" has masked the differentiated legal, economic, and social status between farm husband and wife, between farm son and daughter, and even between adult farm son and mother.

The term agrarian feminism is problematic. Even Carbert acknowledges that agrarian feminism "might more accurately be called petty-bourgeois feminism" because of its specific application to the peculiar economic arrangement which defined farm women's work and family lives.[91] The term agrarianism, generally defined as "the belief in the moral and economic primacy of farming over other industry," and as a "celebration of farming and farmers," is itself slippery.[92] As Deborah Fink demonstrates in her historical study of farm women in Nebraska, "the ideology of agrarianism underlay an undifferentiated farm policy that did not address the reality of gender and class inequalities."[93] The character and goals of agrarianism relied on, and most often acted in opposition to, women on the farm. It necessitated "a subordinate woman, usually concealed and peripheral" who, in her primary role as farm wife, was the "helpmate" of her property-owning husband, and submitted to the paramount needs of the farm.[94] This "agrarian vision" does not accurately reflect the real lives of farm women – nor does it recognize their concerns apart from the ideology's singular focus on agrarian issues: as Fink writes, farm women's concerns "touched on broader issues of economic and social justice."[95]

Carbert concedes that the term agrarian feminism does not readily acknowledge women's concerns apart from agriculture. Clearly, the tool of social feminism is useful in denoting these wide-reaching interests. For Ontario farm women, then, agrarian feminism and social feminism worked in conjunction with one another, with the former heavily informing the latter. As Carbert notes, and as is understood by my chosen term social feminism, "the maternal discourse of social feminism among Ontario farm women, voiced individually and collectively, is grounded in the petty-bourgeois conditions of agricultural production."[96]

Social feminism and agrarian feminism have much in common. Both have at their core the primacy of the family: social feminism prizes the female values that it nurtures, and agrarian feminism acknowledges its crucial economic and social relations. Both feminisms also recognize a distinct female experience – social feminism through the female values promulgated by exclusively female reform organizations, and agrarian feminism through conditions arising from the sexual division of labour on the farm, and the male ownership of production. In both social and agrarian feminism stir radical possibilities: social feminism, because of its general critique of patriarchal values, politics, and public institutions, and its efforts to effect change in the public sphere by asserting the specific expertise of women; and agrarian feminism, because the farm woman within the patriarchal system of household commodity production risks both her family and livelihood when protesting the conditions of either.

The two feminisms also prove complementary: social feminism is directed outward – it seeks to superimpose the maternal values of home and family onto the predominantly male public sphere; agrarian feminism is largely directed inward – it recognizes the way in which economic arrangements and agricultural conditions help shape work, family, and marital relations in the home. Agrarian feminism, then, may be seen as a "feminism of the workplace, of day-to-day life, a feminist politics directed to the amelioration of women's situation in the private sphere," which, no less than social feminism, presents a "challenge to male privilege."[97] Accordingly, social feminism is "a struggle for power in the public realm" by organized groups of women;[98] agrarian feminism is a feminism through which women seek solutions "in personal ways," and engage in a "discourse independent of the public world of male politics."[99] Together, then, social and agrarian feminism is both public and private, both collective and solitary, and both progressive and constrained.

I contend that social feminism (informed by agrarian feminism) characterized Ontario farm women between 1900 and 1970.[100] As part of the patriarchal farm family and the male-owned family farm, women boldly challenged the female drudgery and oppression to which these very institutions gave rise, and on which their survival and status depended. They sought to improve their lives through women-centred education and organization, and by exerting their female influence over the male "public sphere." Indeed, farm women seemed more "progressive" than "constrained" in their expression of social feminism.

The book is divided into seven chapters. Following this introductory chapter, which explains why historians have ignored or largely dismissed the feminism of Ontario farm women, and which elucidates this feminism's theoretical foundation, chapter 2 offers a brief survey of conditions in pre-World War II rural Ontario, and outlines reasons for the general historical neglect of farm women. Chapter 3, referencing notions of agrarian feminism in particular, explores the contentious relationship between early twentieth-century women and men by revealing women's awareness of their disadvantaged status on the family farm, and their efforts to promote their own interests. Chapter 4 locates the feminist impulse of early home economics, and discusses its appeal for farm women as expressed by Macdonald Institute – the school of domestic science at Guelph's Ontario Agricultural College – and the Women's Institutes, the preeminent rural organization for women, and therefore a necessary and inevitable focus in the study of Ontario farm women and feminism. Chapter 5 chronicles the women-centred programs of the WI during and after the First World War, and documents the rise and fall at that time of the equity feminist UFWO. Chapter 6, focusing on the 1950s and 60s, examines the dramatic changes in rural life that potentially threatened but did not mitigate the social feminism of farm women and the WI. To conclude, chapter 7 outlines why the social feminist character of farm women's activism waned after 1970.

2 "Too important to be forgotten": Writing Ontario Farming and Farm Women into History

The period from 1900 to 1970 afforded Ontario farm women unprecedented and since-unmatched opportunities for social feminist expression. At the turn of the century, the women-centred home economics movement inspired the formation of both the Women's Institutes and Macdonald Institute. The WI, established in 1897, was a farm women's group dedicated to domestic science and social reform. By 1903, the organization already claimed over 4,000 members.[1] That same year, Macdonald Institute, primarily a women's college, was established at the Ontario Agricultural College (OAC) in Guelph, and gave young farm women the opportunity to obtain a university-level education in domestic science. The influence of these institutions held strong throughout the seventy-year period, providing several generations of farm women with an organized outlet for social feminist values.

Historians of twentieth-century rural Ontario who focus on farm men and farming, however, generally look to the century's first fifty rather than seventy years as "a distinctive period."[2] According to community historian John Ewing Marshall, for example, the first half-century "bridged the years between pioneer days and the advent of the new agriculture."[3] This "new agriculture" was characterized by dramatic social, economic, and technological shifts which included the move from family-owned and -operated, labour-intensive, mixed-crop farms to highly mechanized and specialized businesses aimed at maximizing farm size, production, and capital.[4] Certainly these shifts were germane to farm women's lives, but for farm women, specifically, this "distinctive period" must be extended to include the emergence of second-wave feminism whose growing popularity in the 1960s helped launch a new farm women's movement that curtailed the influence of social feminism after 1970.

While some scholars have argued that the early twentieth century signalled the decline of Ontario agriculture, others have claimed that in the century's first years, rural Ontario was on the threshold of modernization, whose limitless possibilities came to elevate the quality of rural life.[5] Indeed, rural Ontario before World War II was a vital and dynamic place. The year 1905, for example, marked the "beginning of the end" of the horsepower age on Ontario farms, which increasingly welcomed the gas engine tractor.[6] By 1921, almost 7,000 tractors were in evidence on Ontario farms; by 1931, this number had close to tripled.[7] Equivalent to the work power of four horses, the tractor required fewer men who exerted less effort in shorter time.[8] The tractor could also pull or power almost any equipment on the farm. David Densmore declares that "the agricultural world hailed the tractor as the single most important farm machine ever invented."[9]

The horse was also subsumed by the automobile. In 1913, Ontario farmers owned fewer than 1,000 cars; by 1920, the number had increased to over 57,000.[10] The automobile relieved isolation on the farm by facilitating family trips, neighbourhood visiting, farmer exchange, and access to urban pleasures.[11] Before 1910, rural Ontario saw the cars in its midst as representing the encroachment of corrupt urban ways, and accused them of frightening horses and creating excessive dust harmful to farmers, crops, and foodstuff consumers. After 1910, however, this hostility began to dissipate, so that by 1914 it had all but disappeared.[12]

Along with the tractor and automobile, hydro-electricity revolutionized rural Ontario.[13] While hydro-electricity serviced only 2,627 rural homes by 1922, of which only 737 were farms, by 1930, it claimed 44,436 rural customers, of which 16,011 were farms.[14] By 1940, these numbers had risen dramatically to 121,801 rural homes, of which 58,727 were farms.[15] As a power source both within the barn and farm house, electricity superseded wood, coal, and kerosene, as well as the all-purpose gas engine generator, and inspired the creation and use of a host of labour-saving farm and domestic devices.

The modernization of turn-of-the-century rural Ontario also took the form of mixed-crop farming and expanded farm acreage. Mixed-crop farming was the choice farming strategy during a time of widening urban markets, and would prevail until the advent of crop specialization after 1945.[16] In mixed-crop farming, wheat, the staple crop of nineteenth-century farms, might have been only one of several grain, vegetable, fruit, and/or livestock cash crops tended on farms now increasingly engaged in dairying.[17] As the number of farms steadily declined after 1911, when there were just over 200,000 farms, their average size steadily rose.[18] In 1911, the typical farm claimed 110 acres; by 1941, it comprised about 20 acres more.[19] The increasingly fewer farms with their expanding acreage reflected a shrinking farming population throughout the first half of the century. The 1931 census, which was the first to specify the proportion of rural dwellers who resided on farms, reveals that the farm population for that year consisted of 786,000.[20] By 1941, this number had dropped to 695,000.[21]

Despite these dramatic transitions, and the fact that Ontario's rural population exceeded its urban population until well into the start of the twentieth century, historians have paid little attention to Ontario rural life after 1900.[22] Dufferin County chronicler John Ewing Marshall seems a minority voice when he declares that the last century's first fifty years of farming "are too important to be forgotten."[23] The historical neglect of rural Ontario, contended D.A. Lawr in 1972, may be attributable to Canadian economic historians who, "always in search of a staple product and a transcontinental economy," looked to the wheat economy of the West, and contrasted it to the manufacturing economy of the East.[24] Accordingly, agriculture has been synonymous with Prairie wheat: historians interested in the social and political ramifications of agriculture inevitably survey the West to find them, leaving social and political histories of the East almost exclusively urban-focused.

More generally, twentieth-century rural life has been disregarded by many historians because of the prevailing assumption that country living is simple, virtuous, serene, and unchanging.[25] "It is difficult," notes one American writer "to think of country life without illusion ... rural folklore, shamelessly exploited, intensifies images of idyllic simplicity and bedrock values."[26] Historians, especially those who write community-sponsored local histories, have taken little care to correct this romanticized image of farm life. Both those inclined toward a rural or urban bias, in fact, have a stake in perpetuating the mythology: for agrarians, it glorifies the civility of the country; for urbanites, it elevates the cosmopolitan ways of the city. The apparent sophistication of the city may, for agrarians, indicate a certain decadence and corruption, but at the same time, it favourably casts urban life as complex, dynamic, disparate, and advanced. This contrast is rooted in theories of modernization which espouse that "a population 'develops' as it moves from rural to urban, from farm to factory, and from religious to secular."[27] Whether perceived with a rural or urban eye, a nostalgic image of rural life necessarily obscures its complex realities, and precludes it from serious attention.

Romanticization of the countryside and its inhabitants has had serious ramifications for farm women in particular, whose subjugation and disaffection with life have rarely been addressed by historians.[28] Granted, the paucity of personal papers by farm women has contributed to their idealization, and to their more general invisibility.[29] Aside from being too occupied with their work to write extensively about their lives, and being furnished with little of the privacy which writing requires, many farm women undoubtedly believed that their thoughts and activities, whether dutiful or defiant, were not worthy of recording.[30] In existing diaries by farm women, this shortage of time, privacy, and/or a sense of self-importance translates into brief passages that variously document weather conditions, chores, visitors, outings, and illness, entries which rarely offer personal reflections revealing ideas, opinions, and hopes.[31] Nevertheless, historians seem to have exerted little effort in locating these papers, and other primary sources, which can help, even nominally, to elucidate the thoughts and lives of farm women. What has resulted are books like a 1978 local history of Dufferin in which a photograph of a churn has as its gender-neutral caption "Farm Folk had to churn their own cream."[32] That churning was virtually a female responsibility, as is evident in farm women's journals, merits no mention, rendering the fact of this female labour historically invisible. It has largely been the WI, not historians, who have recognized the rich history of farm women. While the WI's reverence for the past is best known through its Tweedsmuir Histories – written and pictorial chronicles of towns in which WI branches thrived – it has also over the years documented, studied, celebrated, and commemorated the lives of farm women.

Institute records are a valuable resource for the historical examination of farm women, yet they are also not without their limitations. Because the WI claimed hundreds of local clubs, and existed at both the district and provincial level, it was far from monolithic. None of its records taken individually, then, can be understood as entirely representative of the group and its members. But at every level, and even when used selectively as I have done, they can illuminate meaningful trends in the concerns, goals, and pursuits of Institute women. Another liability of Institute documents is that the experiences of minority women are virtually imperceptible. The WI, in its attempt to attract a diversified membership, was attentive to issues of class; the organization was negligent, however, in its consideration of race and ethnicity, and this bias is reflected in the records. Despite the WI's apparent snobbery in having educated, professional women as provincial organizers, and affluent rural wives as local leaders,[33] the organization intended that Institute involvement be accessible to everyone with regard to class. Institutes established a modest fee of twenty-five cents "so that membership would be within the means of all who wished to join."[34] This policy allowed Mrs McDougal of the Maxville Institute near Ottawa to boast in 1917 that within the WI she had "seen women, separated by mountains of class distinction … grow quite chummy over a new recipe for Johnny Cake."[35] The predominantly white, Anglo-Protestant WI, however (its composition reflective of the larger farming population in Ontario), was possibly exclusionary in other ways. Margaret Kechnie writes that, in the early years of the organization at least, black women, for instance, did not participate in the WI. Even in the rural areas of Amherstburg in Essex County and Buxton and Dresden in Kent County, where vital black communities had long been established, there is no indication that black women joined existing branches or initiated clubs of their own.[36] The absence of black women from the WI begs consideration of whether the organization made any effort to either exclude or attract black farm women, or whether black farm women deliberately avoided the WI. In terms of religion and ethnicity, the WI was similar to the Women's Christian Temperance Union (WCTU) in that it "did not insist on church affiliation as a condition of membership, but it would have been awkward for anyone of non-Protestant persuasion to join."[37] The WI, despite its restriction on sectarian issues,[38] advocated a "purposeful devotion to the great ideal … a constructive, practical Christianity," and desired that meetings as an expression of "spiritual values" open with the singing of the "Lord's Prayer in unison."[39] Issues of ethnicity found a place in early Institute records, but only within the context of the WI's commitment to assimilating foreigners. Mrs George Edwards, president of the Federated Institutes of Ontario, asked conference delegates in 1922 to consider the WI's role in "Canadianizing" the post-war immigrant: "the stranger within our gates, what of him or her? Some sixty nationalities are represented; a hundred or more languages are spoken. Our work is indeed great. We want all the people within our boundaries to *think Canadian, see Canadian* and live good Canadian lives."[40]

Because of this loyalty to the dominant culture by the WI, as well as by the mainstream agricultural press, minority women, including black, aboriginal, and francophone women, receive, regrettably, virtually no attention in this study.[41] As the first extended historical work on the feminism of Ontario farm women, its priority is to examine the feminism of "majority" women – of white, Anglo-Protestant women (who lived in the most populated farm regions[42]). This focus on majority women, however, should in no way preclude analysis of how issues of race, religion, and ethnicity informed their feminism. Although I have attempted to consider such factors, my treatment of them is admittedly cursory. In this way, I regard my work as a crucial jumping off point from which scholars can pursue more nuanced treatments of the feminism of all farm women, including detailed consideration of their various racial, religious, and ethnic backgrounds.

A fundamental reason that historians might not have bothered to probe the experiences of farm women is that defining them is difficult. The meaning of "farm women" is complex due to the "intertwining of family, market, and farm work."[43] The term "farm women" may refer to women who own a farm, or to those who manage and/or work a farm that belongs to them, their families, or somebody else.[44] In Ontario, prior to 1970, however, the term farm women most often referred to the wives of farmers, although I sometimes use the term to include unmarried adult farm daughters as well.[45] Rarely did the term refer to women as farmers themselves. According to the Canadian census, only those few women who owned and operated farms, necessarily without husbands or fathers (or inheriting sons), were farmers. Farm wives and adult farm daughters who performed unpaid domestic and agricultural labour on behalf of the enterprise were not represented by the census as farmers, farm partners, or even as farm workers.[46] Nancy Grey Osterud identifies four major groups of farm women: "inheriting daughters," who came from a long line of farm families and inherited the family farm (a situation that was rare in rural Ontario); "women who married inheriting farmers" who originated from established farm families; "daughters of marginal farmers," who had parents, usually immigrants, who strove to establish their own farms; and "farm partners," who started a farm with their husbands, but who neither shared a past with the land, nor envisioned the farm as a legacy to their children.[47] Of course, the term "partners" is erroneous if referring to women who held no ownership rights to the farm.

If these categories were not complex enough, there remains for historians the difficult prospect of determining class. Historians usually ascertain the class of urban women by looking at the socio-economic position of their husbands or fathers, and this is decided by locating their professions on a scale which, according to certain criteria, categorizes jobs as upper, middle, or working class, and the men as capitalists or labourers. From a feminist perspective, this method is faulty, but from an agrarian perspective, it is untenable. Although agrarians of the past often referred to those living on the land as a "farming class," and various scholars contend that there existed "a shared identification with a single mode of production which overrode class distinctions,"[48] there were, in fact, numerous socio-economic strata within farming itself.[49] The success of a farmer (who was most often both capitalist and labourer[50]) could be measured by how many acres he owned, how many farmhands he employed, the quality of his house and barn, his prospects for expansion, the yield of his crop, the number of livestock, his yearly income, and the extent to which his farm was mechanized.[51] These criteria, however, sufficiently varied and complex as they apply to men, cannot so readily apply to the class characterization of farm women: for the most part, they neither owned the means of production, lived as "ladies of leisure," nor earned a wage for their work, whose description was forever changing with the seasons, mechanization, and the growth of the farm, and with the caretaking responsibilities of growing children and family elders.[52] Accordingly, issues of race, religion, and ethnicity, rural background, class, and life cycle, as well as geography, all render generalizations about farm women, and by extension the WI, somewhat tenuous.[53]

Farm women were essential to the farm economy largely through their unpaid productive and reproductive labour, another reason for the historical invisibility of them and their work. Deborah Fink theorizes that assessing the volume and significance of women's unpaid work on the farm would expose "fundamental contradictions in a system that has used women so fully but evaluated and rewarded them so meagerly," contradictions that would challenge the hegemony of agrarian men.[54]

The general condition of women's unpaid work has led to the assumption that women's labour on the farm was exclusively in the form of production for use rather than for sale, and thus it has gone unnoticed. But these two functions are not so easily separated. The productive labour of the farm woman included "farm enabling" work – she facilitated the sale of crops and livestock through her work meeting the basic needs of her farming husband, her labouring children, and the resident farmhands.[55] She cooked and served meals, made bread, butter, cheese, cream, and sausages, and did the gardening, preserving, cleaning, laundry, milking, and mending.[56] Fink terms her provision of emotional needs as "moral capital." It refers to her job nurturing, consoling, appeasing, and uniting family members, which enabled the farm family to persevere, and the family farm to survive and prosper, especially in times of conflict and crisis.[57] The productive work of the farm woman also included caring for house guests and elderly and infirm family members, as it freed her husband and children to tend to farm work.[58] Nevertheless, farm women are cast as "helpmates" to their husbands, who are considered the true farmers and providers.[59] That farm women might define themselves in this way is based not on the hours that they perform farm work as compared to their husbands, but on the fact that their husbands are essentially the overseers of their labour.[60] Carolyn Sachs emphasizes that "the position of women on a farm [and their perception of those positions] cannot be understood without considering male domination in society and in the family"[61] – another reason perhaps why traditional historians have disregarded serious analysis of Ontario farm women.

Championing this assertion, I examine various forms of male domination, but underscore the efforts of Ontario farm women, as wives, daughters, workers, and club women, to challenge them. Through their deliberate expressions of female specificity, solidarity, separatism, and reform, farm women critiqued, even subverted, the androcentrism of agriculture, knowledge, and politics, and sought to elevate their status both on the farm and within the "public sphere."

3 "These self-made men make me tired": Gender Conflict on the Farm at the Turn of the Century

In early twentieth-century Ontario, the survival of the family farm · enterprise necessitated interdependence and cooperation between women and men, who assumed differing roles on the farm. The presumption that this mutuality nurtured an egalitarian partnership between wives and husbands, however, not only overstates women's power within the patriarchal farm and family, but implies that little or no conflict existed between women and men within the farm family. The alternative view that women martyred themselves for the sake of the farm, a disempowering conception of women, also suggests the general absence of gender discord. Women were indeed dedicated to the success of the farm, but they themselves recognized their disadvantaged status there, and discerned that their interests and needs often opposed those of their men. Indeed, farm wives and daughters decried their unmerciful workload and the devaluation of their labour, and in so doing asserted a shared recognition of female oppression for which many of them impugned farm men. Accordingly, gender conflict, a necessary condition for a feminist impetus, was in no way rare on the farm, where women expressed self-determination, hope for women-centred reforms, and a well-spring of informal coping strategies, all which spoke to their efforts at agency.

Most of the farm wife's time was consumed by arduous household demands. These included domestic, productive, and reproductive work, and the care not only of husband and children, but of infirm relations and farmhands.[1] A 1912 article in the *Farmer's Advocate* entitled "Is Marriage a Failure?" chronicled the farm woman's typical

day: "up in the morning early, breakfast over, hurry to milking, sepa-
rating milk, washing dishes, (minding babies in intervals), tidy
house, get dinner [lunch], wash dishes, do mending, sewing, gardening, berry picking, helping in field if necessary, washing, ironing,
baking, with the thousand and one interruptions, which come
through the day; get supper, put sleepy babies to bed, milk, wash
dishes, sew or mend again till bed-time."[2] These daily chores were
usually organized around a weekly routine: laundry on Mondays;
ironing on Tuesdays; baking, housework, or sewing on Wednesdays
and Thursdays; baking on Fridays; selling at market and shopping on
Saturdays; and church and visiting on Sundays.[3] Work weeks, in
turn, were somewhat influenced by the seasons: major house cleaning in spring; gardening in spring and summer; canning in summer
and fall; and extra baking in winter.[4] Reflecting upon her work,
Frontenac County farm woman Helen Campbell declared that "on
the farm, I emulated a camel – the original beast of burden."[5]

It was, in fact, a widely held belief in early twentieth-century Ontario that because of interminable monotony, overwork, and exhaus-
tion (vacations from the farm were rare and brief), countless farm
women had gone hopelessly insane, and were alarmingly over-
represented in the province's lunatic asylums.[6] This topical issue
appeared in farm journals of the day such as the *O.A.C. Review*,
which in 1912 detailed the farm woman's descent into madness:

during the [childbearing] years when she is entitled to a certain amount of
care and rest, the woman on the farm struggles along, bearing burdens
which should only be borne by those who are physically strong. She is unable to cope with her work, and she lets some of it go. There she shrinks
within herself, lest some neighbor should drop in and find her unprepared.
Her appearance begins to suffer. Her shoulders stoop and her whole figure
assumes the attitude which she adopts most frequently when working
hard, and it is usually an attitude neither graceful nor proper. Her clothes
wear out and she has little time to spend on having them replaced. Her
teeth go, and she cannot leave the babies long enough to have them attended to. ... And all this comes in the nine or ten years which follow her
courtship and marriage. Is it any wonder that many a young woman finds
the change from girlhood to such strenuous wifehood too great for her
mental or physical strength? She succumbs. She is laid away in the church-
yard or she is taken to the asylum for the insane. ... If she is dead they lay
flowers on her grave. If she is insane, she gets care and rest: She is surrounded by green lawns and flowers. ... But it is too late. One year sooner
the care and rest would have saved her, and from a financial point of view,
if from no other, she would be worth the saving.[7]

In describing the way in which insanity impeded the ability of women during their childbearing years to keep house, maintain their appearance, and repair their clothes, this account ignored the general symptomology of insanity, and underscored its gender-specific manifestations as they related to the distinctiveness of women's work.

It is true that the rigours of farm life took an emotional toll on its women, and were sometimes too overwhelming to bear. Louisa Good, for example, experienced excessive strain and fatigue in her unsuccessful effort to attack the staggering workload at Myrtleville, her parents' large farm near Brantford. She was acutely aware of her inability to conform to the demanding domestic role which was expected of her as a woman – especially a farm woman. These feelings no doubt contributed to her stay at a small private hospital in Toronto in 1911; in 1912 she was committed to the Ontario Hospital in Hamilton. She suffered from various "nervous" conditions, and endured these ailments for the remainder of her life.[8] Selina Horst of St Jacobs, outside of Kitchener, remembered that after the birth of her youngest sibling, the family's ninth child, "my mother had sort of a breakdown." The children were sent to live with various relatives during the summer months. Horst cited too many people to care for and too little privacy as the reasons for the collapse.[9] At the height of the Depression, farm woman Dorothy Franklin of Brechin, near Orillia, wrote to Prime Minister Bennett of her farm and family's financial plight, conveying her feelings of hopelessness and despair: "'we were taught to believe God put us women here for the noble cause of Motherhood. I wonder how many would have suffered what we have, had we known our children were not even going to have the necessities of life. ... I'm so discouraged. I wonder which requires the greater courage, to carry on knowing how much we are all needing and cannot have or to end it all as that poor woman did this week in Oakville by sticking her head in a pail of water and drowning.'"[10]

Conversely, however, doctors in a 1905 *Farmer's Advocate* article entitled "Farmers' Wives and Insanity" testified to the fact that farm women were no more prone to mental collapse than other groups of people, especially given their "idyllic" surroundings. Dr Groff, of the Pennsylvania Board of Health, wrote that "'less farmers' wives become insane than of any other class, owing to the joyous elements of country life.'"[11] Dr C.K. Clark, superintendent of the asylum in Kingston, asserted that he had "'a great deal of faith in the level-headedness of the farmer's wife, and cannot understand why she should develop insanity more readily than the city woman surrounded by more artificial conditions.'"[12] And Dr Daniel Clark, superintendent of the Toronto Asylum, declared: "'it is my opinion that farmers' wives, as a rule, are a healthy class with healthy work in the fresh air, and who are, as a whole, contented.' "[13] Farm women were largely represented in insane asylums, these doctors believed, only because they comprised one of the largest occupational groups.[14]

In their effort to dispute the myth about the pervasiveness of insanity among farm women, however, these doctors might have overstated their case. Many farm women found few "joyous elements of country life," and hardly felt "contented." But most did not go "insane," nor did they stoically suffer in silence. Rather, farm women expressed with much clarity and candour their displeasure about the volume and nature of their work, and in so doing presented a challenge to the connective gendered family and work relations on which farm women's very survival depended. In a *Canadian Countryman* article entitled "Lo! The Poor Farmer's Wife," for example, one resolute farm woman testified to her lot by actually tabulating the hundreds of baked goods that she made for her family over six months.[15] A forthright Mrs Hopkins of Russel County outlined the most distressing issues for farm wives in her 1912 letter to *Farm and Dairy*. She declared that "in no other occupation are we offered so great a contrast between the superior advantages of the male and the acquiescent humility of the female ... so poorly paid, so complacently considered as only a chattel, a mere machine, a possession valuable only according to her work and childbearing capacity."[16] The frustration expressed by Ontario farm women led author John MacDougall to address the topic in a book chapter entitled "Social Causes of Unrest," and also prompted a writer in the *Farmer's Advocate* to declare in 1920 that "this 'restlessness' [among farm women] that we are reading and hearing about all the time is not growing any less throughout the country, to put it mildly."[17] As this chapter will indicate, rural sociologist Nora Cebotarev is mistaken when she asserts that Ontario farm women "accepted the undervaluation of their work."[18]

Sympathy for the plight of the overworked farm woman was evident in the women's pages of the agricultural press, where "women's issues" were consistently addressed.[19] Indeed, the editor of "Home and Fireside," the women's page of *Canadian Farm*, recognized that "women do love to hear about how other women do their work, care for their children and manage their husbands."[20] Comprised of contributions by farm wives and journalists, these women's pages revealed the extent to which farm women's domestic labour went unappreciated on the farm. Certainly they never intended to highlight the adversity of farm life for women; in fact, they, like the doctors previously mentioned, seemed committed to touting its healthfulness, morality, and beauty. That these pages lamented the farm woman's difficult lot is a reflection of this problem as a pervasive concern among rural women.

Women's pages put the devaluation of women squarely on the shoulders of farm men. One presumably female author in *Farm and Dairy*, frustrated by their relative privilege and arrogance, summarized the prevailing sentiment: " 'I am a self-made man.' How often we hear this assertion now-a-days made with great pride and satisfaction by men who in a comparatively few years and with few opportunities have raised themselves from poverty to affluence. ... The self-made farmer – and we have many of them in this country – boys who came here with nothing at all and now have splendid farms well stocked and paid for, owe more to their wives than any other class of self-made men. ... These self-made men make me tired. Why cannot they tell the whole truth and give to the woman in the case her due credit?"[21] One article written by a man, and seemingly directed to male readers, warned them of the possible repercussions of their neglect:

have you ever thought what the result would be if all the farmer's wives and housekeepers in this country were to form a sort of labor-union and then go out on strike, for something under an eighteen hour day and a pay-envelop [*sic*] every Saturday night? ... the fact that the 'female of the species' has always been more faithful to her home and family in the past than she has been to any 'union' or organization is no argument proving that she will always remain in that attitude, or frame of mind. ... Surely, we say, let the woman of the farm go out on strike. There are a whole lot of things in this world that are hers by rights, and she hasn't been getting them.[22]

While farm wives and their supporters believed that "the chain of farm life is no stronger than its woman who keeps the home ... going,"[23] they knew that the productive work of farm wives, however extensive, and however integral to the survival of the farm, did not render their sexual equality within the enterprise or within the legally sanctioned patriarchal farm family.[24] Indeed, while reciprocity was evident between farm husband and wife, "family relations could stress hierarchy and control as often as mutuality."[25]

Sympathy for the plight of farm women could rarely be found among urbanites. If the urban authors of the *Harper's Bazaar* 1912–13 series on rural America are an indication, city dwellers were critical and condescending of their complaints:

It's making a revolution in values to have the farm woman perched like a bird on a bough, ready to sail into the blue if her convenience isn't studied. But it isn't by running away that the country woman can solve her problems. ... Gas, electricity, and alcohol [cookstoves] are all of them easier fuels to use than wood or coal, and since the farmer's wife no longer believes that there is virtue in perspiration, she is turning to one or the other of these. For it's all very well to go around pitying and commiserating the farmer's wife – laying a soothing hand on her shoulder and saying, 'Poor thing, how hard it is for you!' The truth is, the farm woman who plays the martyr is like the aggravating woman who, getting into a street car and finding no seat near the door, are [sic] too stupid to go farther up where there is room, and so stand unnecessarily in the presence of seats to the discomfiture of everybody. For the things that the farmer's wife needs are hers to take.[26]

The article's vigorous condemnation of the farm wife could not have helped urban-rural relations, which were already strained.

The assumption of the passage that farm women had unlimited access to newly available labour-saving devices was incorrect. Indeed, the lack of these conveniences in the home was at the core of the farm woman's frustration with farm life.[27] In particular, many farm women were infuriated by the fact that the barn, viewed by their husbands as the "real soul" of the farm,[28] was better equipped with labour-saving devices than was the kitchen, and that, by extension, men's labour could be done in a more timely and efficient fashion than could theirs. Farm women did not anticipate at this time that domestic "labour-saving" equipment could potentially increase the standards and pace, and thus the time and amount, of their work. Indeed, with their awareness that "women were the last to get anything for the household,"[29] feminism for farm women, asserted a *Farmer's Magazine* article, was defined by their struggle for and acquisition of modern appliances for the home: "feminism in the city may mean things. It may mean a combination of short hair and knickerbockers or of babies and jobs. It may mean equal pay for equal work and equal pay for equal misbehaviour. But on the farm and homestead from the east to the west, feminism means something else. To quote 'The Declaration of Independence' recently drawn up and published by the farm women of Nebraska, it means: A power washing-machine for the house for every tractor bought for the farm. A bath-tub in the house for every binder on the farm. Running water in the kitchen for every riding-plow for the fields. A kerosene cookstove for every automobile truck. A fireless cooker for every new mowing-machine."[30] As this passage indicates, farm women and their supporters consistently drew analogies between the requirements of the barn with those of the home. Advocate Ethel Chapman, for example, asserted in her 1918 article "Machinery For Women – Why it Pays" that machinery for women has not kept pace with labor-saving equipment so rapidly coming to farms. We have a lot of bank barns with warm, comfortable stables ... yet a furnace that would keep every room in the house at a livable temperature is a rare luxury in many neighborhoods. Every year sees more well-ventilated, well-lighted stables, but it seems a lot of trouble to cut an extra window in an old house. ... More and more we find running water in the barn for cattle, while the water for the house is still pumped and carried from the well. ... All over the country barns are well equipped with litter-carriers and feed chutes, but women carry things up and down cellar without anyone ever suggesting that the farm could afford a ten-dollar dumb-waiter, or a dinner waggon."[31]

Chapman pointed out that the warm, well-lit environment that modern technology offered the barn prompted many farm women to complain that barn animals lived a more comfortable life than did the farmer's own family.[32]

While there was some sense that the lack of modern conveniences was attributable to the farm woman's fear of machinery, and to her reluctance to try new ways, many women claimed that it was the fault of the notoriously conservative and frugal farmer who had the power to sanction the purchase of devices for the home, but who underestimated their value in easing his wife's work.[33] His ignorance in this regard was problematic for his wife who understood that "the installation of machinery in most farm homes will have to come through a man's understanding of its need and in the case of power machinery, his teaching on how to operate it."[34] Women, then, knew that their acquisition of labour-saving devices was dependent upon both the tenuous goodwill and earned capital of men, and upon men's presumed knowledge of domestic machinery about which they likely knew little.

Many women felt cheated by "such outrageous discrimination," and although they intellectually understood the survival strategy of "the Barn First school of farming," they demonstrated some resentment to this dictum.[35] Guelph-area farm woman Mrs Cragg acknowledged the priority of the barn, but felt shortchanged when it received plumbing before the home. As her son recalled, she tried to cope with this inequity by enlisting her husband to help alleviate her continued drudgery: "she bought two extra water pails, four in all, and ranged them beside the kitchen door. She trained father and the hired man to take the empties out, hang them on hooks she provided at the windmill and never to come in, for meals or anything else, without a pail of water. It took training, but mother, if nothing else was persistent."[36] Even with this assertive, self-styled scheme, however,

Mrs Cragg could not help at times feeling "bitter about the inconveniences of the average farm kitchen." She cursed those men who designed and constructed farm homes, hoping that one day "a woman – 'no man would have sense' – would plan a big, useful farm kitchen, that would still save women's steps."[37]

The gendered opposition set up between the barn and the farm house at this time masks the fact that while farm men seldom assumed responsibilities in the home, farm women, although absorbed first by domestic concerns, were very much involved with the workings of the barn.[38] Kenneth Cragg recalled that when his father told his mother to " 'keep your nose in the house where it belongs and I'll look after the barn,' Mother's unfailing reply to such advice was: 'A lot of looking after the barn would get if I weren't around.' "[39]

Poultry-raising was deemed the most suitable barn work for women.[40] Ontario farm women seemed to have agreed with their American counterparts that poultry-raising was " 'a nice ladylike branch' " of agriculture – one in which inherently female attributes proved more advantageous than those of men.[41] Women's ability to nurture (especially small creatures) and to keep house (coops had to be cleaned), and their attention to detail and fondness for order all served poultry-raising well.[42]

Farm women enjoyed the personal and financial benefits that poultry-raising brought them. Mrs Jull of Oxford County found that " 'to take care of poultry is really nice work.' "[43] It allowed farm women to contribute directly to the profits of the farm, and, along with dairy and garden work, provided them with some financial independence.[44] In an article entitled "The Farmer's Wife as a Partner[:] How to Cash in on the Woman's Intuition, Common Sense and Power of Argument," one farm wife boasted that her egg and butter savings grew into " 'quite a little sum, which I keep in the bank until I have the chance to use it.' "[45]

More often than not, however, the farm wife's earnings from the sale of poultry and eggs went immediately to household expenses, which left her little or no money by the end of the year. This scenario prompted Mrs Dawson, who had resided on a farm for six years, to assert that the husband "claims that he supports her, but he is mistaken. The truth of the matter is that she supports him." In contrast to the farm wife, her husband "comes to the end of the year with a nice bank account to his credit. He has sold his grain, his cattle, his horses, his pigs, and the proceeds are all his ... Then what about the wives and daughters?"[46] MP Agnes Macphail, herself of the farm, quipped that " 'in farming women break fifty-fifty with the men ... fifty dollars to the men and fifty cents to the women, and I doubt if that is overstating the case.'"[47] Mrs Dawson recommended that "either the farmer should recognize the fact that his wife and daughters have made his large bank account possible and should give them some tangible interest in that bank account, or he should pay his share toward the board and clothing of his family and allow his wife and daughters the privilege of starting a bank account of their own."[48] Even a male contributor to *Farm and Dairy* stated in a rare confession that "we farmers too often share the profits with our partner in a grudging spirit as if we were giving them something that belongs rightfully to us." He called for "more true cooperation. Let us divide the profits of the firm graciously and justly."[49] The significance of this entire issue was not lost on one woman who saw feminism to mean "our share of the farm income."[50]

Milking cows was another barn job farm wives performed, although the care of cattle was work they did less often. A notable exception to this convention was Mrs Lawrence of London who, instead of boarding men as impoverished urban women did, "boarded" Jersey cows. She was quoted as saying "that she 'would rather wait on Jersey cows than on men any day,'" a statement that "may be construed as very complimentary to the cows, or extremely uncomplimentary to the men."[51]

Whether or not farm wives should engage in barn work involving livestock, and should labour in the fields alongside men, was a contentious matter of gender in rural Ontario. An article entitled "What is a Woman's Work on the Farm?" referred to the issue as "this Oft Times Burning Question."[52] Tradition dictated among white North American farm families of Western European origin that the care of large animals and labour in the fields were men's work, while tending garden, small animals, the household, and children was women's work.[53] Only during times of financial and/or labour crises did women temporarily assume men's labour, an indication that women's usual absence from the fields was based more on convention than on the presumption that women were simply incapable of the work.[54]

There was a handful of wives who enjoyed barn and field work for a variety of reasons. Some were keenly interested in agricultural issues, and wanted to experience all aspects of the farm.[55] Others simply welcomed the opportunity for outdoor work, and freedom from domestic drudgery. One farm woman from Louise in Grey County observed in 1918 that "the farm men are the objects of a great amount of sympathy, and they seem to look for it, but really I don't think they deserve as much as they get. This spring, on account of scarcity of men, my husband is alone on 300 acres. I tried to help, by harrowing sometimes, and one day rode the three-horse cultivator. Really it was just fun."[56] Elizabeth Davis of Tottenham, near Barrie, recalled that she "just love[d] being out on the tractor ... you could just be thinking about things and looking around and enjoying nature and the fresh air, and there was a sense of rhythm, just going up and down the fields with the tractor, working. To me it was a real outlet." Davis regretted "having to come back into the house and face the mess there and to clean up later. I think I would have been quite happy just to do that type of work [field work] if somebody else had been there tidying the house and getting meals for me."[57] Farm women especially appreciated that field work, unlike housework, had a beginning and an end.[58] John Cairns of Ameliasburg in Prince Edward County insisted that his wife performed barn and field work partly because "she got a lot [sic] of pleasure out of helping me."

But Cairns himself hints at the public disapproval of women's demanding barn and field work. He was clearly defensive when he claimed that "she didn't lose anything by it; she lived a good long age and it didn't hurt her to work."[59] Indeed, it was precisely this attitude of men which infuriated women such as Mrs T.H. Bass, who, like the majority of farm folk, opposed women's outside work. She caustically declared that "real men prefer to do their own work themselves," adding that "it is quite possible to train a man to expect a woman to do the 'chores' outside the house. I have seen this done, but it never struck me that the gratitude of the man was proportionate to the energy expended by his 'other half.' "[60] Mrs Bass would have approved of one agricultural speaker who, when asked at a meeting if his wife milked cows, bitingly replied " 'my wife, sir, does nothing on the farm that a man can do for her.' "[61] In fact, many men supported this viewpoint, deriding those members of their own sex who turned their wives into "the pack-horse of the family ... a sort of upper servant or slave": "there are some women physically strong, or regular Amazons, who do enjoy that life, and speak from that viewpoint. Then, let them live their own lives, and find their own happiness that way. Or perchance, a leech-like husband, who has no more manliness about him than to suck his wife's life-blood by such a slavish life."[62]

Men and women who opposed female barn and field work, however, seemed to do so for different reasons. Women's objections largely pointed to the fact that farm wives, whose domestic obligations would not be reduced in exchange for their outdoor labour,[63] were already overworked and physically taxed:

Why should the women on the farm have so much more to do than the average city woman? ... No woman can do the work in the house and field also, and no wonder a woman is dissatisfied who trys [sic] to do both.[64]

I consider woman's work in the farm home as in the city home [to] be housekeeping and homemaking. She should neither be a hewer of wood nor a drawer of water, for her real work lies indoors, just as the farmer's lies out of doors. Either one, however, should lend a helping hand as necessarily requires.[65]

Generally speaking, there is a strong opinion in Canada against women undertaking manual work on a farm. Nothing which has happened so far during the war indicates that this opinion is to be changed. It is agreed that country women have enough to do without helping in the fields, barns or stables. ... anything which tends to alter the standard with regard to women not undertaking manual work on farms will be strongly resisted by Canadians.[66]

Carolyn Sachs sees farm women's repudiation of field labour as "one avenue of resistance" to their overwork, and notes that within the confines of the house, farm wives "were able to claim their own realm" free from supervision by men.[67] While often sincerely directed at women's welfare, men's concerns about outdoor work were generally rooted in the primacy of women's reproductive role, and in the work's possible emotional and financial cost to farmers. Men felt that the outdoor work of mothers threatened the fitness of the human race.[68] One man wondered, "what will the offspring be if a wife and mother has to do a man's work and what care can a mother give to her young family under such circumstances? I would like to hear the opinion of a good, sensible, medical practitioner. Why are the young women (I mean farmers' daughters, principally) not as strong as our grandmothers were? I think it is because our mothers and grandmothers had to work too hard in their pioneer life, had to do men's work. I believe that is the principal reason that there are so many weaklings in these days." This "Householder" also feared the potential problems and expense of women's outside work: "if the farmer's wife is to become a slave by working in the fields to help produce more, what will become of her health? She will be a wreck in a few years with no pleasure for herself or those around her. And further, if by working so hard her health fails and a doctor has to be called who will come good for the expense? We will have to face that question ourselves and pay a hired girl if one is to be had."[69] The status-minded farmer preferred to pay farmhands whose presence in the fields, unlike that of his unpaid wife, announced his prosperity to the neighbours.[70]

Underlying both male and female arguments against women's barn and field work was the shared belief between the sexes that a wife's rightful place was in the home.[71] But, ironically, and as many women knew only too well, the home itself exposed them to the heavy labour and emotional stress and strain it was thought they would experience outdoors. Indeed, despite the proposed correlation between women's overwork in the home and insanity, many farmers failed to realize that women's taxing workload in the house posed as much of a health risk as their "male" outdoor work.[72]

While women were told that farm men should share in the concerns of homemaking,[73] many wives felt that husbands did little to lighten their household burdens: "in speaking of 'Woman's Work on the Farm,' we are dealing with a difficult problem for reasons that are obvious – lack of help, lack of convenience, and lack of consideration of the husband";[74] "in days gone by there was a happy slavery practiced by our dear old grandmothers. There was very little machinery then, and they were away to the field and barn after their husbands trying to help all they could. All honor to them; but it has evolved a generation of men, our cousins and uncles, who in this age of 'a machine for everything' still want to be mothered."[75] Clearly, in this writer's view, technology advanced to a greater extent than did the attitudes of men, who, although living in a modern world, remained as old-fashioned as ever in their perceptions of women.

Farm wives also complained that husbands rarely acknowledged their labour.[76] Two presumably male contributors to *Farm and Dairy* recognized this problem, and advised men to express appreciation to their wives, highlighting not the congeniality of such displays, but the economic advantages of this gesture and their work: "surely the women are deserving of at least words of appreciation; these seem to have big value and they cost nothing. We all may give them without stint";[77] "some [women] are working close to the breaking point. Their load may be lightened greatly by a little appreciation, expressed before it is too late, by those for whom they work. In the enumeration of statistics housewives are not wage earners; but when a woman dies and it is necessary to employ someone else to take her place, she must be paid $4 to $5 a week for doing the work the wife did. Many of us farmers need to give expression to a greater appreciation of the great work these wives are doing for us."[78]

In an era that promoted the companionate marriage, farm women complained that husbands as a whole made phlegmatic partners. In March of 1923, Ethel Hillier of Vyner, near Sarnia, attended a "Literary Evening" which entertained the following debate: "Resolved[:] that books are more companionable and of more use to a woman than a husband."[79] Kenneth Cragg remembered his mother's frustration over her husband's excessive time in the barn, away from his family: "'you'd think enough of your own family to spend some time in the house besides when you're eating,' mother would say. ... The way he would hang around the stable at night was a constant annoyance to mother. 'I've given up trying,' she would tell her relatives in her resigned way. 'If he has no more respect for his wife and family than to spend all his time with his horses' ... Sometimes she tried sarcasm. 'Well have you at last got the horses tucked away for the night?' "[80] Mrs Cragg was not alone in her frustration. David Densmore confirms that "for farmers, a house was a place to rest between workdays, and many a farm wife over the generations has lamented that her man seemed to prefer the company of the barn to that of the house."[81]

The personal deficiencies of the farm husband were blamed on several sources. They included both his lack of marital training and his position of privilege: "how often we are warned to train our girls to be good housekeepers and wives, but whoever heard of training boys to be good husbands; and the happenings of the wife depend on the husband. If the tables were turned and the boys taught to dance attendance on sister and mother our farmers, at least some of them, would be more thoughtful."[82] Others blamed the faults of the farmer on his parochial and subservient wife. The article "Is Marriage a Failure?" insisted that "many women are much to blame themselves for their husbands regarding them as mere household servants. After they become wives and mothers, apparently their interest in the outside world vanishes, and all their thoughts are concentrated on the human beings in their own homes. They only get to town once a year; what they wear does not matter so long as it is clothes; society is a dead letter; books and papers nonexistent, newspapers only for the men, and the conversation of the women limited to butter, eggs, husband, children and gossip. They become narrow-minded and quite often fretful, so the man and woman having no outside community interests drift apart." The same article asserted that "if a woman makes a meek mop-rag of herself you can hardly blame a man for wiping his feet on her (figuratively). I am sure no self-respecting woman would get out in the morning, milk, light fires, get breakfast, feed chickens, pigs and calves, all before she ate her own breakfast." Instead, advised the article, she should recruit the men of the farm to perform these tasks.[83] Indeed, another article instructed farm women that "a woman's duty to her husband and children does not mean that her individuality be so stunted by conditions that she becomes a mere machine, losing interest in things that make life worth while."[84]

If living at home, the adult farm daughter helped her mother with much of the domestic work. For Galt-area daughter Roxie Hostetler, and most young women like her, it meant "housework!: raising children; scrubbing floors; milking cows; making butter; baking bread and coffee cakes and pies. We used to bake fifteen pies every Friday."[85] As the eldest of four children and the only girl, Ethel Hillier performed countless household chores, and often remarked in her diaries that she was "very busy," "real busy," and "busy as usual."[86] When asked if Ethel's parents employed a hired girl, her daughter laughingly replied years later, "she was it!"[87] Ethel was so consumed by domestic work that she was obliged to forgo high school, and only left her parents' farm when she married relatively late at age thirty-five.[88] Unlike Ethel, who in fact married a farmer, one group of country girls, repelled by the prospect of continued domestic drudgery on the farm, "declared out and out that no farmer need propose to them."[89]

The farm daughter who had no older brothers or no brothers at all, however, was often exempt from domestic work to help her father outside. While some girls viewed themselves as "tomboys," and preferred "the role of a farmer's son,"[90] some daughters like Beatrice Snyder from the Kitchener area, who was designated her "father's hired man," regretted that she "missed all the opportunities of becoming knowledgeable of work in the house." Her relegation to outside work also meant little time spent with her mother. Only when Beatrice visited neighbouring farms to assist on "Butchering Day" could she "take the women's part; just in my own home is where I had to do the manual labour."[91] As the eldest of ten children, and ten years older than her nearest brother, Beatrice performed all barn work and many aspects of field work and butchering.[92] In fact, when her father played cards with the two male farmhands, Beatrice, as "hired man," was "the fourth."[93] As she grew into adulthood, the workload, as it did for the maturing farm son, became much more intense. At seventeen, she suffered a stroke which the doctors attributed to hard labour.[94] Partly paralyzed, she was prescribed a one-year reprieve of bedrest and quiet. In 1921, at nineteen, she married, partly to escape the demands of farm life under her father, but only to perform similar work while her farmer husband managed a trucking business.[95] Jean Lozier, in describing her mother's 1911 wedding at her parent's farm near Stratford, wrote that "it was said years later that Mother's father was so 'put out' when she got married that he went to bed for a week. I guess he figured he had lost a good 'work horse.'"[96] As a young woman, Beatrice herself was acutely aware that her outside labour in lieu of a hired man's meant not only needed help for her father and grandfather, but also their increased savings.[97]

Indeed, most adult daughters provided savings for their fathers by performing unpaid domestic work in place of the "hired girl," and, like Beatrice, were cognizant of their economic function and lack of reward. Alice Ferguson, asking "Should Daughters be Compensated for Their Labor?" in *Farm and Dairy*, observed that "money is always forthcoming for the payment of hired help, but apparently little for the daughter who does the same work. The girl feels this is not just to her."[98] Kingston-area farm daughter Jennie A. Pringle, in a letter to the *Canadian Countryman* addressing "What Girls Need Most in a Rural Community," firmly pointed out that "the hired girl and man get wages. If she were working in the city, she would be paid. Why not on the farm? ... Fathers, why wait to give us our share on our marriage or your death?"[99] The disparity between the economic treatment of farm daughters and sons intensified the resentment of daughters. It prompted one outspoken woman to proclaim that "the girls who stay at home should be paid for their services. Why not? When the son comes of age, if he stays at home, he enters into a business like agreement with his father as to the wages he shall receive, and is not regarded as mercenary in the least. Why should the daughter be regarded as a minor child, a ward of her father or of some male relative, till legally delivered over into the care and keeping of her husband? ... Have changes in economic conditions made a place for this woman on the Canadian farm?"[100] Farm daughters agreed that the absence of an income was "the bane of the farm girl's life": "as she grows older and realizes that she is holding up her end of the farm life, she wonders why she is not allowed a definite share of the income, or the proceeds from the poultry, pigs, garden spot, or whatever has been her special care. It hurts her self-respect to ask for spending money continually."[101] Farm daughter Edna I. Brown confirmed that "the lack of any such provision in most farm homes is the chief reason why Daughter leaves; almost the only reason why she is discontented if she stays."[102]

In response to her appeal for earnings, and to prevent her migration (and thus the boy's migration) from the farm,[103] suggestions for how to compensate the farm girl appeared in rural journals. Considered were a set allowance (for those looking after the household), income from one particular (female) branch of the farm (such as gardening), and a fixed share of the profits, especially as they related to her extensive dairy and poultry work.[104] Certainly Ethel Hillier, for example, was deserving of the $1,614.27 that she earned in 1924 selling butter, eggs, roosters, hens, and turkeys.[105] Reaping rewards for her contributions to the farm, noted observers, would make the daughter feel independent, responsible, and mature.[106]

For older, "spinster" daughters who had long remained on the farm, poverty and dependence were a consuming fear not readily felt by sons or even their wives. "Floy" explained in her essay "The Stay-at-Home Daughter" that "we older girls who stay to care for parents, nurse the sick ones, take over just a little more of the home burdens, do it all so gradually none of the others notice how feeble the parents are growing or how expenses must be cut down. Every day comes the thought, will this home be ours long – one day more, one year, or by reason of great strength will father be spared us ten years, and what then? The horrors of an auction sale, no home, little money! Can we find a job? Can we stand it to live in a house that isn't a home? How such questions can haunt a woman by the time she reaches forty."[107] Elizabeth McCutcheon, in her article "The Single Woman in the Country[:] Can the Spinster Remain on the Farm and be Independent?," declared that dependence is "a thing which every self-respecting woman shuns." She told the story of her Aunt Mary, a "country spinster," who for years was imposed upon by her sisters and brothers to care for their children and clean their homes. When elderly, Aunt Mary, like other unmarried farm women who were "expected to serve without recompense," could claim no assets of her own, and was forced to rely on others. McCutcheon then compared Aunt Mary to Flora, who was also a spinster, but who lived in the city and worked as a nurse. Like Aunt Mary, she was asked by her married sisters to care for ill children, but, although she was no more competent at childcare than Aunt Mary, "her sisters have not the face to ask her to drop her work and come to their assistance ... without recompense. They expect to pay her regular salary, and Flora expects to get it, and does." In contrasting rural and urban scenarios, McCutcheon's story underscores the country spinster's vulnerable status at the hands of her self-serving family. The story also points to the fact that country spinsters were not solely those who declined offers of marriage in favour of "self-sacrificing devotion to their parents"; they also serviced the needs of their married siblings, and managed the homes of bachelor or widowed brothers. McCutcheon asked "if those who choose this self-sacrificing sphere are not paid for their labor, what have they ahead of them? ... When old and helpless, their existence may be a continual misery because of the ingratitude of those whom they have served."[108]

This ingratitude was no more profoundly expressed to the devoted and overworked spinster daughter than in the pages of her father's will which unjustly and consistently provided far better for the farmer's son than for his daughter. In an article entitled "A Plea for Farmers' Daughters," J.R. Black explained that "where the property is disposed by will, the common practice is to give more to the boys than the girls. Indeed, the cases in a neighborhood are not so rare as to be regarded as strange where a testator in a bequest aggregating several thousand dollars, leaves a hundred only to each of the daughters, while to each son is bequeathed an amount requiring four figures to express it."[109] Indeed, "A Farmer's Daughter" wrote that she knew of "one case where a daughter came home and tended her father for years, giving him every loving attention, and when he died he left his daughter one hundred dollars, and the son a farm and stock worth thousands."[110]

The son's favoured treatment was further highlighted by his wife's share of the pot. Mrs M.C. Dawson relayed the story of farm daughter Mary, "a good faithful girl," who, as the eldest in the family, carried the burden of work for most of her thirty-five years. Her father's will provided her with only $100 and a cow, while her brother John received the farm, and "John's wife has the comfortable home which John's mother and John's sisters helped so materially to earn. Mary can live with John and care for his babies or go out to service. This is one thing about the average farmer that I can never understand. Why does he prefer to see some other man's daughter well provided for than to see that his own daughter has a home and a means of support?"[111] Dawson and others recognized that wives in this case, despite their precarious financial status, were economically privileged by the institution of marriage as compared to those farm daughters who never married at all – women who were essentially penalized for not aligning themselves with men.

Some contended that the entire system of gendered inheritance was "all wrong," for farm daughters contributed as meaningfully as did sons to the success of the farm.[112] The farm girl, therefore, should not be kept at home, noted one embittered daughter, "working and earning a farm for the boys."[113] With little or no provisions made for the daughter in her father's will, farm daughters asked "and what of the girl? She is left wholly defenseless. … She must either marry or go to a factory or domestic service. … Think of the shame and disgrace of being forced into a marriage for the sake of a home. Can anyone imagine a worse fate?" They suggested that if fathers "cannot leave their daughters enough to keep them, they should at least take a little and provide them with the means of learning some life-work. … the daughter could in time come to be a credit to her parents, instead of, as is often the case, being a stranded wreck on the shores of time."[114]

Both farm wives and daughters did more than lament their mistreatment by farm men. Wives, for example, employed various strategies to guarantee that they exerted influence and agency on the farm. Given that mutuality best served the security of farm women, some of these strategies were more moderate than others, but all of them challenged the patriarchal conventions that governed family and farm. While shared decision-making about all aspects of the farm was rare, for instance, most farm women ensured that they governed virtually all of the decisions in the home.[115] Goderich-area resident Marjorie Jean Pentland "heard it said that if you're driving through the country and you see a barn and all the out-buildings in real good condition and painted up, well, the man is the boss there. But if it's the house that's all in good condition, well, it's the woman that's the boss on that farm."[116]

This is not to say, however, that women lacked influence in other areas. In fact, when their opinions differed from those of their husbands, women employed clever strategies to get their own way. Kenneth Cragg remembered, for example, that when his mother disagreed with her husband over the sale of a cow, and he protested before a farmhand that "her place was in the house," she "really rebelled," and went on strike: "she didn't come out when the next load came in and father seemed surprised. She didn't go out to help with the milking and by this time father caught on. Neither said anything about mother's strike, but father gave in first. The second day, at noon, he said, kind of casually, that he had decided to keep the cow, and mother her face saved, helped that night with the milking. It was a heady experience a woman of lesser calibre might have taken advantage of. Not mother. She had a new knowledge of power and content."[117] Galt-area farm daughter Jessie Beattie recalled that while farmers "held the purse," often it was women "who made the final decisions as to what should be bought." Jessie's mother ensured this by seemingly "seeking his [her husband's] approval, and allowing him to do the ordering." If her parents disagreed on what should be purchased, her father "was usually submissive if Mother protested."[118]

Farm women were often consulted about the borrowing and spending of money, partly because they held the job of bookkeepers on the farm.[119] Accordingly, they were often the first to seek help when financial problems struck. Ethel, a financially troubled mother of one, consulted her doctor when her husband rebelled against the demands of farm work.[120] Destitute farm wife Mrs Stewart Nolan of Chadwick, without her husband's knowledge, wrote to Prime Minister Bennett in 1935, informing him of her family's illnesses and requesting that he send directly to her " 'anything in Parcel or money.' "[121]

The decision-making powers and influence of farm wives, however, did not alleviate their undervalued status in the home, a problem which invited a variety of solutions. One idea was for women not to get married, a somewhat radical notion given that they were raised to anticipate marriage. In an article entitled "Independence for the

Daughters," "A Farmer's Daughter" declared that "all girls do not care to marry, although the men profess to doubt the assertion."[122] The "doubt" of the men underscored the modernity of this option for women, and the extent to which men disbelieved the desire of some women to live independently of them.

Another solution that farm wives discussed was divorce. It was an issue about which they expressed a surprising degree of support. At a literary club debate ouside Sarnia which addressed whether or not "divorces are detrimental to Humanity," the affirmative won only thirty-nine to thirty-four, a close margin given the rarity of divorce at this time.[123] Kenneth Cragg remembered that his mother "was motivated deep down by a militant conviction that men were no good. In later years it colored deeply her attitude to divorce, so that, to the amazement of some, she had the conviction that grounds for divorce should be broadened to include anything that would give good and sound reason for a legal separation. 'Why not,' she would argue with simple clarity, 'get rid of them once and for all? There isn't a man alive worth what women have to go through.' "[124] In 1896, Mrs Bavin filed for divorce because her husband, "an affluent farmer," had frequently assaulted her over a thirteen-year span. When the judge in the case ruled that Mrs Bavin not receive alimony because she had condoned the violence (by continuing to live with her husband whose violence she at times forgave), she successfully appealed the ruling.[125]

In very rare cases, farm wives remedied severe mistreatment at the hands of their men by resorting to murder. The stress and hardship of farm life, and the alcoholism among farm men which these conditions sometimes spawned, created an environment ripe for wife abuse.[126] As Kate Aitken knew, a farmer could be "a stern [and] forbidding ... man," with a "heavy-handed over-all authority that made life almost unbearable."[127] In one combative marriage of an older farmer and his neighbour's daughter, the woman retaliated. One year, she uncharacteristically marked his birthday with an elaborate homemade cake. The following day, the farmer was dead. While he reportedly died of a heart attack, the community suspected the wife of his murder: the druggist recalled her buying strychnine to poison the rats in the barn, and the doctor recollected that he had been called to the scene rather late, whereupon he noticed the corpse had been washed and the bedding changed. With gossip circulating among her neighbours, the coroner ordered an inquest. A jury of farmers examined the case, which was soon after dropped and largely forgotten.[128]

Agency among farm wives found expression not only in their condemnation and attempted alleviation of overwork and marriage troubles, but also in their efforts at birth control – while farm women generally prized motherhood, believing it their true and God-given role,[129] their patterns of childbirth gave them reason for pause. Although overburdened farm wives knew that more babies meant more work for women in particular, they were generally inclined toward large families.[130] In Dufferin County, for example, farm families at the turn of the century averaged more than ten children.[131] Women, accordingly, experienced successive pregnancies well into their forties. Orison Howe's wife, for example, had twelve children less than two years apart, with two sets of twins among them.[132] Beatrice Snyder's grandmother bore so many children that the last of them were born when her older children were having babies of their own.[133]

Not uncommonly, farm women became pregnant long after the birth of their presumed last child. One day in 1896, doctors told forty-two-year-old Mrs Beattie that she suffered from a stomach tumor. Two weeks later they determined she was pregnant. She had previously given birth to six children, two of whom had died as toddlers. Her two sons were about twenty years of age and her two daughters were fifteen and eleven when her seventh and last child Jessie was born.[134] Mrs Howe, a neighbour of Mrs Beattie, became pregnant with her thirteenth child ten years following the birth of her second set of twins.[135]

Situations such as these prompted more married women than single women, by one account, to consider abortion, an illegal option of last resort.[136] Mrs Howe revealed her desperate situation when she lamented to Mrs Beattie "'ten years and I thought I was finished. I'm not. *And I don't want it.*'"[137] Mrs Howe carried through with the pregnancy,[138] but Lucknow doctor William Johnston knew of many women in his Bruce County practice who did not. Johnston remembered that, as abortion was neither legally nor morally sanctioned, women often underwent the procedure in distant locales: "a farmer's wife, thirty years old, was pregnant for the third time. She had two robust sons in their teens at home and she didn't want another child. … In spite of my advice of caution, she insisted that she have an operation somewhere and if necessary would go to Detroit. … She did."[139] Dr Johnston also recalled that "another farmer's wife with several children came in with the same request. On my refusal to assist, she declared her determination to interrupt the pregnancy and had already decided to call on a doctor some forty miles away who had a well-known reputation as an abortionist. … The abortion had been performed."[140] Refused abortions by Dr Johnston, some women might have been just as happy to seek them elsewhere for fear that their plan would be impeded by contesting husbands, disparaging family, and gossiping neighbours, and in order to inhibit the discovery of the procedure by those (possibly husbands) who had been kept in the dark.

Dr Johnston's rural practice indicates that farm wives sought abortions with some frequency. Having refused one woman "pleading to be rid of her unwanted child," Dr Johnston gave her iron pills to help reverse her anemia. When she suffered a miscarriage several days later, he remembered that "within a month no less than three women from different localities asked for tablets similar to those I gave Mrs. S. to bring on her abortion."[141]

Not all women relied on doctors when they desired abortions. With the assistance of family, some oversaw the procedure themselves. Dr Johnston recalled that "an emergency call at daybreak ... took me to a farm home seven miles into the country. The mother of two children was in shock for a miscarriage at seven months. She was as white as a sheet and gasping for breath at intervals. Her life was in danger from loss of blood. ... It looked suspiciously like deliberate interference by someone."[142] Dr Johnston conceded, however, that rarely could he determine "whether the miscarriage was accidental or induced. The women wouldn't talk." What characterized those women who desired abortions, concluded Dr Johnston, regardless of the method, was "their coolly calculated willingness to resort to desperate measures even at the risk of their lives."[143] It is unclear whether Dr Johnston perceived this quality positively or not, and it certainly did not matter; these farm women knew that action, no matter how dangerous, or how contrary to legal and social dictates, was necessary to their own sense of personal welfare and agency.

Women were very much aware that childbirth for them could be just as risky to their health.[144] Mary Tom, the matriarch of the Good family at the turn of the century, bitterly opposed the prospect of her five daughters marrying, possibly because "she was terrified of childbirth (she had certainly had plenty of grim experience with it), and hated to think of it for her daughters." In September of 1909, her son's wife Jennie almost died giving birth to a stillborn baby.[145] It is little wonder that those women who experienced easy births, like Dr Johnston's patient who a day after childbirth was up milking the cow, could be the object of envy and awe by others.[146]

It was the fear of childbirth, whether difficult or not (as well as abortion, no doubt), that often moved women to initiate preventative birth control efforts. Dr Johnston recollected two women who "refused to become pregnant again" because of arduous first labours.[147] Jessie Beattie alluded to the abstinence practiced by her forty-six-year-old mother who by 1900 had borne seven chidren: "there was a brief period following my birth when I believed that my mother may have been affected by fear of another conception. During this time, I was aware of an altered relationship between my parents. Could this have been the effect of my mother's state of mind? In recollection, it appears to be a natural explanation for her cooling attentions to my father and a withdrawal into herself which was apparent even to a small child."[148] Although abstinence strained the Beattie marriage, Mrs Beattie felt compelled to assert control over her own sexuality and reproductive fate.

The successive and strenuous pregnancies of farm women necessitated that much of their domestic work be shouldered by older daughters – a burden that prompted many young women to leave the farm. Mrs Tomin, for example, bore thirteen children, one about every fifteen months. As she was always pregnant or convalescing, her daughter Roxie, by the time she married in 1912, had "raised more kids than my mother did."[149] Many daughters in Roxie's place, who witnessed or bore the burden of their mother's lot, and whose families could eventually spare them, had every intention of leaving the farm for new opportunities elsewhere. Indeed, between 1900 and 1910 alone, 205,000 young people in Ontario left the countryside for the city, and most of these were women.[150] By 1914, men outnumbered women in rural Ontario by 86,000, leaving bachelors struggling to find brides.[151] This mass migration of daughters from the land also left mothers bereft of household help, which further contributed to their drudgery. If finances allowed, they employed a hired girl who was most often a neighbouring farm daughter who had not yet migrated or married.[152]

Overwhelmingly, those daughters who left the farm sought in the city, if only temporarily, the privacy, money, and sociability that they were deprived of on the farm.[153] While the domestic service, factory, clerical, and sales jobs which the city offered were often no more satisfying than farm work, they were less physically taxing, and, because they were urban-centred, held the promise of wages, independence, new friends, and excitement.[154]

Daughters who aspired to higher education and professional careers, incompatible with the routine of farm life, were also among those who left for the city. They were likely influenced by the rhetoric of the club and suffrage movements, by talk of the "new woman," and by their contemporaries pursuing careers of their own. Jessie Beattie remembered, for example, that in 1914, her sister Lillian's "success as a career woman [as a hospital dietician] had brought to our attention the need to consider a similar opportunity for [elder sister] Jean." Jean's decision to cultivate a career was in fact influenced by her stay with female cousins in California who were teaching school and studying music.[155]

Mothers and aunts did not seem adverse to daughters' plans to leave for an education and career. They supported the modern view that "farmers' daughters should receive the best education possible,"[156] and hoped, likely because of their own limited opportunities, that "the country girl will get more education in the future than she has had in the past."[157] Quoting her best friend Louise, Lillian Beattie declared to her mother that " 'we'll never get anywhere if we stay in this old dump [the village].' " When Lillian's mother asked her daughter what career she wanted to pursue, "one could see that she had expected opposition from Mother and was taken by surprise."[158] The Good family assumed in the 1890s that "Tom Good's daughters were to be educated for professions," and their Aunt Clara "repeatedly wrote her 'dear girls' at Myrtleville, that they must stick to their studies, and avoid all the difficulties she had had in earning a living."[159] When Anne Henry began nurse's training in 1910, her mother "was very much in favour of it," while her father "wasn't so keen."[160] Similarly, Beth Latzer wrote that when she enrolled at the University of Toronto in 1932, her mother "who had not gone to college, was as determined as I was that I should go; my father protested mildly that I could educate myself at home."[161]

Daughters who aspired to careers were determined in their goals. Jessie Beattie, for example, knew that she would "become an author at all costs."[162] Lucinda Allendorf of the Kitchener region, first an apprentice seamstress and then manager of her own dress shop, turned down two marriage proposals before the age of thirty-three because she was intent on becoming a "business girl."[163]

Like most progressive career women during the first part of the century, farm daughters pursued careers in fields that generally conformed to feminine codes of behaviour.[164] Teaching was the most common career for farm daughters, proving attractive because in addition to there being a teaching shortage early last century, training was not overly costly to fund.[165] Moreover, within farming communities, a woman schoolteacher, while poorly paid and subjected to trying working conditions and little privacy, "was always considered a good catch."[166] In 1904, two of the five Good sisters (Fanny and Ethel) attended Ontario Normal College in Hamilton, and graduated in 1905. That same year, a third sister, Louisa, took a short course in teaching at Moyle's School in Toronto. In 1909, a fourth sister, Carol, also attended a teaching short course.[167] Farm daughters who aspired to be musicians also set their sights on teaching. Family and farm obligations would prevent a regretful Louise Ritz from attending normal school, but she took piano and organ training in Kitchener, and received her diploma in 1922. She had practiced ten hours a day, squeezing in her farm and domestic work, but refusing to do any labour which could damage her usually protected gloved hands.[168] After 1922, she launched her career teaching piano in Baden, ouside of Kitchener. Her teaching led to positions playing piano and organ at silent movie theatres, at Sunday morning church services, at Women's Institutes meetings and conventions, and at numerous weddings and funerals.[169]

Nursing, which the National Council of Women deemed "important work," and "so essentially a work for women," also attracted farm daughters.[170] Janet McPherson of Bruce County, for example, wished very much to become a nurse, and in the 1920s only took a job as a hired girl for a bachelor because she had the opportunity to care for his elderly mother. Janet always regretted that she never pursued professional training, although she did take nursing courses through the Women's Institutes and the Red Cross.[171] Anne Henry began nurse's training at Guelph General Hospital in 1910, and after graduating in 1913, she enlisted in the army and served as a nurse in England. She eventually settled in New York, and, never marrying, nursed there for forty years.[172] Feeling dissatisfied with teaching in the summer of 1911, Carol Good enrolled in nurse's training at the Brantford General Hospital, and eventually graduated at the top of her class in 1919.[173]

Bookkeeping was also a female-dominated career that attracted farm daughters.[174] Unlike those girls whom one article urged to do "Bookkeeping for Papa,"[175] Emma Johnston attended business college "to get out and see something more." She left the domestic and barn work of her father's 900-acre farm near Wingham for a position in Toronto as a shorthand clerk, and later worked as a bookkeeper at a local creamery. Jobs such as bookkeeping, which for some were temporary distractions from farm life, and for others long-held ambitions, enabled farm daughters, loath to replicate their mothers' lives, to avoid burdensome domestic work on the farm. Indeed, asked why when in the city Emma avoided domestic work, she replied "If I wanted that I could [have] stay[ed] home."[176]

Plagued by drudgery and the devaluation of their labour, farm women were neither equals, nor martyrs, nor mad. They were dissatisfied workers who, as the wives and daughters of the male farm owners who undermined them, felt the sting of their oppression all that more keenly. The intimacy which characterized this work arrangement meant that farm women, who articulated their concerns about a variety of problems, were obliged to combat their oppression with much care and finesse, and in clever and resourceful ways. They indicate that while farm women were duty-bound to the needs of the farm, this obligation did not preclude their demand for dignity, opportunity, and fairness. This appeal garnered sympathy among female contributors to the agricultural press, who publicized the plight of both farm wife and daughter – a plight which finally drove many daughters to leave. But it was the domestic science movement and the Women's Institutes which forcefully took up the farm woman's cause, and transformed it into an organized and widespread lobby for change.

4 "We old-fashioned folk do not put enough science into our domestic lives": Home Economics and the Inception of Macdonald Institute and the WI

The home economics movement which pervaded North America at the turn of the century addressed the nature of women's work in the domestic sphere. Home economics arose from women's increasing dissatisfaction in the home, the veneration of all things scientific, and a mood of social and educational reform, and it grew into an influential movement embraced by professionals and homemakers alike.[1] For Ontario farm women, its emissary was Adelaide Hoodless, Canada's leading advocate of home economics, who conceptualized the field as a female-centred and separatist study that would elevate the quality of women's professional and domestic lives. The feminized character of domestic science appealed to farm women who had long valued female networks and rituals. Hoodless delivered her brand of domestic science to farm women by helping to establish Macdonald Institute at the Ontario Agricultural College in 1903, and by launching the Women's Institutes in 1897. The social feminist ideas of Hoodless and the home economics movement captured the imagination of progressive farm daughters and wives who responded to Macdonald Institute and the WI in the century's early years with a vision to bettering themselves, and the lot of farm women as a whole.

Instruction of women in the household arts had existed for some time. Religious and philanthropic organizations throughout the nineteenth century had provided training in domestic skills to young working-class women in the hopes of imbuing their homes with order and virtue, and of grooming qualified domestic servants for the middle-class.[2] By the turn of the century, however, urban married middle-class women, confined and isolated in the private sphere, and left sole custodians of the home, were also thought in need of domestic instruction. Economically dependent on husbands, most conformed to the expectations of their sex: they bore babies, reared children, and performed mundane household work. Homemaking marked women's days, but lacked the worth and regard accorded women's pre-industrial domestic production, as well as its diversity and creative flavour.

The home economics movement of the early twentieth century, which catered largely to these middle-class wives, as well as to their career-minded, single, middle-class sisters, differed from the earlier, religiously inspired efforts. It sought "to integrate the ethics of the home with the economics of the market,"[3] and thus claimed a more theoretical and systematic approach to domestic labour. "Economics" denoted, as in business and industry, the expedient "use of time, money, or energy," and was intended to convey the mutuality and similarity of the home and market, and their need for corresponding management techniques. These strategies were rooted in the laws and principles of the natural and social sciences which were revered as thoroughly modern, functional disciplines, and which were regarded by home economists as pertinent, indeed imperative, to the efficient operation of the home.[4]

The priority of home economics reformers was scientific research into housing, clothes, and diet that could serve to elevate standards of physical, as well as mental and moral health.[5] Physics, chemistry, and biology were the mandatory courses for most upper level home economics programs, although other fields of study included hygiene, economics, sociology, and history.[6] All were to be examined through the prism of the home, a perspective that promoted an ethical, pragmatic, and women-centred approach to knowledge.[7]

This perspective was in reaction to a new culture of knowledge that was increasingly abandoning the late nineteenth-century woman. She was " 'outstripped by new knowledge, ... [and] was less able to cope with what it produced. A new culture was emerging – a cosmetic, mechanical culture created by man's exploitation of advancing knowledge. By detaching woman from its new processes and functions, he was creating a new environment with new human values in which the female's point of view was missing.' "[8] Moreover, men claimed that this male-centred system which venerated science was inherently objective and neutral.[9] The home economics movement of the early twentieth century, dismayed by this neglect of female priorities, necessarily recognized what feminist Dale Spender would elucidate in 1981: " 'the invisibility of women is ... a structural problem which has been built into the production of knowledge. Because it has been primarily men who have determined parameters, who have decided what would be problematic, significant, logical and reasonable, not only have women been excluded from the process but the process itself can reinforce the 'authority' of men and the 'deficiency' of women.' "[10] Home economics was the first women-centred field of academic study, calling for women to formulate knowledge for and about themselves. In so doing, it challenged the assumption that women were anti-intellectual, and inept or disinterested in science, and belied the notion that science was objective.[11]

Home economists shared several basic and related convictions. They believed that women bore the primary responsibility for the home; that women were disadvantaged because the home was devalued; that the home was the true guardian of one's "moral and physical" health; that formal education was essential for social change; and perhaps most importantly, that the status and nature of women's household work, both paid and unpaid, needed to be upgraded.[12] Homemakers, it was agreed, then, required homes designed and built from a female perspective, with women's efficiency, time, and safety in mind; a scientific education to remedy their ignorance and the drudgery of their work; time and energy to pursue opportunities for self-betterment; elevated status for the private sphere and the labour performed within it; and recognition that they created "human capital" in their reproductive, caretaking, and "connectiveness" functions.[13]

Yet, as reformers varied widely in age, education level, occupation, class allegiance, political conviction, club membership, and nationality, the home economics movement promoted what could be regarded as contradictory tenets: the movement espoused both ethics and economics; practice and theory; liberal individualism and cooperative housework; woman's role as producer and her job as consumer; her beautification of the home and the evils of excess; her obligation to her family and her right to a career; and her woman-centred studies and her education alongside men. As well, it promoted the instruction of servants for proficiency on the job and the training of wives to replace them; technology's ability to decrease household work and its dangerous hold over housewives; and its role as champion of tradition and as advocate for change.[14]

Whatever their ideological conflicts, however, domestic science reformers were united in their resolve to protect and affirm female interests. As a "woman's movement," home economics, like the suffrage cause, sought "emancipatory goals for women."[15] Unlike suffragists, however, who pursued power via the public male world of politics, home economists, recognizing that women endured more than political inequity, sought access to power through knowledge – knowledge which women could selectively adopt to meet their everyday needs, and which could fortify the private sphere of the home. As such, while other women's rights campaigns appropriated the standards, values, and tactics of men, home economics, although inspired by male-defined economics and science, was resolutely women-centred, and an expression of "women's activism" on behalf of their domestic and family concerns.[16]

To deny home economics its feminist character is to ignore the fact that many of the issues that preoccupy contemporary feminist activists have been consistently explored by home economists since the turn of the century. These issues include domestic labour and child care, and the systemic problems of female subordination, exploitation, exclusion, and neglect.[17] Patricia J. Thompson advises that home economists today "would do well to note that where the feminist shoe fits, they should wear it!"[18]

Adelaide Hoodless, Canada's foremost home economics promoter, was born Adelaide Sophia Hunter in St George, Brant County, on 27 February 1858. One of twelve children in an Irish Presbyterian farm family, her father died shortly before her birth. She attended the local rural school and a ladies college, but never received a university education. In 1881 she married John Hoodless, an affluent furniture manufacturer in Hamilton, with whom she had four children.[19] Tragically, Hoodless's youngest child died as a toddler from consuming contaminated milk, and it was this misfortune in 1889 that inspired her to promulgate the cause of domestic science and hygiene.[20]

Hoodless became active in a variety of volunteer organizations in which she promoted domestic science, most notably the National Council of Women and the YWCA. In 1893, she helped establish a Council of Women branch in Hamilton, and then assumed the post of the National Council's first treasurer until 1901. She sat on the executive of the organization until 1908, presiding over its Home Economics Committee. Between 1890 and 1902, Hoodless was also president of the Hamilton YWCA. Under Hoodless, the facility offered extension education classes in homemaking which trained some of the city's young and poor female factory workers in cooking, sewing, and housekeeping. Hoodless' association with these working-class women proved cursory, however; her true ambition was to establish a teacher-training centre in domestic science.[21]

Initially, Hoodless equated "domestic science" for girls and "manual training" for boys, simply reasoning that the manual training of girls should find expression through domestic work, given their future position as homemakers. For poorer young women, the purpose of domestic science education was three-fold: to instill upstanding qualities, such as a strong work ethic, organization, and loyalty; to produce good cooks who could entice husbands to stay at home, and thus keep families intact; and to create, as an alternative to over-crowded factory and clerical work, a traditional female labour pool of skilled milliners, dressmakers, and especially domestic servants, who by the end of the nineteenth century were in short supply.[22] Hoodless tirelessly asserted that these women were entitled to a vocational ed-ucation that would ensure them a living wage. She argued that do-mestic science for girls, and to a lesser extent other areas of technical training, had to be given preference over industrial arts for boys, as fewer than one-third of girls entered high school, and too many of those who did not (one-half to three-quarters) obtained factory jobs. She felt that trade schools should be established " 'to put into the hands of every girl the knowledge and skill so that she might enter a clean, healthy, profitable employment, for which she has a natural ap-titude.' "[23]

By 1900, however, Hoodless approached domestic science with consideration for the uncertain status of middle-class women.[24] Hoodless, like many domestic science reformers, believed that their position had been undermined both by industrialization and an infe-rior educational system. According to Hoodless and others, industri-alization usurped the sanctified role of women in the domestic sphere by promoting the emergence of factories, consumerism, and the dis-tinction between the private and public realms. With men as the pri-mary wage-earners in the workplace, and with the mass availability of goods their wages could buy, women were robbed of their once pivotal role as domestic producers in the family economy. They were now consumers, who were disengaged from their homes and who bothered less – and simply knew too little – to communicate home-making advice to their daughters. The outcome was that daughters, who perceived no opportunities in the household arts, looked to fac-tories and offices for work – places, believed Hoodless, which threat-ened women's physical and moral health. Hoodless maintained that for society generally, the erosion of women's domestic role, and the breakdown of the family which necessarily followed, meant moral decay, an increase in crime, and a climbing divorce rate.[25]

Hoodless argued that the education system had also failed women. It "represented a male-defined education which was antithetical to women, denigrated a domestic role by ignoring it, discounted expe-riential learning by institutionalizing knowledge, and established a hierarchy which alienated women in traditional roles from their edu-cated daughters and peers."[26] The intellectual and theoretical bent of traditional, male education needed to be modified to make room for more practical instruction relevant to everyday life. For women, this meant an equally challenging but more useful education geared toward homemaking. Instruction in mathematics, for example, would address household monies and grocery budgets, and would therefore instill proficiency in both the finer points of math and home management. Domestic science, argued Hoodless, encompassed elements from each and every subject, and thus was the ultimate achievement in higher learning.[27]

For middle-class young women, then, domestic science education proved a lofty calling. At its best, domestic science was about much more than character building, the preparation of meals, and manual training for paid labour; it was a systematic approach to the "scientific" matters of the home: nutrition, ventilation, time management, economics, citizenship, disease prevention, sanitation, and health care.[28] Such an approach was not the cause of women's waning traditional folk knowledge, but a necessary response to it. By rationalizing domestic labour, Hoodless sought to raise the status of the work that women did. She maintained that the " 'aim of the Domestic Science movement was to secure for women's work equal consideration with man's work,' " in order that women would cease to be " 'the drudge of the family.' "[29]

The disparity in Hoodless's vision of domestic science as practiced by working-class women and by middle-class women reveals her own middle-class allegiance. The career options of millinery, dressmaking, and domestic service that she outlined for working-class women would clearly benefit those members of her own social standing who could afford such services, and who had for a long time expressed a demand for them. Hoodless had little regard for the fact that these traditional areas of female employment often proved the most exploitive for women.[30] But she also never considered that the elevated status that she envisioned for middle-class housewives encouraged their vulnerability as unpaid workers, their isolation and arduous work within the privatized domestic sphere, and their tenuous position within the patriarchal nuclear family. As well, her scenario did not allow for unmarried women's access to education and professions beyond the confines of domestic science, whose reputation, because of its female and practical orientation, would remain inferior to that of the traditional science disciplines.

As such, the question of Hoodless's feminism generates disagreement among her biographers. In 1952, Mary E. Whelan insisted that Hoodless had been "in no sense a feminist," and thirty-eight years later, historian John Weaver agreed that "the modern label of feminist hardly applies to Adelaide Hoodless."[31] Historian Robert Stamp, however, justifiably proclaims Hoodless a "Champion of Women's Rights," and author Cheryl MacDonald refers to her as "an important figure in Canadian feminism."[32] In fact, premised as it was on the primacy of the home, and the valuable work of women within it, Hoodless's seemingly conservative brand of feminism was generally not unlike that of most early twentieth-century women activists:[33] "even the most rebellious of Canadian feminists was reluctant to deny her primary responsibility for the preservation and well-being of her home."[34]

Indeed, Hoodless was often derided by her contemporaries for her "extremism." Although at least one critic thought her outlook obsolete, and felt that she had "very little regard for the precious, up-to-date, twentieth-century girl,"[35] Hoodless, for the most part, was branded a "radical" and a "new woman" by the press, and was accused of forsaking her family in favour of her work. Patricia Saidak describes Hoodless as having been "vilified" for "violating the passive, submissive conventions expected of her sex."[36]

There is irony in the fact that Hoodless espoused the virtues of domesticity while pursuing such a noteworthy career, for she truly believed, as did other home economics reformers of her time, that the locus of women's influence and power rested primarily in the home – not in public life – and especially not in the attainment of suffrage.[37] As one newspaper explained upon her death in 1910, "she knew that though women had no votes and never got them[,] they could secure all the power, all the privileges they desired, by queening it in the household."[38]

Hoodless did acknowledge the possibility of women's role in politics, but insisted that it was women's lack of education, and their devalued status in the home – not the inaccessibility of the vote – which prevented their more meaningful influence in public life.[39] Hoodless noted that " 'any girl or woman who has been brought face to face with the great truths presented through a properly graded course in domestic science and Home Economics in its wider interpretation,' " would, in fact, feel little need to " 'be found in the ranks of the suffragettes.' "[40] This ardent anti-suffragism has no doubt contributed to the perception of Hoodless as anti-feminist, but at least one admirer in 1910 recognized this faulty correlation: "Her life and character and achievements are a rebuke to those weaker and lesser sisters who hold that woman, in order to be truly useful, must obtain political equality with men."[41]

Indeed, Hoodless arguably held "radical separatist beliefs."[42] They included her conviction that women were defined by their sex, and that experience was as crucial a consideration as intellect when formulating theory.[43] Hoodless' separatism was also evident in her belief that men should be excluded from the discipline of home economics, specifically as home economics "experts" in their capacity as administrators and supervisors of curriculum and courses.[44] According to Hoodless, "education has been organized from a man's point of view, and everyone knows that it is utterly impossible for a man to see a question from the same point as a woman."[45] She maintained that " 'school boards are not reliable enough, made up as they are of all sorts and conditions of men to trust to arrange a course in Domestic Science,' " and that " 'it is woman's work and must have women associated in its development.' "[46] Not surprisingly, Hoodless's Ontario Normal School of Domestic Science and Art was managed by an exclusively female staff.[47] Perhaps most significantly, she saw men as appropriating the cause once it garnered success, and resented the higher salaries that they received, as well as the goals that they were given room to accomplish.[48] She wrote in 1901 that " 'it seems hard that women have to fight for every inch of justice for their work, and when men ask for a thing it is granted without our side being so much as consulted.' "[49] While middle-class women activists did solicit the requisite male support for the domestic science movement, this pursuit "did not obviate their own objectives or obscure the anti-masculist feelings of women like ... Hoodless. ... If their social position and/or education gave these women vested class interests, it also gave them access to insights about the abuse of power by middle-class males."[50]

In the late 1890s, despite the movement's apparent urban bias, Hoodless delivered her home economics message to rural women. The problem of women's declining status as domestic producers was less a rural than urban trend at this time, and the promotion of separate spheres had little relevance on the farm, where the farmer and his wife both laboured, and where farm women compromised their unpaid domestic pursuits with some farming and income-producing work. Nevertheless, in December of 1896, Hoodless gave a speech to the Ontario Agricultural College in Guelph entitled "The Relation of Domestic Science to the Agricultural Population." In it, she articulated the right of farm wives to formal instruction in domestic science, and to modern appliances in the home: "and now that our Legislative bodies are giving attention to the question of providing scientific training for the farmers, it is only a natural sequence, that something should be done for the farmer's wives and daughters. ... Is it of greater importance that a farmer should know more about the scientific care of his sheep and cattle, than that a farmer's wife should know how to care for her family, or that his barns should have every labour saving contrivance, while she toils and drudges on in the same old treadmill instituted by her grandmother."[51] Hoodless also advocated that farm daughters, like their urban sisters, were entitled to a university education. She argued that they should be taught not the same material as men, but " 'on the same level as men, the principles of horticulture, dairying, poultry production, and learn also of bacteriology and the chemistry of the soil.' "[52] As the first three branches of agriculture were the traditional domain of the farmer's wife, Hoodless's vision was generally in keeping with both her own domestic science priorities and the realities of rural life. By 1897, Hoodless had been quoted in a newspaper as insisting that " 'the Agricultural College at Guelph must be thrown open to the young women on the same terms as to the men. There is no reason why the young people of our sex should not be taught there.' "[53]

In February of 1897, Hoodless also addressed a small group of Stoney Creek farm wives at a special meeting of the Farmers' Institute (FI), a government-sponsored agency which apprised farmers of new and efficient agricultural techniques. She was invited by Erland Lee, an organizer within the FI, who had heard Hoodless speak in Guelph about the death of her son due to impure milk, and about her campaign to elevate the standards and station of homemaking. Hoodless urged the farm wives to create the more needed female equivalent of the FI – an educational and social association which could facilitate formal instruction in modern, systematic approaches to homemaking.[54] Hoodless's suggestion was indeed provocative, especially given that the government, which had always conceptualized farming as male, had hitherto funded only men's agricultural training and education programs.

Hoodless premised the need for this organization on the apparent isolation of farm women whom she believed were typically deprived of opportunities for education and sociability. She reasoned that " 'the natural tendency, when people are isolated, as they are more or less on the farm, is to sluggish indifference. This tendency is more pronounced in the case of women than men, because the women are largely confined to the home, while men do get out in the fields and on the roads. For this reason there is more presising [*sic*] need for the organization of institutes for women than there is for like organizations among the men. The value of the intellectual quickening and social influences of such an institution on the women of the farm cannot be over-estimated.' "[55] In her effort to sell the idea of a domestic science women's group in rural Ontario, however, Hoodless might have exaggerated the solitude of farm women, for it was precisely because the potential for isolation was so great in the lives of farm women and men that both were mindful of their domestic, kin, and community ties. Women assumed the primary responsibility for cultivating these interconnected relations, and perhaps due to the androcentrism of rural life, likely cherished same-sex company more profoundly than did men.[56] Linda Ambrose points out that "the value" which rural Ontario women accorded female friendships "cannot be over-stated."[57] The united effort by farm wives and daughters to sustain these family and friendship networks created "intimate ties among women,"[58] and nourished the sense of specificity, solidarity, and sep-aratism that facilitated, not derived from, the home economics move-ment and the establishment of the WI.

Farm women participated in distinctly female activities, and con-tinued the women-centred rituals of their mothers and grandmoth-ers. These most often revolved around the church women's auxiliary, which devoted much time to sewing and quilting.[59] Mrs T.H. Bass confirmed in 1912 that "it is not good for women to live without soci-ety altogether. … It must be an extremely scattered community that cannot support a Sewing Circle."[60] The church sewing and quilting bee, an exclusively female activity, was a welcome (and socially ac-ceptable) distraction from marriage and home life.[61] It also afforded women the opportunity to exchange local news of particular interest to them: Mrs Nichol Mackie of Cochrane District in northern Ontario remembered the quilting bee as "an important event" because "be-fore telephones were common, the meetings were a channel through which the neighbours spread news."[62] Talk at the bee most often cen-tred on community happenings and homemaking matters, but dis-cussions also tackled political issues of national concern; according to quilt historian Mary Conroy, bees sometimes entertained debate about women's rights and suffrage.[63]

Regardless of what was actually discussed, however, these meet-ings were often thought of as unabashed forums for gossip. Mrs Bass revealed that "sewing circles are spoken of as gossip centres … by the male portion of our community," who, by her inference, perceived gossip unfavourably.[64] That gossip was understood by some as a friv-olous female pursuit belied its constructive socializing, networking, and news-gathering functions, and encouraged the pejorative associ-ation between women and female-specific activities. Ironically, the disparagement of gossip also underscored its power, in that those who felt compelled to degrade it were perhaps those who had most reason to fear it.[65]

Quilting bees were more than an occasion for talk and news: they were also a rite of passage for women new to the community, and for local young girls. Helen Richards Campbell, from Frontenac County, recalled that as a new rural teacher at the start of the century " 'how are you at quilting?' [was] more than a kindly invitation to partici- pate: it was a responsibility tendered on the generous tray of genuine friendship. ... Few teachers living in such a closely knit community could stand idly by and look on. From the feeling of an imposition, we gradually accepted this involvement as a way of life – a privi- leged way of life."[66] When old enough, farm daughters and grand- daughters were also expected to attend the neighbourhood bee. Their placement around the quilt marked their coming-of-age in a specifi- cally female way.[67]

Threshing bees during the autumn months also united women, who together prepared elaborate meals for their husbands and field hands. Kate Aitken, who grew up in Beeton, Simcoe County, remem- bered that "when threshing time came around[,] Mother always went to the Smith Farm to help prepare and serve the enormous meals con- sumed by the threshers."[68] The quantity and quality of the food, and the threshers' enjoyment of it, were a source of collective pride for the farm woman, whose ambition it was "to set such a table as would sat- isfy the hungry men, and send them away saying, 'You should see the meals we had at the Gosley farm.' "[69]

In addition to church and farm gatherings, wedding rituals brought women together. On 14 July 1926, for example, the women of Vyner, near Sarnia, honoured bride-to-be Ethel Hillier with a wed- ding shower, and named her "bride-elect of this month," a title which suggests the frequency with which women met to celebrate this mile- stone together. The town newspaper reported that she was presented with beautiful silverware "which showed the esteem in which Miss Hillier is held."[70] In the days that followed, until the wedding the following week, Ethel noted in her diary that at her parents' home in Plympton Township there was "company all the time."[71]

As Ethel's diaries indicate, there was in rural Ontario, especially among farm women, "a compulsive need to visit."[72] This practice of visiting had its origins in childhood. When Jessie Beattie was con- fined to her home with scarlet fever early in the century, her best friend Tillie arrived every day after school "to flatten her nose against the outside of my window and blow kisses to me."[73] At Myrtleville, the Good farm outside Brantford, both daily and long-term visitors in the early twentieth century were the norm, not the exception. In fact, farm daughter Fanny Good noted in retrospect that her mother's penchant for visitors, and the domestic work that it produced, caused much " 'stress and strain' " at Myrtleville.[74] Sadie O'Keefe of eastern Ontario remembered that two or three families always visited without notice at the end of the week. Women, in particular, O'Keefe noted, "walked many miles to visit friends or relatives."[75] Vera Dahmer remembered that her friend Emily frequently rode her bicycle from nearby Galt to visit and help with the ironing.[76] Women valued female company to such a great extent that those few who rebuffed it were themselves rebuffed. Adult farm daughter Jean Beattie told her father that she hoped the travelling minister "would move away, and stay away. His wife doesn't mix with other women in the community."[77]

Visiting often took the form of long-term stays by the adolescent daughters of female family and friends. During the winter months of 1897, for example, seventeen-year-old Louisa Good lived with the unmarried Wye sisters who were long-time farm friends of her mother.[78] Jessie Beattie recalled that in the early twentieth century, a village girl named Sophia "came and went at our house almost as an extra daughter of the family."[79]

Farm women also cared for each other's children in order to aid new mothers. Mrs Nichol recalled that after a quilting bee early in the century, " 'one of the ladies stopped at the farm where the new baby had arrived and 'borrowed' the next older child for a few days to give the new mother a little help. When the child was 'returned' several days later, he likely had an extra pair of socks, a new pair of hand-knit mittens and perhaps a toy of some kind ... One of the ladies on reaching home, packed a box of homemade bread, fresh butter and a jar or two of homemade pickles and jam to help the new mother in caring for her family.' "[80] In the years after Ernie Morris and Maphilda Lacroix married in 1921, she gave birth at home to six children, all of whom were tended by two women who came to help.[81] Nancy Grey Osterud notes that in nineteenth-century New York State female neighbours "were bound together in intricate networks of mutual assistance."[82] Evidence suggests a similar trend in early twentieth-century Ontario.

Non-farming rural women took their cue from farm women that children and their mothers were the responsibility of a female community. When Jessie Beattie was ill, for example, her teacher's wife arrived to relieve a spent Mrs Beattie, whereupon the guest stayed until dawn.[83] Rural school teacher Helen Richards Campbell was struck by the expectation that while a teacher's day ended by late afternoon, "evenings, Saturdays, and Sundays belonged to the community." Campbell was enlisted for child care and domestic duties: "the first time I was asked to assist at a 'birthing,' I wondered seriously just what was my role in the community. Although I understood the need, I resented, at first, this intrusion into my private world. Knowledge came quickly, albeit harshly. Very soon, I recognized and was very grateful for the compliment." Eventually, Campbell grew accustomed to the community involvement expected of her. When beginning a new school year, she expressly saw each student home, ate dinner with her/his family, and stayed the night.[84]

Farm women went out of their way to assist these community newcomers. Kenneth Cragg remembered that when the new minister's wife dried her risqué silk underclothes on the parsonage clothesline, his mother immediately came to her defence. Over tea, she advised the woman on how to conceal the drying undergarments, and once home, instructed her husband that when in the company of his inquisitive male friends he was to side with the right of the minister's wife to wear what she chose.[85]

The relationship among sisters was especially prized – sisters tended to each other when ill, eased the transition from girlhood to marriage, and provided treasured assistance once children were born. Jessie Beattie remembered that in 1909, when she was a sickly thirteen-year-old and sister Jean was twenty-seven, "Jean slept beside me whenever I was ill, alert to every move which I made on occasions of restlessness." When Jessie entered the Hospital for Sick Children in Toronto that same year, Jean was by her side for the entire six-week stay, and she continued to nurse her at home for years after.[86] When Louisa Good was in the hospital in Walkerton with typhoid fever, her sister Mamie helped nurse her there, and in 1906, their seventy-six-year-old Aunt Annie spent most of the winter as companion to her sister Charlotte who suffered from loneliness, anxiety, and arthritis.[87] Louise Ritz, who never married, looked after two of her sisters for most of her life, and after 1943, when her parents died, was never without her blind sister Ina.[88] Vera Hood recalled that it was her older sister Mildred in whom she confided her thoughts about marriage and men; once married and having babies, Vera could rely on her mother and sister to care for her older children.[89] Mrs Howe looked to the kindness and needle skills of her unmarried sister to keep the twelve Howe children in stockings and socks.[90]

Sisters acutely felt one another's absence, therefore, if career or family obligations took them away from home. When Fanny Good left the family farm, for example, to teach in Manitoba, Louisa "brood[ed] on how far away her little sister was."[91] As a child, Jessie Beattie wondered how she and sister Lil could do without California-bound sister Jean, as she was "the confidante of Lil and the one person to whom I had, from early childhood, poured out strange thoughts and questionings." Indeed, when Jean arrived home after three months, Jessie rejoiced that she continued "to be the strong influence and support of us all and to contribute the quiet devotion which made her presence necessary to our happiness."[92]

Naturally, not all relationships were congenial. Generational conflicts were especially evident, particularly between mother and daughter-in-law. If they resided in the same house, their differing approaches to housekeeping, child care, and cooking, and the issue of who reigned supreme in the kitchen, could be a persistent source of tension.[93] As well, as seen in chapter 2, a woman could certainly resent her sister for exploiting favours of cleaning and child care, and her brother's wife for reaping the rewards of the family farm.

But regardless of these conflicts, same-sex friendship and kinship networks clearly demonstrate that many farm women were neither entirely isolated nor exclusively aligned to their men. For farm women, then, home economics was a reasonable and welcome extension of entrenched female community and ritual. It was this tradition of friendship and kinship among farm women, not their isolation, that actually worked in Hoodless's favour.

Ontario farm women endorsed and popularized Hoodless's home economics vision for several reasons. First, unlike urban women who were commonly consumers, farm women "had a shared identification ... with a home which by definition had not been removed from economics."[94] The movement's emphasis on women's productive domestic work, therefore, affirmed what they had already known was their indispensable role in the home.

Second, farm women believed that home economics could remedy the distress of overworked farm wives, and the mass migration of farm girls to the city.[95] They supposed that domestic science would elevate the status of housekeeping, ease the burden of housework on the farm, and provide equal access of the farmer and his wife to scientific knowledge and methods which had heretofore been available only to him. In this way, domestic science would make rural domestic life attractive to all women, and would, it was hoped, keep the young ones on the land.[96]

Because the migration of farm girls had depleted rural areas of domestic servants, farm women felt comfortable using home economics to modernize their work "for the sake of efficiency."[97] The amelioration of their domestic labour through the time- and labour-saving strategies of home economics could, theoretically, make them more readily available to assist their husbands in income-producing farm work.[98]

Farm women, no doubt, also relished that many of the movement's leaders had been born and bred on the farm.[99] Adelaide Hoodless, American Ellen Swallow Richards (1842–1911), and Briton Alice

Ravenhill (1859–1954), for example, all had agrarian backgrounds. Their shift from rural to urban ways highlighted for the leaders that the home's general devaluation was attributable to the dissolution of household production that was evident in urban homes.[100] The farm home's divergent emphasis on domestic production, farm women likely surmised, meant that these once-rural folk would be especially appreciative of farm women's labour. Arguably, this reasoning would later hold true in the case of home economist Ethel Chapman.

The movement's emphasis on education also appealed to farm women whose older population in particular had been denied opportunities for formal learning. Farm women took to Hoodless's concept of "intellectualizing domesticity," and of opening university doors to women in an academic field which was "now socially sanctioned in the name of the family."[101] Accordingly, they supported the establishment of home economics at Macdonald Institute, and would later press for a degree program there.[102]

Macdonald Institute, which was established at the Ontario Agricultural College in Guelph in 1903, was a teacher-training facility offering a co-educational program in Nature Study, a Manual Training Division for young men, and, most significantly for farm women and their daughters, a Department of Home Economics exclusively for young women, who could obtain a teachers' certificate or a nonprofessional diploma in Domestic Science.[103] By 1911, the home economics programs at Macdonald Institute, the University of Toronto, and McGill University would collectively claim 20 per cent of all female post-secondary students in Canada.[104]

The home economics program at Macdonald Institute had its beginnings in October of 1894 when Hoodless, under the auspices of the Hamilton ywca, opened Canada's first teacher-training school of domestic science. It attracted about 110 women to its one-year program.[105] For these turn-of-the-century women with few career options at hand, teaching home economics rated as a sensible pursuit by the audacious and traditional alike: "it held the promise of better than average remuneration, expanded geographical mobility, and advancement free from male competition. In addition, it combined the domestic skills expected of women with the financial independence of an employment in service to a female culture, free from the questionable propriety attached to clerking and typewriting by cautious middle-class parents."[106]

Hoodless's dream for a teacher-training college stemmed from her work championing domestic science in Hamilton public schools. With endorsement from the National Council of Women, she and other women had appealed to the City's Board of Education in July of 1894 to implement a new curriculum which included domestic science education for girls.[107] In 1896, the board agreed to provide one hundred teenage girls in 1897 a half day a week of domestic science education at the Hamilton YWCA. These sessions afforded Hoodless's teachers-in-training an opportunity to gain first-hand teaching experience.[108]

With the establishment of a school, and a successful arrangement with the Hamilton Board of Education, Hoodless secured the backing of George W. Ross, Liberal minister of education under Oliver Mowat. Ross supported Hoodless in publicizing the initiation of domestic science courses in schools throughout Ontario, and in 1897, his ministry developed guidelines which outlined the substance of course curriculum, and allowed for the examination of would-be domestic science teachers.[109]

Widespread support eluded her in Hamilton, however. Undoubtedly, this was due in part to the Conservative leanings of the Board of Education and the Hamilton *Spectator*, both of whom regarded Hoodless's promotion of domestic science as a Liberal platform.[110] As well, Hamiltonians took note of the elitist character of Hoodless's work on behalf of middle-class women on the one hand, and the philanthropic mandate of the YWCA on the other. In 1896, when a fundraising drive for a staggering $15,000 was launched in order to improve domestic science facilities, criticism abounded. It convinced Hoodless to divorce the Domestic Science School from YWCA programs, although the teacher-training program remained in the YWCA building. Upset by the controversy surrounding Hoodless, the Hamilton Board of Education rescinded its arrangement with her in 1897.[111]

Hamilton's political climate aside, other women and men opposed or misunderstood Hoodless's domestic science cause. First, there were women who felt insulted by the presumption that homemakers were deficient at their jobs, and ill-equipped to instruct their daughters at home.[112] Second, there were men who feared that domestic science, with its practical-over-theoretical approach and its repudiation of conventional (male-defined) curricula, would lower the standard of education, and, due to elaborate equipment, prove expensive to fund.[113] And third, and perhaps most injurious to Hoodless, there were men who simply undermined the significance of the movement. Carolyn Sachs maintains that in the United States at this time "men were glad to support women who wanted to teach other women the moral value of staying in the home. At no time did these men take seriously the scientific claim of the [domestic] scientists, however."[114] The impressions of one Hoodless observer validates Sachs' assertion that men's interest in the movement was undeniably flip and self-serving. In 1898, Dorothy Drew wrote "I have no doubt a great ma[n]y of them [men] would be quite in favor of converting the entire school curriculum, so far as it is taught to girls, into a vast cook book out of which the coming woman may be taught to minister to the stomachic rights of man. So the privileged men who listened to Mrs. Hoodless [last year] pondered the matter in their hearts and dreamed dreams of a golden age when every woman would be able to cook like mother used to."[115]

During these difficult times, Hoodless continued to address audiences throughout southwestern Ontario. She fashioned herself a domestic science "'missionary'" who had the full endorsement of a minister rallying behind her worthwhile reforms. The committed, eager, and well-spoken Hoodless proved enormously proficient in this work.[116]

In the late 1890s, Hoodless intended that her own school become the pre-eminent teacher-training facility in Canada. To this end, she received annual funding from Hamilton City Council and the first Ministry of Education grant for a project of this kind. She was also given government approval to amalgamate her school with the Ontario Normal College in Hamilton. In 1900, she again consulted George Ross who consented to the certification of her graduates as domestic science teachers. Graduates from other schools, including the Toronto School of Domestic Science, were not yet acknowledged in this way.[117]

In February of 1900, with Hoodless as school president, her upgraded, ministry-sanctioned teacher-training school opened as the Ontario Normal School of Domestic Science and Art. It occupied the former YWCA building rather than a new facility, which had been the goal of the unsuccessful fundraising drive four years prior. The school, unlike others, offered both one- and two-year programs. Students majored in either the scientifically oriented area of foods, or in the needle arts, and were instructed by domestic science and medical experts from Britain, the United States, and Canada.[118]

But the school soon met with its demise. To blame were the tremendous restrictions governing acceptance into the programs. Hoodless expected nothing less than excellence in her graduates, and felt that it could only be achieved with the help of high entrance grades; a solid science background, which few young women had; and respectable social standing.[119] The exclusive, elitist nature of Hoodless's school prompted the Hamilton Board of Education to revoke its 1901 grant, and, as a result, Hoodless experienced difficulty maintaining the facility. She also felt overwhelmed by her duties to raise money, and to locate teaching jobs throughout Ontario for her graduates.[120]

Dispirited, and worried about the survival of her Hamilton school, Hoodless contacted the affluent Sir William Christopher Macdonald. Macdonald, born the son of a Prince Edward Island politician in 1831, was a Montreal millionaire who, in addition to financing the National Council of Women, funded the establishment of schools, particularly manual training facilities for boys.[121] Hoodless knew of Macdonald through OAC president James Mills, who himself had approached the philanthropist to help fund a domestic science program at the OAC.[122]

Mills, lamenting what he perceived as the declining state of rural homes, and women's inefficient role within them, supported domestic science. Mostly, he sympathized with those men forced to flee hearth for tavern to escape "'the must[y] smell, the untidiness, and the filth'" of the home, which were "'sufficient to drive the average man to desperation.'"[123] Mills took note that in the midwestern United States many agricultural colleges offered home economics programs for rural women, and expanded these courses to include instruction in the farm woman's usual barn and outside work of dairying, breeding fowl, and tending garden.[124] Canada provided for no such arrangement. Indeed, an OAC alumnus, in an article titled "Giving the Girls a Chance," observed in 1900 that "while it is true that Canada's institutions of higher learning in the arts and sciences have opened wide their doors to the women of the land, who wished to stand on the same professional plane as their brothers, it is also true that there is not in the whole Dominion a single school or college offering such a course of study and training as would tend to fit the farmers' daughters of to-day to be the farmers' wives *par excellence* of to-morrow. The question is far from being one of narrow individual opinion." He noted of the OAC that "her gloomy halls have never yet been enlivened by the joyous laugh of the *coed*," and awaited the day when the OAC will be "the great Woman's University for the rural population of the Province."[125] Mills, too, had realized that his agricultural college would serve as the perfect place for a domestic science course, as the school already possessed teachers and facilities equipped for both science and farm work instruction.[126]

Macdonald, however, showed little interest in the OAC, even though two of his nephews had been schooled at the college, and his education consultant, James Robertson, had been a professor there. Not to be put off, Mills set out to include Hoodless and Robertson in his bid to lure the benefactor.[127] "'I quite agree with you,'" Mills wrote Hoodless in 1900, "'that it will be necessary for us to continue our agitation in getting a Department of Domestic Science at the College.'"[128]

In 1901, however, Hoodless contacted Macdonald with the hope of trying to save her own Hamilton school. James Robertson had told Hoodless that Macdonald was looking to fund a training facility for girls similar to his manual training centres for boys, and this proved encouraging to Hoodless. With her trip subsidized by the education department and with the support of James Mills, Hoodless conferred with Macdonald in Montreal in October of 1901, who agreed to rescue Hoodless's school of domestic science by incorporating it into the OAC.[129] In 1903, Hoodless's financially troubled school relocated from the Hamilton YWCA to the new Macdonald Institute. Mary Urie Watson (1866–1950), who had been the principal of Hoodless's Hamilton school, became the first lady principal from 1903 to 1920, and was also its first director of home economics.[130]

As part of the OAC, the Department of Home Economics at Macdonald Institute was to contribute to the betterment of rural Ontario education and life. Government funding for "Mac" came, in fact, not from the Department of Education but from the Department of Agriculture.[131] Indeed, Hoodless in her written pitch to Macdonald to affiliate with the school, had paid special attention to the larger interests of rural Ontario, which she knew were of special concern to Mills and Robertson: "I discussed the question of establishing a training department for teachers, who could … give scientific practical instructions to the inhabitants of rural districts without the necessity of [the inhabitants] leaving home and acquiring a taste for city life etc. … I mentioned the amalgamation of the Normal School of Domestic Science at Hamilton, so as to provide the necessary training for young women without whom agriculture cannot be advanced."[132]

Hoodless's remarks reveal the ambiguous goals of the home economics Department as related to the nature and priority of the education of farm daughters. Hoodless alluded to farm daughters both as the disciples of teachers who trained there, and as collegians who would continue with farm life. But initially, there was a question of which, if any, program – advanced teacher-training or domestic science for farm daughters – Macdonald Institute would make its chief focus.[133] Unlike the OAC's annual report of 1901, for example, which stressed equally the college's training of public school teachers and the " 'practical education for … farmers' daughters,' " education consultant James Robertson insisted that the primary purpose of the facility was " 'the training of teachers for rural schools' "; only after that was it " 'instruction and training for farmers' daughters … in household science etc.' "[134] Farm daughters, however, some of whom had already attended the OAC for short courses in dairying,[135] and others without aspirations of teacher-training, were determined to acquire a practical domestic science education at Macdonald Institute. Soon, the emphasis of the home economics department was on the two-year Normal Course and Professional Housekeeping Course, which specialized in training domestic science teachers and institutional housekeepers respectively; however, by 1906, the department offered a one-year Homemaker Course "planned for girls who look forward not to earning a living away from home, but to living at home and who desire to be prepared for a home-maker's duties."[136]

For farm daughters and others whose work their families could not long forgo, the department also instituted in 1906 a three-month version of the Homemaker Course.[137] It was intended for women such as Galt farm daughter Jean Beattie, who enrolled in the course in 1914. At thirty-two years of age, and living at home, Jean tended house and nursed her frail sister Jessie. Jean feared abandoning their aging mother to attend the school, an indication that even a comprehensive course of three months was regrettably too long for some. Jean's sister Lillian, however, urged her to go, forewarning that should she not seize this chance, " 'there may not be another.' "[138] This comment revealed what many daughters knew: that caring for ill and aged family too often prevented them from pursuing opportunities off the farm.

Young women, and their mothers, were excited by the thoroughly modern idea that farm daughters could receive a college education, and possibly a career, in a field as progressive as domestic science. When Brantford-area farm daughter Ethel Good, for example, grew discontented with her job as a mother's helper in 1903, she declared in a letter to her brother, " 'I want to be a B.A., a trained nurse, a Domestic Science Graduate, and a musician. What shall I do first?' "[139] Ethel, no doubt, attached much significance to being a " 'Domestic Science Graduate' " – she capitalized each word, as one does a title, and ranked this goal alongside some lofty career ambitions.[140] Edna I. Brown of Paisley, Bruce County, advised in a letter to the *Canadian Countryman* in 1926 that a girl should routinely set aside money in the event that she may "some day wish to take a course in domestic science or other branch of helpful knowledge."[141] In a letter to the *Farmers' Sun*, a York County mother wrote that she wanted her children "to have more than a common school education," insisting that her daughters "must have a domestic science course." She no doubt perceived the course as modern in approach when she regretted that "we old-fashioned folk do not put enough science into our domestic life."[142]

Macdonald Institute, which by 1921 housed only the home economics department, was throughout the early part of the century upheld by advocates for the farm daughter (and by itself) as a bastion of progress and modernity.[143] Alice A. Ferguson, for example, in an article entitled "What Education Should Farmers' Daughters Receive?," boldly proclaimed in 1914 that "farmers' daughters should not be slaves, but free." Emancipation for them can best be achieved, she said, through education, particularly through a domestic science education at Macdonald Institute. It was training, she argued, for which they, in contrast to their urban sisters, had a particular aptitude: "in their earlier years, farmers' daughters are imbibing knowledge at first hand, of sanitary science, household economics, and of outside life." For this reason, the farmer's daughter, Ferguson concluded, "should be worthy of any man, and is often too good for most men."[144] Macdonald Institute, asserted another supporter in 1927, provided "the opportunity to study under the direction of women of wide culture; the opportunity to make congenial friends; the opportunity to broaden the whole social and mental outlook; the opportunity to secure definite training for some chosen work – Macdonald Institute offers one opportunity after another."[145] In 1930, Junia, the advice columnist of the women's page in the *Farmer's Advocate*, told her readers in an article entitled "Independence for Farm Daughters" that she would have the farm daughter "try her wings in a larger world, preferably with a preliminary period of study at some such place as Macdonald Hall. ... This experience will give her many benefits – a knowledge of the world and of business, poise in handling the affairs of adult life and confidence in herself. These are the things in which the girl who stays always at home so often has no chance to improve, remaining rather shy and diffident and in some ways too young for her age."[146]

This promotion of Macdonald Institute as a fashionable, pioneering, educational facility offering necessary instruction for women struck a chord with the farm daughters of Ontario. Indeed, Director Olive Cruikshank informed the *Farmer's Advocate* in May of 1927 that "there is never room for all who wish to enroll as students at 'Mac,'" and that many had been on a waiting list for three long years.[147] In 1928, while the OAC claimed only thirty-four graduates, Macdonald Institute degree graduates numbered an impressive eighty-two.[148] Lillian Beattie wished desperately to enrol in domestic science at Macdonald Institute. When she discussed the idea with her father, and he debated her plea to go, she branded him "'old-fashioned ... just plain old-fashioned.'"[149] In 1911, twenty-seven-year-old Lillian and her best friend Louise made application to the two-year Professional Housekeeping Course, and "waited patiently for a reply." Lillian later recalled that "we were very happy, after a suspense of three weeks, to find we were accepted. When I asked Dad for a loan to take the course, he was more than surprised. 'You will get married,' he said, 'and it will all be wasted.' I assured him that Home Economics could never be wasted, married or single."[150] Confident "Mac" graduates also praised the benefits of their alma mater. Minutes of a Wilton Grove Women's Institute meeting reveal that Miss May Williams gave "a very interesting account of her life and experiences at the McDonald [sic] Institute – showing the advantages of a course there both socially and educationally."[151] Jessie Beattie remembered her sister Jean extolling the school when years later she "appealed to ... father for permission to design the [new] house. 'I learned house planning when I took the three months' Homemaking Course at Mac Hall,' she told him. 'We had long discussions on the way to save space and steps at the same time, and each of us had to draw a plan for what we thought was an ideal house ... I thought about the kind of home we should have ... please trust me, Da,' she ended, 'for I really know what will make housekeeping easier for Mother.' "[152]

In this climate of enthusiasm, however, there was a sense in rural Ontario that the opportunity for farm daughters to attend Macdonald Institute was reserved for the privileged few. Jennie A. Pringle, for example, asserted that farm daughters like herself required community centres for social and intellectual growth because, she lamented, "so few of us can attend MacDonald [sic] College!"[153] Not only did farm daughters have to abide waiting lists and sometimes resistant parents, they also had to be able to afford costly tuition fees,[154] to free themselves from their work on the farm, and, if not living in residence, to travel the sometimes lengthy distance between the school and their homes. As well, the college, in keeping with middle-class standards of female propriety, insisted that girls be of sound "moral character" – praised by a minister, teacher, or distinguished family friend as having "a very pleasing personality," and as being "very cooperative" and "quite wholesome and honourable."[155] The school also obliged girls to write college entrance exams in English, geography, and math, subjects which only a select number would have mastered.[156]

These obstacles no doubt contributed to the modest enrolment of farm daughters. Their exact number is difficult to determine due to the catch-all description "rural," meaning farm or non-farm, which was indiscriminately used to distinguish these young women from their urban counterparts. Nevertheless, the *Farmer's Advocate* stated that in 1926, rural girls comprised only 42 per cent of the school's enrolment. Moreover, many of these young women were taking not the one- and two-year programs but the condensed three-month short courses. Aware of the inadequate representation of farm girls, the college placed some of the blame for this problem on the women themselves for not acquiring "the necessary schooling," and on the lack of facilities in rural areas offering the requisite education programs.[157]

Nevertheless, Macdonald Institute made an effort to be more inclusive of farm daughters. In September of 1915, for instance, Macdonald Institute asked "why not carry the Short Course out to the girls who cannot come to us?" and opened an "off-campus" location outside of Cambridge, calling the Ayr public school classroom Macdonald Institute Branch No 1. The short course attracted twenty-two young women, seventeen of whom were farmer's daughters.[158] In 1927, Macdonald director Olive Cruikshank maintained that true to its original mandate (which was, as mentioned, somewhat uncertain) Macdonald Institute "sought first to serve the girl from the rural home. Applications from rural girls are given preference, provided they are received in sufficient time."[159] Even by the mid-1940s, hopeful applicants to the proposed four-year degree program in home economics were informed that "our accommodation is limited, and preference must be given to farm girls."[160]

The popularity of Macdonald Institute at the OAC speaks to the fact that agricultural colleges were where home economics met its greatest success.[161] It was largely the farm women of the WI who cultivated domestic science at the OAC, given their desire to integrate home economics with post-secondary education.[162] Indeed, in 1902, one year before the opening of Macdonald Institute, the pioneer branch of the WI wrote Sir William Macdonald that his support of domestic science as an academic discipline "affords us great satisfaction."[163]

This first official branch of the WI formed in Stoney Creek just one week following Hoodless's urging in her 1897 address that the area's farm women create their own club. Approximately one hundred women (about sixty-five more than anticipated) assembled at Squires Hall to form the Woman's Institute of Saltfleet.[164] Minutes from that meeting and several which followed reveal that from the very beginning WI members made the cause of home economics instruction their own. After all, as journalist Marjorie MacMurchy declared, "many women at home are skilled it is true, but they are self-taught, and their experience and discoveries are not available to other women ... why should all classes of workers and students feel the need of conferences and discussion, except home-makers?"[165] Accordingly, the WI Constitution declared that "the *object* of this Institute shall be to promote that knowledge of Household Science which shall lead to improvement in household architecture with special attention to home sanitation, to a better understanding of the economic and hygenic value of foods and fuels, and to a more scientific care of children with a view of raising the general standard of the health of our people."[166] The Constitution also allowed for six standing committees related to home economics concerns: "(1) Domestic Economy. (2) Architecture, with special references to Sanitation, Light, Heat etc. (3) Physiology, Hygiene, Medicine, Calisthenics, etc. (4) Floriculture, Horticulture. (5) Music and Art. (6) Literature and Sociology, Education and Legislation."[167] Research papers delivered by Saltfleet members at their first several meetings included "Proper Food for Children," "Housekeeping versus Homemaking," "The Science of Keeping Clean in the Household," and "Domestic Science and the Modern Home."[168]

Similar topics were evident at meetings of the Wilton Grove WI, founded by women of Middlesex County in 1909. At the first official meeting, members delivered papers on "Easy Methods of Housecleaning" and "Home Nursing." Subsequent meetings entertained lectures about "The Care of Milk in Warm Weather," "Canning and Preserving," and "Economy and Household Waste." As well, "Miss Maggie Munro and Miss Anna Harris read splendid papers on 'Labour Saving Devices and Kitchen Conveniences' showing how by making use of all inventions along these lines our house work could be reduced to minimum drudgery"; "Miss Katie Murray read a very … instructive paper on Simple Meals Well Cooked and Their Refining Influence showing the effects of good meals on the health and morals of a family"; and "Miss Munro read a carefully prepared paper on a 'Girl's Duties in the Home,' showing the home as a training school preparing the good daughter for the good wife of the future."[169]

WI meetings combined issues of home economics with those of farm life for women. Initial meetings of the Saltfleet WI included addresses on "Butter-Making," and "The Country Home."[170] The Wilton Grove WI discussed "Ideas of a Plain Country Woman," "Women's Place in the Finance of the Farm," "The 20th Century Farmer's Wife," and "How to Make Farm Life More Attractive."[171] These topics belie the notion of cynics that the WI neglected issues of relevance to farm women in favour of urban concerns.

That the WI sustained its almost singular focus on home economics in the years prior to the First World War was attributable in part to the Ontario Department of Agriculture which, having supervised the FI, adopted the WI in 1902. The government encouraged the WI's home economics concerns for various reasons: it saw the organization's emphasis on domestic production, household integrity, and community welfare as an expedient way to augment the economic productivity of farm wives, to prevent the rural depopulation of farm daughters, and to improve social conditions in the countryside, respectively.[172]

The government assisted the WI in a variety of ways. It provided the group with regular, albeit minimal, grants to supplement its twenty-five cent annual membership fee; it supplied clubs after 1903 with visiting home economics lecturers and demonstrators; and it helped fund domestic science short courses, which were held at branch locales and/or at Macdonald Institute.[173] In return for this help, it seemed to some, the WI was to adhere to government-dictated policy controlling aspects of conduct and content at all group meetings.[174]

The speakers and courses that the government sponsored eventually came to supersede the practice of members delivering their own domestic science papers. It was a change which some members saw as a subversion of the original WI plan, and others welcomed as a relief to their already excessive responsibilities.[175] Hoodless promoted the new arrangement: "these [Women's] Institutes have been intensely popular, but now they have got beyond the stage of discussion, and are clamoring for teachers. Two of our students went to the O.A.C. and took the dairy course and are now travelling teachers, but what are two, where hundreds could be employed?"[176] For the ever-enterprising Hoodless, visiting speakers and professional courses meant that WI members would not only receive a more credible education, but that there would be a greater demand for the graduates and resources that few but she could provide.

With support from the government assured, the WI received less than favourable reviews from rural men. In fact, "male attitudes to women's organizations were among the biggest obstacles facing the young movement."[177] Anxious husbands of early WI members foresaw expensive additional membership costs, women's preoccupation with Institute activities over domestic concerns, and growing discontent among increasingly politicized women.[178] As well, men almost certainly feared the potential threat of an organization that rendered them somewhat superfluous, as suggested by their disparagement of the group at that time and for decades to come.[179] But these men were heartened by the certain prospect of female in-fighting, and by the lack of active male leadership, both of which, it was assumed, would break the WI before long.[180] In the face of this opposition and scepticism, the WI "spread like wildfire,"[181] challenging patriarchal prescriptions and stereotypes, and ultimately proving wrong all predictions of an early demise. By 1919, with the formation of the Federated Women's Institutes of Ontario, there existed 900 branch Institutes in Ontario, with a membership over 30,000 strong.[182]

In making the women-centred field of home economics the *raison d'être* of the wi, organizers necessarily asserted its exclusively female membership, declaring its regular monthly meetings for women only. In fact, doors to meetings were sometimes locked "to prevent unwelcome male intrusions."[183] These meetings which assembled women in a female-only space encouraged the forging of new friendships within a social setting. In the early years of the wi, branch meetings most often took place at members' homes, where time was reserved for informal conversation over lunch or tea.[184] Unlike the church, which negotiated the membership of women through that of their husbands, and rural church groups, which sought to unite women according to shared religious beliefs, the wi endorsed the independent membership of women, and promoted their solidarity, as Linda Ambrose asserts, "on the basis of gender alone."[185] In so doing, these women dismissed the relevance of their men to their organizational lives.

The home economics agenda which dictated the single-sex character of the wi also allowed for the discussion of other female-centred issues to which rural women might have never otherwise been exposed. At early meetings of the Saltfleet wi, Mrs McNeilly gave an original paper on "Clubs for Women," and Miss Fenton delivered what must have been a provocative reading on "How to be Happy Though Married."[186] At meetings of the Wilton Grove wi, members read history papers on "Woman Through Different Phases of her Existence," and "Some One of a Kind Canadian Women."[187]

For farm daughters and wives, the female specificity of home economics was not its weakness, as some scholars suggest, but its strength. Building on the familiar bonds and rituals of a female culture among farm women, it allowed for the creation of Macdonald Institute and the wi. Both addressed the "intellectual famine of farm life"[188] by providing women with access to education, information, and a new vital female network. During World War I and after, the wi would also offer its members the opportunity to participate in matters of citizenship and social reform, a fact which buttresses the claim that "separatist organizing, in women-only activist groups, can provide a basis for transforming society."[189] The members of the wi, as proponents of Macdonald Institute and of their own organization, in some ways resembled "most feminists" in the early twentieth century who "preferred to retain membership in a separate female sphere, one which they did not believe to be inferior to men's sphere and one in which women could be free to create their own forms of personal, social, and political relationships. The achievements of feminism at the turn of the century came less through gaining access to the male domains of politics and the professions than in the tangible form of building separate female institutions."[190]

Those Ontario farm daughters and wives who attended Macdonald Institute and/or belonged to the WI embraced domestic science as progressive, elevating, and advantageous for women because Adelaide Hoodless had defined it in this way. It sought to raise the status of homemaking so it could be considered a valuable contribution by women to society; it encouraged and supported the productive role of women, from which many derived their sense of independence and self-worth; it advocated safer and more efficient working conditions for women in the home; it provided a vehicle by which women could obtain a university education; it capitalized on the pervasive notion of women's private sphere in order to create careers for women as dieticians and home economists in the public sphere; and it advocated the truly radical notion that domestic skills were not inherent in women, or even easily taught, but, like other skills, needed to be studied and updated – an innovative concept, especially in rural areas. Perhaps most importantly, the home economics movement acknowledged the values and experiences of women, and made them a subject for academic consideration. Hoodless's conception of home economics so impressed prospective WI members, in fact, that she was appointed honorary president of the organization upon its inception, and would be canonized as the group's beloved founder and model of womanhood.[191] This support for Hoodless, and for her vision of home economics as meliorative, female-specific, and separatist, spoke to the social feminism of many reform-minded farm daughters and wives.

5 "Think something else than kitchen": The Failure of the UFWO and Equity Feminism in the Inter-War Years

The United Farm Women of Ontario, a self-professed rival farm women's group established in 1918, espoused an equity feminist platform, but never enjoyed the popularity of the WI among farm women. The WI during World War I had subordinated its domestic science agenda to projects related to war relief, and while home economics re-emerged as an Institute priority in the post-war years, progressive reform work, particularly as it related to women, took centre stage. In social feminist fashion, WI members believed that, as women, their superior morality and special domestic talents and skills made them especially qualified to redress the social ills created in part by male politicians in the public sphere. Some of the most vocal proponents of the UFWO held contempt for the social feminist work of the WI, but locally, UFWO clubs resembled, indeed emulated, WI branches in their women-centred activities and social reform goals. That the failure of the equity feminist UFWO has been blamed in part on the conservatism of farm women negates both the similarity of the WI and the UFWO at the local level, and the progressivism of the WI.

In 1914, the WI, which comprised 888 branches and almost 30,000 members, shifted its focus from domestic science and the home to assisting the war effort.[1] Wartime meetings of the Wilton Grove WI near London, for example, entertained only the occasional address on "The Fine Art of Cookery" or "Health and Home Remedies." Even lectures on homemaking as it related to wartime conservation or recycling were rare.[2] Like most other WI branches, Wilton Grove was consumed by charitable war work. Indeed, at its August 1915 meeting, as many as one hundred women came to hear an address on Red Cross initiatives. Wilton Grove itself acknowledged in 1916 that "the object of all the [year's] meetings was Red Cross work."[3]

Across Ontario, WI branches contributed to the war effort in numerous ways: they sewed garments, knit socks, canned fruit, and made jam for shipment overseas to Allied soldiers and civilians. The Wilton Grove club, for example, reported that in 1916 it had made 265 garments, knitted 164 pairs of socks, and raised $116.87. Moreover, clubs initiated aggressive fundraising campaigns through countless socials, bazaars, and fairs.[4] By war's end, in fact, WI members in Ontario had become artful fundraisers, contributing over $1,560,000 "in cash and goods."[5]

Despite the success of the WI at this patriotic work (or perhaps because of it), the group's sudden and dramatic shift from a rural homemakers' club to a fundraising society unsettled some members who felt that the WI had strayed from its original purpose to educate farm women and improve rural life.[6] Indeed, by 1920, the WI had gained the dubious reputation as a "money-making society" (WI clubs had engaged in fundraising pursuits before the war, but they were on a smaller scale, and, for the most part, were for projects related to domestic science).[7] To counter this perception, the Federated Women's Institutes of Canada, which formed in 1919, passed a resolution in 1921 which recommended that "institutes endeavour to guard against the danger of degenerating into money making machines."[8]

That the WI had lost its way and needed time to reinvent itself for peacetime is evident by the Wilton Grove WI, whose membership had dropped significantly by war's end. At the Wilton Grove gathering in May of 1918, members decided to call meetings only for administrative reasons or if they could arrange for speakers. Two years later, reflecting upon its inertia, the club decided to disband at least temporarily.[9]

Although the WI's patriotic effort distracted the organization from its original work, it provided farm women with a rare opportunity to connect with the larger world beyond the farm. It introduced them to a complex network of charitable and reform agencies and women's groups, including the Red Cross, the Belgium Relief Fund, the Women's Patriotic League, and the Prisoners-of-War Fund.[10] It trained them to be fundraisers, activists, and organizers. And perhaps most significantly, it made them acutely aware of political structures, and of systematic social, economic, and legal injustices. These gains would benefit WI women in the post-war movement, which urged them not only to return to their homemaking roots, but to work toward social reform.[11]

With war's end, there was a renewed emphasis on homemaking by the WI, a trend which signalled its continued belief in, and promotion of, the specificity of women and their female-centred domestic pursuits. The minutes of the Norton WI (the former Wilton Grove WI[12]) reveal that while "the science" in domestic science had been subverted at the local level by more artistic pursuits (demonstrations and lectures at the Wilton Grove Institute, for example, addressed table bouquets and paper flower-making[13]), the provincial executive reaffirmed its commitment to homemaking by promoting the domestic science of the pre-war period. In an article in *Home and Country*, the official organ of the Federated Women's Institutes of Ontario first published in 1933, the provincial convenor of home economics proclaimed that "to raise the standard of homemaking as a profession is highly important. Bringing efficiency into the home is a well worthwhile project for any branch. After all, this was the purpose in organizing Institutes forty years ago. We surely do not think the home less important today than at that time."[14] Indeed, young women at the local level like Miss Laurena Rutherford of Woodbridge, outside Toronto, also supported this sentiment. As a guest at a club meeting, she professed that "one of the highest and noble desires of any girl today is that she may become a well informed, efficient Home-Maker."[15] The provincial WI continued to emphasize the physical sciences, household efficiency, and the elevation and professionalization of household labour:

woman's greatest accomplishment is being a perfect home-maker. Notice, not merely housekeeper, but much more than that. ... Sciences that centre in or relate to the body and the physical health ... are ... essential to every woman. ... Certainly, she who knows and practices good housekeeping and the divine art of cookery, has better claim to be considered an educated woman.[16]

In the past housekeepers ... knew nothing of domestic science. ... How different, how complex is the housekeeping of today. ... but there is much yet to be done before it is recognized as one of the most dignified professions open to women ... Most men have theory [*sic*] that ... women should be born housekeepers and should take it as her natural vocation in life. Never was there a more mistaken idea.[17]

The WI also continued in the post-war years to promote home economics training at the OAC's Macdonald Institute. Thamesford's Miss Nettie Babb, in a *Home and Country* article entitled "A Young Woman's Accomplishments," lauded the school's usefulness: "it may well be said that the knowledge to be attained in Macdonald Institute is of such practical value, dealing as it does with the first principles of housekeeping, that the student may not only learn what other cultivated women do, but she is given an opportunity to become proficient in some line of work, and if needs be self-supporting."[18]

The provincial wɪ's interest in the connection between homemaking and the farm also resumed after the war, controverting suggestions that the organization was more urban than rural.[19] The wɪ, for example, helped organize agricultural fall fairs, and sponsored and manned the homemaking exhibits.[20] Notable wɪ member Ethel Chapman pointed out in 1926 that "the women's department at fairs offers a rather exceptional opportunity for educational work in home economics – for exhibits that teach something."[21] In 1934, Mrs J.D. MacMillan linked homemaking, the farm, and business in her *Home and Country* article "Training Future Housekeepers." She insisted that "probably no time in the history of the world has housekeeping – good housekeeping – been regarded as such a rural business occupation as at the present time."[22] In 1937, in fact, the Ontario wɪ, in conjunction with the federal and provincial governments, offered numerous short courses in home economics to farm daughters who desired training in domestic science for use in part-time work. Of the 622 young women who enrolled in the short courses, 62 per cent of them were from farm homes.[23] Miss L.A. Row rejoiced in 1934 that housework on the farm "has been revolutionized wherever the hydro lines are extended," but lamented that "too many farm women ... are still denied this service and must do a great deal of work not lightened to any great extent by modern invention."[24]

The installation of hydro in rural areas was just one of many concerns of the inter-war wɪ. Indeed, with branch, district, and provincial standing committees on Social Welfare; Health and Child Welfare and/or Community Activities and Relief; and Legislation and/or Citizenship, the organization lobbied the municipal, provincial, and federal governments for a variety of reforms that would elevate the standard of rural life and improve the welfare of rural children and women.[25] And when these governments proved slow or unwilling to act, or when needed reforms were small and specific, the wɪ stepped in to help enact changes.[26]

For wɪ members, women had "a unique role to play" in public life.[27] "Women of vision and earnestness," noted one member, "saw that ... in addition to their home duties[,] Community housekeeping demanded their attention."[28] The wɪ gave women "a sense of their responsibility for building a better community, a better province, and a better world, and a realization that on them, the homemakers of the nation, depends the type of citizenship we are going to have in Can-

ada in the years that lie ahead."[29] Women were obligated to participate in public affairs because "the social standards, activities, and
ideals of the community influence ... each home in the community,"
and, as WI women were " 'the mothers of the community,' " they
" 'should have a guiding hand in community affairs.' "[30] As homemakers and mothers with a special contribution, women were reminded in 1935 that "we ... do not arrive at our fullest competence
when imitating man."[31] The rhetoric of these women, which justified
women's participation in the public sphere based on their status as
mothers, which utilized domestic and maternal imagery when referencing their public role, and which emphasized women's unique,
if not superior, approach to reform, was the language of social
feminism.

Consistent with the Institute urging that "we must at all times be
progressive," the WI facilitated many groundbreaking reforms.[32] In
the area of public health, clubs initiated medical inspection in
schools, established clinics, arranged for district public health nurses,
oversaw the immunization of schoolchildren, and funded and/or
served hot lunches at schools.[33] Related to these reforms were those
which addressed sanitation: clubs provided individual drinking
glasses for children at school, and ensured its clean water supply.[34] In
the area of public works, branches lobbied for heat and lighting at
country schools, for the building of efficient and accessible roads,
and, of course, for the availability of hydro-electricity for use in rural
homes.[35] WI efforts for "rural beautification" included the painting of
classroom walls and the purchase of park benches and swings.[36] As
well, for the purpose of community reform and charitable works, the
WI continued to fundraise, so much so (despite the 1921 resolution
that fundraising ease up) that a 1928 article about the WI claimed that
"real community welfare and neighborliness is [sic] being swamped
by too great a zeal for money-making."[37] Clubs collected money to
help support hospitals, to build public memorials, to maintain ceme-
tery grounds, to purchase books for libraries, and to establish
women's rest rooms.[38] For needy farm families during the Depression, when government welfare programs were still in their infancy,
members of any one branch might perform housework and child care
tasks (especially for new mothers), sew quilts, hire a nurse, take up a
collection, or donate Christmas gifts.[39]

Of particular concern to the WI during the inter-war period was reform related to the political representation of women. With its increasing focus on matters outside of the home, and with its belief that
women's influence was needed in political affairs, the WI wanted to
help ensure increased public appointments for women. It insisted, for

example, that women be appointed to the Senate, that a woman be named to the Ontario Censorship Board, and that women secure seats as Board of Education trustees.[40] The absence of female trustees had in fact long exasperated some farm women. Back in 1912, for example, Mrs W. Buchanan of Ravenna, Grey County, wrote "I have known of cases where men put in as trustees and secretaries of school boards, and their wives had to do the work for them. Why could not the women have been put in at first? We women are tired of sending 'deputations,' and praying his 'lordship-man' to condescend to let us have this or that needed reform."[41] Mrs Buchanan recognized the power disparity between women and men in political circles, and was resentful that the politician's wife was denied the privilege and influence of political office, but only she cared enough to initiate the worthwhile reforms. Buchanan continued by condemning men who offered insincere promises of educational reform, and who mocked the women who approached them for change.

The WI also emphasized the importance of education and reform with regard to laws and legislation as they related to women. The organization expressed "keen interest" in issues of property inheritance, wills, child custody, pensions, mothers' allowance, and banking.[42] Indeed, Miss Jean Ross of Lucan, near London, reported in 1934 that numerous branches studied excerpts from the book *Legal Status of Women in Canada*, and held contests, discussions, and mock parliaments on the subject.[43] At the Islington club in York County, a lawyer was secured to inform members about women's property rights and joint ownership, topics to which they responded with "definite interest." A lawyer was also invited to the Norton WI, where he "gave a very interesting and instructive talk on the laws of Ontario as they effect [sic] Women, dealing with Wills, property rights, women's dower, divorce, and alimony and many other interesting facts, after which questions were asked by the members."[44] That branch farm wives and daughters were so receptive to information about these laws suggests their desire to protect themselves under a system that they more than suspected was unfair to women. Indeed, exposing members to rules of law was part of an Institute campaign to redress unjust or insufficient legislation regarding women and children. In 1919, for example, the provincial WI lobbied the government for mothers' allowance, testifying to "the importance of children being brought up under their mothers' care." The confident, albeit idealistic, convention chair boasted that "we have only to let our Government know our feelings, and we will have mothers' allowances."[45]

The WI's concern for women's disadvantaged status under the law had its roots in the suffrage debate, an issue which proved contentious for the WI. One problem was that Ontario farm women were not united in their feelings about the vote.[46] Certainly for many, it held limited appeal.[47] Abigail Shearer, who grew up on a farm in the Grand Valley, Dufferin County, and became an Oxford County farm wife in 1921, was unimpressed by the perceived militancy of the movement, and questioned the credibility of suffragists. She recalled that her friends and family "just took ["the suffragettes"] with a grain of salt. ... We wondered what women would get up and transfer up and down the streets for a cause." Relatively contented farm women such as Abigail also believed that they had done just fine without suffrage, and that it would not necessarily better their lives. As Abigail noted, "I never would have fought for a vote. I was living comfortably and ... I never felt the lack of a vote."[48] Others maintained that men rightly accorded respect to women based on their own actions and deeds, so that it need not be won by women through the vote: "it is idle to put up a cry for political rights, as the suffragettes do. Men usually have and usually will accept women at their own valuation. They always believe in powers that demonstrate themselves by results."[49] With regard to social reform, many rural women believed that "as the housekeepers of the nation," they could effect change without the vote, especially through women's associations like the WI. Historian Margaret Kechnie asserts that after the suffrage victory, "the women of the countryside ... did not embrace the vote as the single most important instrument to achieve change in rural Ontario. While they recognized that voting rights could be used to alleviate some of the problems the community faced, many also saw politics as a destructive force."[50]

Nevertheless, other farm women did support suffrage, as evidenced by the numerous letters on the subject which appeared on the women's page of a 1912 issue of the *Farmer's Advocate*. Taps of Wentworth County, for example, declared in her letter that "certainly women should have the franchise if they want it, and it seems very apparent that they do by the efforts they are putting forth to have it. ... the woman bears an equal share with the man in making the home. She does at least half of the work; spends herself, in many cases more than the man, to keep the home together; and bears a great deal of the responsibility. ... keeping the suffrage from woman is one of the last traces in our Christian civilization of the dark days, when she was little better than a servant or slave. ... Women are as able mentally as men ... they are surely as sensible. Why, then, can they not vote?"[51] Mrs W. Buchanan opened her letter by asking "Should the Suffrage Be Given to Women?," whereupon she answered "yes, undoubtedly, yes."[52]

Like many farm women, both Taps and Mrs Buchanan based their arguments for the vote not on sexual sameness and equal rights, but on women's distinctly female priorities, abilities, and roles. Taps premised her argument on the female-centred reforms that only women would pass into law: "the very strongest reason why women should have the franchise, is that, in all probability, they would pass temperance measures."[53] Hardly conservative in their goals, women like Taps hoped that temperance would inhibit men from squandering their earnings on drink, and from beating their children and wives. With the suffrage victory in 1919, Mrs M.C. Dawson, who believed that women too "timid" to vote ultimately did so for the welfare of their children, agreed with Taps' assessment that the vote would create female-centred laws. In her article "Politics, Woman and the Boon She Will Crave," Dawson reflected that for women voters there was "a realization of what their place in politics must be. ... The man is interested in making a living. The woman is interested in the making of lives. Each has a distinct part, and neither interferes with the other. ... in the future, there shall be more laws dealing with the child, with life, with women and girls. ... these laws are not already incorporated in our statutes. Man legislated about the things in which man was interested directly."[54] Mrs Buchanan also acknowledged men's neglect of women's legal protection: "legislation in the past has made many laws which do not grant equal privileges to man and woman. Because they are wholly made by men, they are made from man's standpoint, and to suit themselves."[55]

Farm women also justified the vote by pointing to women's calling to morally elevate public life, and/or by emphasizing their distinct role as mothers. Taps asked "would not the purity and truth, all the beautiful characteristics of the fairer sex, help to uplift politics and make a higher standard?", and then responded that they would.[56] The presumably female author of the article "Should Women Have the Suffrage" also affirmed women's moral highground: "the presence of women purifies politics, and is proved by a reference to any country or state where they exercise the franchise. Political life is purer, and dealings are straighter, than elsewhere."[57] Mrs Buchanan argued that it was women as mothers who, more than men, were deserving of influence in political affairs: "he [the father] is the guardian of the children according to law. ... But why is it that women who are mostly responsible for their children's moral and religious upbringing have no say in their public or social life?"[58] The author of "Should Women Have the Suffrage" agreed that women as mothers merited the vote because it only made sense that they "should help make the laws to protect the home."[59]

Consistent with the views of Institute founder Adelaide Hoodless, some WI members believed that if women claimed and used the natural influence that was theirs, they would not have the need for the vote,[60] but generally speaking the WI did not disagree with Taps and Mrs Buchanan's support of suffrage (nor would it have disagreed with the justifications that the two women offered). Indeed, support for suffrage was pervasive among Ontario Institutes, especially in the years preceding World War I.[61] In 1917, for example, when the president of the Women's Canadian Club told Institutes "that they [women] become more worthwhile when they have the vote," members responded with a burst of applause.[62] The Central Dumfries WI, near Waterloo, requested in 1918 that the provincial organization lobby the government for the federal vote, if only for the reason of temperance.[63] At an evening meeting in December 1910, the Wilton Grove WI members and their husbands held a debate which addressed the question " 'Should Women Have Votes.' " Arguing for the affirmative were two Institute women, and for the negative, two of the invited men. Those propounding the affirmative were declared the victors.[64]

That members even discussed suffrage, whether for or against it, was another problem for the WI. Government policy governing the WI dictated that religious, ethnic, class, and political interests would in no way shape Institute agenda or play a part at club meetings. The government informed branches in 1916, for example, that "you may discuss whatever subjects you think well, but we strongly advise, and we are very sincere in our advice, that you avoid all controversial or political questions. There is such a large field of work without taking up these questions."[65] The government particularly urged that discussion of these issues be avoided in the presence of Departmental speakers because "you can readily understand that no Government, no matter what its complexion, would be justified in spending public money to provide instructors when the time which should be devoted to instruction is taken up with controversial and debatable questions."[66]

Although the WI overtly disregarded the government dictate at times,[67] "controversial" subjects, including politics, were largely avoided at Institute meetings, WI women appearing to heed the government's wish for them to "think nationally, not politically."[68] At the 1918 provincial convention, for example, the WI's Committee on Resolutions predictably recommended that "the resolution of the Central Dumfries Women's Institute asking this Convention to petition the Government to grant universal suffrage to women before the next election be laid aside as not coming within our jurisdiction."[69]

The government expressed concern that subjects "so peril-fraught as 'woman's suffrage'" would threaten Institute cohesion, and would distract members from their common purpose of addressing the problems of rural life.[70] But it no doubt feared that discussion of potentially volatile issues could invite rural dissention and/or insurgence which could very well prove politically ruinous. The government discouraged political discussions more fervently than those related to other issues, appearing to feel especially vulnerable to the frustration potentially fuelled by this kind of debate, as well as to the political opportunists (now voters) it perceived within Institute ranks: "it is a mark of development and intellectual activity for citizens who have the franchise to make careful study of political issues, administrations, etc., but where there is a likelihood of dividing the people by introducing such discussions, and the likelihood always exists, those interested should be advised to join an organization which has for its object the furtherance of the interest of some particular party or policy."[71] It was this silencing of political debate that so infuriated the executive of the United Farm Women of Ontario, which perceived the government's financial support of the WI, and its accompanying control over policy, as a deliberate strategy by urban politicians to stifle the potentially defiant voice of the farming class.[72]

Formed in 1918, the UFWO was an auxiliary farm women's organization that existed alongside the WI. The appeal of the UFWO among farm women, however, despite its determined efforts, would never approximate that of the Institutes. Unlike the immensely popular WI, which articulated the priorities of social feminism, the provincial UFWO espoused an equity feminist platform.[73] It sought integration with, and relied on acceptance from, the United Farm men, emphasizing an equality between farm women and men based not on their equally valuable but distinct roles, but on their shared experiences as part of the farming class.[74]

The UFWO grew out of the United Farmers of Ontario (UFO), a populist farm organization founded in Toronto in 1914 by farm activists W.C. Good, J.J. Morrison, E.C. Drury, and J.Z. Fraser. When these men met in 1913, Ontario's farm movement "was never at a lower ebb."[75] Although discontent among farmers had long been raging, the so-called movement, with the notable exception of the successful WI, consisted of a somewhat fractured array of languishing associations.[76] According to UFO founders, this loose network of groups was not sufficient to promote the welfare of agriculture, which, as the UFO asserted, necessitated that farmers fight rural depopulation, urban interests, the evils of capitalism (including competition and exploitation), political corruption, high protective tariffs, the denigration of farmers by big business, intemperance, and militarism. Fundamental to this offensive was co-operation, a business philosophy for which UFO men like Good exhibited an "unfaltering evangelism,"[77] and, most significantly, the creation of a class consciousness among farmers that would move them to oppose their disfranchisement with a strong collective voice. Also essential to this struggle was "the raising of the rural people to a higher plane of citizenship," and giving the farmer "a knowledge of public questions, and an influence on national life commensurate with his importance."[78]

The success of the United Farm movement came quickly. By February of 1917, it claimed 200 clubs and 8,000 members; by December of 1918, these figures had climbed dramatically to 2,000 clubs and 25,000 members. By 1920, membership of the movement totalled 60,000 men, women, and children.[79] This terrific increase in members beginning in 1918 was attributable not only to the formation that year of the UFWO, but to the somewhat unexpected foray of the UFO into party politics.[80] Farmers were furious with Ottawa for revoking the military exemption of young men who laboured on Canadian farms. This injustice prompted the UFO in May 1918 to lead a protest on Parliament Hill of 6,000 farmers, who ultimately were turned away from the House of Commons. UFO chronicler Melville Staples asserted in 1921 that "this literal shutting of the door in their faces did more than any one thing to cause the political upheaval which has since taken place."[81] Incensed by urban politicians repeatedly dismissive of rural concerns, and caught up in the progressive political fervour following World War I, branch delegates at a UFO meeting in Toronto in October of 1918 agreed to run United Farmer candidates in rural by-elections. Surprisingly, forty-four out of sixty-four UFO candidates swept to victory in the 1919 provincial election, forming a coalition government with Labour.[82] With this, UFO founder and president E.C. Drury would distinguish himself, between 1919 and 1923, as Ontario's first and only United Farmer premier.

Although farm women contributed little to the election process, the mission of the zealous UFWO was to educate them on how to make the most of their newly acquired right to vote.[83] Essentially, this procedure involved reinforcing the UFO position that rural demands for dramatic reform could be achieved only through farmer solidarity, partisan affiliation, and agrarian political power. That these tenets necessarily disregarded or demeaned the distinct priorities and experiences of women helps explain why the UFWO was shortlived and small in membership, and therefore an impotent political force.[84]

Nevertheless, the UFWO believed that its focus on political discourse and activism, particularly as they related to the farming class, distinguished it from the WI. Future vice-president Mrs J.N. Foote of Collingwood found a decided tendency at Women's Institutes conventions to stifle any sign of "independent thought on the part of the women," and "to shut off discussion, or at any rate to control it."[85] Most UFWO supporters maintained that the apparent political neutrality of the WI was simply a manifestation of government control, and of Institute deference to the party in power: UFWO activist Margery Mills declared that "inasmuch as it [the Women's Institutes] is a Government-owned and controlled institution, it is wrong in principle, for in a democratic country the people should mould the ideas of the government, and not vice versa."[86] A.K. reported that at the annual meeting of the western Ontario branches of the WI in London, the speakers "'were so offensively partizan [sic] that a great many members who did not see eye to eye with the Government in all its vagaries, were incensed that an organization with such ostensibly high ideals for 'Home and Country,' should have deteriorated into a mere Government machine.'"[87]

The UFWO believed that the unspoken arrangement between the government and the WI, which in the UFWO's view allowed for government funding in exchange for political compliance, compromised the integrity of both institutions. The UFWO insisted in 1920 that "'we do not want to be in a position where the Government can dictate to us. We want to maintain our independence and, if necessary, dictate to the Government.'"[88] As late as 1929, when the provincial UFWO had all but disappeared, the secretary of the organization recommended that the government release its hold on the WI so that it could thrive as an independent society. At the same time, however, she outlined the UFWO proposal for a Women's Bureau so that "'the services now rendered exclusively to the Women's Institute membership be made available to all women's organizations on equal terms.'"[89] Clearly, with its demise imminent, a practical UFWO, while remaining unwilling to compromise its political character, wanted access to public funds: "'our Provincial Government already expends annually a large sum of money in organizing and maintaining one group of women – the Women's Institutes Branch. ... Surely, when such a huge sum is already being expended by the Government on a department for women, it is only reasonable to ask that the services of such a department should be made available, not to the Women's Institutes only, but also to the United Farm Women and any other organizations who so desire.'"[90] Provincial monies meant not only government acknowledgment and financial support, but, in the case of the WI, a sense of entitlement and privilege that the UFWO resented.

The time was ripe, believed UFWO supporters in 1918, for a politicized, independent alternative to the impassive, government-funded WI: "since women are now becoming citizens instead of wards, we must have some means whereby we may qualify for citizenship, and since the W.I. shuts the doors on all matters pertaining to citizenship, it will have to make way for other organizations such as the U.F.O."[91] After observing the WI's partisanship during an election campaign, United Farm woman A.K. declared " 'I feel now that it is high time that farm women united without being responsible to any party.' "[92] Of course, like the United Farm men, United Farm women aligned themselves to the UFO party, belying the jab at the WI by UFWO president Mrs George Brodie of Newmarket that " 'we're going to be political ... but we're going to leave party out of politics.' "[93]

Because the UFWO was resolutely agro-centric, its distrust of the WI was rooted not only in what the UFWO saw as political acquiescence, but in the WI's acceptance of non-farm women members, and its alleged indifference to urban exploitation.[94] In a letter to the *Weekly Sun*, UFWO supporter Muuver declared that the WI "is not filling the bill" because "every trade and profession [is] in the Institute."[95] Another UFWO adherent claimed that the Institute member was "letting herself be used by the urbanite influence against the interest of the rural woman."[96] In response to these kinds of accusations, the district secretary of Bruce County Institutes insisted that the combined rural and urban membership had "brought the town and country together as no other organization has done. It has been a boon to the life of our farm women and given them a point of social contact with the town women which we would otherwise have missed."[97] She could have also made the point that although WI membership was not exclusive to farm women, a significant number of farm women belonged to the WI.[98]

The most vocal critic of the WI was Miss Emma Griesbach, a Collingwood farm woman and teacher who was the first provincial secretary of the UFWO, and the opinionated editor of Sun Sisters' page, the women's page in the *Weekly Sun*. Griesbach was born in 1864 in Collingwood, Ontario, to Johanna Baker and Charles G. Griesbach, a Prussian immigrant who established a successful farm just outside Collingwood. Griesbach trained as a teacher, and held teaching posts in Ontario and in western Canada. In 1907, the year her father died, she held the position of school principal in Okotosh, Alberta. By 1910, presumably to assist her widowed mother who died in 1913, she was back in Collingwood, where her three brothers managed the family farm.[99]

Interestingly, many of Griesbach's most controversial and provocative views appeared in a regular editorial which did not bear her name. Readers knew the women's page editor only as "Sister Diana" or "Diana," Griesbach's pseudonym,[100] and only occasionally would readers be privy to information about her. Their suspicions that she herself was not of the farm likely prompted the *Weekly Sun* in April of 1918 to reveal that "Sister Diana is a farm woman. She lives on a farm in one of the large counties of Ontario, and her weekly budget of editorial matter comes very much in the nature of a hobby with her. It is a work of love."[101] That Diana, a farm woman, had time to devote to an editorial, even as "a hobby," drew scepticism from some readers. Indeed, curiosity about the identity of Diana moved several Sun Sisters' page readers over the years to request that a photograph of her be printed in the paper.[102]

Although the *Weekly Sun* not surprisingly ignored this request, the paper otherwise responded to the interests and concerns of the farming class. Founded by Goldwin Smith, and directed to farmers, the newspaper was bought in April 1919 by the Farmers' Publishing Company (FPC), a branch of the United Farmers' movement. The paper was then renamed the *Farmers' Sun*, and for use as political propaganda was declared "the Official Organ of the United Farmers of Ontario."[103] Indeed, while the FPC had a separate executive and treasury from the UFO, shareholders of the FPC were almost all UFO members. Staples described the inherent bias of the paper: "that the policy of the FPC and the *Weekly Sun* would run contrary to the policy of the UFO could hardly arise."[104]

Even before the purchase of the paper by the FPC, however, the *Weekly Sun* was promoting the interests and goals of the United Farmer movement, with Sister Diana, the UFWO's most strident voice, and some would argue its leader, endeavouring to politicize its women allies.[105] In addition to spouting the UFO party line, Griesbach's Diana repeatedly outlined for readers the goals of the UFWO. They broadly included educating farm women in political affairs, mobilizing farm women for political action, elevating the status of farm women's labour, and generally expanding farm women's horizons. In her often scholarly, impassioned expositions, the cerebral and self-assured Griesbach addressed all the finer points which these goals raised, offering high-brow references to literature and art, and moralizing about the import of various political, economic, and historical trends. Her commentaries were so varied and so efficiently researched that when W.C. Good suggested in a letter to Griesbach that she consider the seemingly benign topic of "the ridiculous and harmful french [*sic*] heels," she was able to boldly reply "I have [already] written on it. I went to the Manufacturers of the 'Natural Tread' footwear in Toronto and gave my readers (of whom you appear not to have been one) the philosophy of *heels* – likewise toes – from the point of view of both hygiene + of good sense. ... This was some time ago, and I assure you it was a very good article." She then challenged Good "to mention *any* subject of interest to women from any point or angle whatever, on which I have not written."[106] Admittedly, Griesbach could be critical, condescending, and dogmatic, but she had an abiding concern for farm women, and sought only that they better their lot.

Diana was first introduced in the *Weekly Sun* on 7 November 1917, when the women's page was known as the "Home Page" or "Home Department," and was focused primarily on household matters.[107] By 20 February 1918, however, the section had been renamed the "Sun Sisters' Page," "a page for women, Edited by 'Sister Diana,' to which all women readers are invited to contribute."[108] In welcoming women to make submissions to the page, Diana created a democratic platform in keeping with the populist values of the UFO.

While the women's page continued to offer "Recipes," "Cooking Hints," and "Household Suggestions," and would add features such as "Fashion Hints" and "Training the Child," its emphasis would be not on domestic concerns, but on issues of greater political, economic, and intellectual significance.[109] The male editor of the *Weekly Sun* boasted that it would prove "distinctive from all other 'women's pages'" because Sister Diana "is showing herself a THINKER" (as opposed to most women, he implied, who presumably didn't think, or at least not as much or as often as men did). He foresaw the page as "a great Women's Forum where opinions will be expressed and views will be exchanged by the Sisters."[110] Indeed, by 16 October 1918, the Sun Sisters' page regularly featured Diana's weighty editorials, and opinionated letters to her from female readers. As well, a column entitled "The Corner" offered a summary of UFWO activities and events; it was compiled by none other than Diana's alter ego, Emma Griesbach.[111] The Sun Sisters' page, according to Diana, proved popular among the newspaper's women readers.[112]

Griesbach's Diana editorials and letter replies (as well as her "Corner" column) unabashedly promoted the United Farmer cause, and women's participation in the movement. Only with the full participation of both farm men and women, she declared, could solidarity among the farming class be achieved. Accordingly, with women's involvement in the UFO, Griesbach and other female leaders envisioned a modern, fully integrated movement in which men and women were admitted as equals, were united in their convictions, and worked together side by side. Unlike the male superintendent of the WI, UFO men would be brothers to their female members.[113] Thus, at the local level, women could join an existing UFO men's club or form a corresponding UFWO club which met on its own and/or in conjunction with UFO gatherings.

UFWO leaders emphasized that its exclusively female organization was not intended to mimic old-fashioned, separatist, same-sex societies like the WI, which invariably divided the farming class.[114] Although the UFWO executive maintained that women's problems "can be best discussed and solved in our own meetings," it declared that UFWO women "are one" with the UFO, "whether we meet jointly or separately."[115] Accordingly, Diana dissuaded her readers from emulating the pattern of gender segregation endorsed by Prairie women's organizations: "the Western [Canadian] women have gone on record ... as believing it to be useless to look ... to the men's organizations for relief in their labor problems, and that they must depend solely on their own organization. I do not think this attitude is altogether right. Who are these men anyway? They are members of our households. They are inhabitants neither of the moon nor of the air nor the sea. They live right alongside of us, and it should be clear to them that our interests and theirs that our welfare and theirs are interwoven so that there is no time of separation."[116] Integration of the sexes, Diana asserted, would serve farm folk best: "we have before us one objective, a strong union of the farming men and women of Ontario. There is work for us to do. ... It cannot be secured by a union of the men alone, or of the women alone. ... It is going to be by a union of the forces of the farming men and the farming women – together."[117] Addressing a joint meeting of the UFO Convention in 1918, UFWO president Mrs George Brodie insisted that a separatist women's group was neither needed nor wanted: "there is no walk on earth ... where the men and women work so closely together as on the farm, and in their own organization there was no desire on the part of the women either for separation or for special privilege: 'We don't want a special women's organization.'"[118] As late as December 1920, UFWO provincial secretary Mrs Meta Laws felt compelled "to emphasize the fact that this U.F.W.O. of ours is not to be understood as an organization separate from the U.F.O."[119] Indeed, in 1924, executive officer Mrs Wyman was of the opinion that the fusing of UFWO and UFO groups in her district was producing more satisfying clubs.[120]

UFWO leaders assumed that in the interest of class solidarity and numerical strength, and by reason of the business "partnership" of farm husband and wife, UFO men would be receptive to the equal standing and participation of women members. After all, the slogan of the movement proclaimed "Equal Rights to all, and special privileges to none." As noted by Meta Laws, "the platform of the United Farmers of Ontario" included a belief in "the absolute equality of the sexes, socially, politically and economically."[121] Griesbach had every reason, then, in October of 1918 to assure a fledgling UFWO that official parity for its members, as granted by UFO men, was no doubt forthcoming. Although provisional status, she proclaimed, is all that it "can legally hold until the U.F.O. constitution is amended in Convention to admit women on the same terms as the men …, we women are not dealing with a hostile body of Shylocks, who will demand their pound of flesh in the way of legal forms, but with our brothers, sons, husbands and fathers."[122] Two months later, President Brodie publicly "expressed her pleasure that the United Farmers of Ontario was the first body of men to admit women to full partnership."[123]

But for the UFO, "full partnership" simply meant that it held title to UFWO monies, which only incidentally made women UFO members.[124] It was early on, in fact, that the UFO denied women use of its provincial head office for their inaugural meeting, and appropriated the women's treasury.[125] Consequently "tied to movement pursestrings, farm women were denied the freedom to set their own agenda, being forced to rely on the benevolence of UFO executives for funding."[126]

Nevertheless, women counting on equal treatment were encouraged by the existence of at least some UFO men who, like the majority of men in the Prairie farm movement, seemed receptive to female membership. Griesbach boasted of one UFO club which recognized that it would not be a "constructive force in the community" as long as it was comprised exclusively of men. "The men of this club," she proudly stated, "are keen to have the women in."[127] The secretary for a Collingwood UFWO, which held both separate and joint UFO meetings, happily reported to Diana that "the men say that the U.F.W.O. has put more life into their organization."[128] One man's enthusiasm for women in the movement was articulated in a poem, by Stratford-area UFO secretary Mr Scott, which Griesbach printed in her Sun Sisters' page:

In this dark age of strife and snub,
Though men we are of many parts,
The success of our Farmers' Clubs
Is the great object of our hearts

But while we put forth all our powers,
and do our level best to win it,
No great success can e'er be ours
Unless we have the ladies in it.

They'll do business without our fuss,
By the exercise of common sense
Great benefit they can be to us,
With their well-known noble influence[129]

The maternal feminist rhetoric evident in the poem's final stanza differed markedly from the equal rights rhetoric espoused by the UFO, and which UFWO women assumed would be applied to their own place in the movement. Even the well-intentioned Mr Scott did not speak to questions of female position and power within the male organization.

Indeed, despite talk of farming class solidarity and "equal rights to all," United Farm men generally proved resistant to women's participation, whether "on the same terms as men" or otherwise.[130] That United Farm women formed their own organization despite their anti-separatist sentiments was likely due to the preference by farm men who wanted to maintain their own association. UFWO executive attended the UFO directors' meeting, but the women were compelled to request that apparently disinterested UFO men "do us the favor of being present at our meeting."[131] Staples himself admitted in 1921 that "the u.f.o. as a whole was not yet seized of their [the UFWO's] importance, and consequently the support of the men was still largely passive."[132] In December of 1919, Griesbach had to concede that despite a request at the UFO Annual Convention in 1918 for men to help establish UFWO clubs, "this appeal may not have met with the full response hoped for."[133] The major cause of the resistance by men was their fear that women would diminish the influence of the UFO and drain its financial resources.[134] Local club women maintained, however, that men rebuffed female membership because of their belief that a woman's place was in the home.[135] Whatever their reasons, UFO co-founder J.J. Morrison observed that UFO leaders paid little attention to eager female provincial organizers until the men deemed women's participation prudent in securing election victory for UFO candidates.[136]

Disgruntled women complained to Griesbach's Sun Sisters' page that men excluded them from UFO clubs and all but ignored the UFWO. Mrs B of Grey County wrote that she was "very much disappointed that the women were not allowed to be present at the u.f.o. meeting last week. I asked my husband to take me but he would not do it." Furthermore, she wished "the speaker had given it to the men for not bringing out their wives."[137] Local UFWO president Mrs A observed that "some of the men are very much against the u.f.w.o., and think we are very much out of place." Mrs A also noted that her

UFWO club was forced to rent a meeting room because the men took over the one available hall.[138] Clearly Mrs A was aware that women were often denied the resources to which men felt entitled.

Accounts such as these drove a disillusioned Griesbach to defy the rhetoric of farmer solidarity with scathing condemnations of farm men.[139] Her antagonism necessarily highlighted the disparity between men and women's lives, so seems inconsistent with equity feminism. Significantly, however, and consistent with equity feminism, Griesbach's hostility towards UFO men was generated by a frustrated need for approval by those very same men. She vilified farm men for their arrogant sense of privilege, and, with brutal sarcasm, informed Mrs B that "accustomed to riding the high horse around the domestic premises, they [some men] are unable to see wife or children on the same level as themselves. The poor men are to be pitied. Seated constantly on the high horse alluded to, and breathing the rarified air of the upper atmosphere, they become peculiarly affected, even diseased. The chief symptoms are (1) Swelled head, (2) Perverted vision, by which they themselves loom very large, and everyone else very small, (3) Ornery disposition. The only way to cure this sad condition is to remove the causes, that is the High Horse. But the patient should have plenty of exercise, and the Secretary suggests – merely suggests, you know – that a Goat be substituted."[140] In the same vein, Griesbach suggested to Mrs A that "[men] think the place for their woman folk is to stop home and calves, while they, the lords of creation, are occupying themselves more agreeably. No doubt they expect a well-cooked meal ready for them when they get back, and a meekly submissive wife to serve it to them. What do you think of such men, United Farm Sisters?"[141] Griesbach similarly targeted the men in her column, "The Corner," in which she threatened to "step into one of these U.F. clubs where it has never been mentioned that the Sisters might belong and cast my eye over the brethren to see what they look like. I bet a dollar they were everyone born a thousand years ago, and they are all dead and don't know it."[142]

Griesbach's biting criticism of farm men also addressed their opposition to women voting, and their lack of appreciation for overworked farm wives. When a farm woman told Griesbach that she overheard some men declare that they "won't let their wives vote," Griesbach wrote a caustic critique of their stance: "one is curious to know what these men are willing to 'let' their wives do. ... Did they refuse to 'let' their wives work hard, pinch, scrape, save, economize, to clear off all indebtedness, cook for them, wash, bring up a family, establish a home and in general promote the welfare of all concerned? ... Luckily, whatever their autocratic powers in their own domestic realm, they will have to 'let' the wives of their enlightened neighbors vote."[143] In an article entitled "The Work and Waste of Women," men were also ridiculed by Griesbach's Diana. In addressing the topic of work, she noted that she was ignoring the issue of labour by men because she was "a little impatient with the attitude of men in general towards women's work."[144] She often condemned men for taking women's labour for granted, referring to them as "our smooth-handed, frock-coated lords and masters," who "not content with our hard service ... shout at us to do more." "If you listen closely," Griesbach added, "you will hear the crack of the whip."[145] There can be no doubt that Griesbach, with her metaphors of bondage and slavery, generally perceived women as victimized by men.

Those Sun Sisters who supported these pejorative portrayals of farm men were, along with Griesbach "and" Diana, criticized by United Farm women who opposed these depictions. In response to Sister Flo's letter about men's selfishness, numerous letters to Diana appeared in which farm women defended farm men. They extolled the virtues of their husbands, and asserted that farmers were consistently used as scapegoats. Like farm women, they argued, farm men, too, were "slaves."[146] When Andrea Thryne announced in her letter that "so far as [the] woman or women are concerned the average Ontario farmer is just plain brute," reader Belinda Bell replied that "your correspondent should either give the locality where she had seen conditions such as she describes, or apologize to the farmers of Ontario for the statements which she makes."[147] Significantly, Diana's disparaging comments about farm men also concerned UFWO president Mrs George Brodie, who publicly censured the editor's propensity "to unduly criticize the men."[148] In a speech at the 1920 UFO convention, Mrs Brodie remarked that men did not read the women's page of the *Farmers' Sun* "because if they looked at it they would see slams at themselves."[149] Brodie's comment that "there are mean farmers, but there are mighty mean women, too" was received with much audience applause.[150]

Indeed although the UFWO was an indisputably staunch supporter of farm women, and lobbied on behalf of their just treatment, particularly in the home, Griesbach and some Sun Sisters tended to belittle, not celebrate, the specific experiences and values of farm women. Griesbach was hardly understanding of the fact, for example, that the enormous demands on their energy and time prevented many of them from becoming more active in the UFWO.[151] When women explained that they were too busy to attend club meetings, Diana responded by asking "don't you think that 'too busy' is an excuse rather than a reason?"[152] Mothers of small children were especially doubtful about whether they could attend the meetings, and asked Diana for advice; Sun Sister Dorothy Wells later wrote that she had not "yet noticed an answer to the query as to how to get to the convention with five small children."[153] Exasperated by the "excuses" of politically inactive farm women, Griesbach sarcastically asked: "does anyone imagine that the women of the U.F.W.O. are of the 'idle rich,' and in this game for amusement? I do not know one woman in the U.F.W.O. who is not a busy household woman, and who does not sacrifice every atom of her leisure and who does not curtail her very hours of sleep, to carry on this work."[154]

The seeming apathy of farm women moved Griesbach and a few Sun Sisters, in the fashion of the United Farm men, to indict these women for their own oppression.[155] Diana scornfully declared that farm women "are the most contented people in the world; they always ask for NOTHING, and they always GET IT." She informed her readers that if they did "not take the only effectual means for general betterment, that is, organized action, they have no one to blame but themselves, for these conditions." Farm women, she said, made "the intensely foolish blunder" of not acting together.[156] Sun Sister Andrea Thryne concluded that the farm woman "is not blameless": she raised her sons to be arrogant men, and became a "moral shirker" who "allowed the soul of a slave" to possess her.[157]

If castigating women for their needless predicament were not demoralizing enough, Griesbach and others credited men with being more committed to female advancement than women themselves. Diana asserted that she had "no doubt ... that the men will co-operate for the relief of the rural domestic situation," and wondered "if the men are not more ready than the women!"[158] In a letter Diana entitled "Are Women Awake?" Sun Sister Betty Brown claimed that she knew men "who show more apparent interest in the questions affecting women than many of the women themselves manifest," while A.W. found "that men on the average are more willing to let women advance than the average woman is willing to step forward."[159]

Griesbach maintained that women held themselves back by focusing too heavily on domestic science and household pursuits. Diana contended that "the domestic science offered to us in the past has been nothing more or less than domestic muddling," and that possibly no labour was "so completely unorganized as all that comes under the general term of 'housework.'" Diana dismissed "the new trend in 'Domestic Science'" as "a huge joke."[160] Indeed, a Sun Sisters' article mockingly asked women if they were "one of those who chase through life, dust cloth in hand, making everyone in the household uncomfortable because of a little dust – upsetting the peace of the whole family, for the sake of gratifying your passion for house-cleaning? Or do you prefer to ... hold their love even above the sacred duty of chasing microbes?"[161] In the *O.A.C. Review*, Griesbach insisted that "we must face the fact that we have allowed ourselves to become household drudges, and that to raise ourselves in the scale of being we must get out of our kitchens often enough and stay out of them long enough to think something else than kitchen."[162] In formulating her critique of domestic science, Griesbach likely took a cue from United Farm men who rejected equivalent notions of scientific farming.[163] More to the point, she perceived principles associated with domestic science, such as consumerism and individualism, as conflicting with the UFO's platform of co-operation. She labelled women's domestic work the "Robinson Crusoe system of household labor" because of its "individualism and isolation," and called for co-operative housekeeping in the form of community kitchens and laundries.[164]

Predictably, many Sun Sisters also censured women's preoccupation with homemaking concerns by berating the WI and its emphasis on these issues. Sun Sister Kintorian supposed that "surely when a room full of intelligent women meet and spread a whole afternoon together, they would be able to discuss something more weighty than 'How to wash dishes' or 'what to make for X-mas gifts,' etc. etc. We have been discussing that kind of stuff too long and accomplished nothing. Why not get after [such] subjects as 'How can we secure Hydro in our homes?' 'How we may help the farm movement along?' 'How best to combat the liquor traffic' 'How best to combine our efforts to help win the Dominion election?' "[165] Sister Fidelis, in a letter revealingly entitled "W.I. Versus U.F.W.O.," confirmed that the WI could accomplish more if it were less consumed by domestic science. She reported that at her Institute lecture on the serious subject of "Simple Meals and their Refining Influence," the women were interested only in exchanging "some new-fangled recipes for cakes or pastries of some kind." Fidelis found the WI's homemaking emphasis difficult to "reconcile," citing that "greater thought [should be] given to the development and expansion of the mental calibre."[166]

But if the UFWO executive viewed the WI as a rival organization whose separatism and traditional focus on homemaking undermined the political reform efforts of the United Farm movement, this meant little to the local UFWO clubs whose activities and work "were identical" to those of the WI.[167] Like WI branches, local United Farm clubs enjoyed separatism, and engaged in domestic pursuits, social reform work, and cultural and intellectual endeavours.

Many United Farm women at the local level endorsed the separatism of UFWO clubs. At a joint meeting in 1924 of the Smith Falls UFO and UFWO, for example, when UFO men proposed to disband the auxiliary and amalgamate all members, "the women quickly vetoed this idea and thanking the men for expressing their views so plainly resolved at least to have a good time and make the third Wed. of the month [designated for separate u.f.w.o. meetings] worth while."[168] Indeed, the Smith Falls women lamented in 1927 that when their group joined the UFO for the annual convention "the men's club monopolized most of the time in discussion," addressing issues of the "shipping of livestock."[169] These women understood that within the mixed-sex environment of the meeting, their voice and priorities were lost to the favoured concerns and interests of men.

Local UFWO clubs focused almost as heavily on domestic science and household concerns as did the WI. Despite Griesbach's efforts to make the Sun Sisters' page an intellectual forum for farm women, they regularly used the page, for instance, to request and share recipes.[170] In fact, when the *Farmers' Sun* editor J.C. Ross informed Griesbach in 1922 that the more domestic-oriented Violet Dickens would replace her as the new women's page editor, he stated that "there has been a growing demand for a distinctly women's page, devoted to home matters such as recipes, patterns ... etc."[171] In March, Ross wrote W.C. Good that "Miss Griesbach has her following and there will be some who will miss her letters and activities, but on the other hand, the majority of our readers found her letters too long and too weighty."[172] UFWO executive officer and Griesbach supporter Alice Webster lamented in a revealing letter to W.C. Good later that month that the new women's page was now a "tiresome repetition" of the Women's Institute platform.[173]

The WI's influence was evident in UFWO clubs across Ontario. At a UFWO meeting in Oxford County, for example, "three interesting and instructive papers were read on 'The Making of maple syrup ...' and 'Gardening,' and 'Marmalades.' Several good recipes were exchanged and [there was] a general change of ideas on the above topics." The Thames River branch of the UFWO sponsored sewing instruction for its members, and "decided to continue the sewing class ... as it was considered too bad to drop such a good movement." At the Listowel UFWO in Perth County, "members answered the roll call by giving a recipe on pickling cucumbers."[174]

The social reform efforts of the UFWO also overlapped those first exerted by the WI. The community work of local UFWOs, like that of the WI, were largely children- and women-centred, and included improving the sanitary conditions of rural schools, providing hot lunches for students, initiating travelling libraries, raising funds and goods for orphanages, hospitals, and shelters, cleaning up cemeteries, establishing women's rest rooms, and, of course, lobbying for hydro-electricity.[175] Like the WI, UFWO clubs also took great interest in legislative reform as it related to women, entertaining issues such as property, wills, divorce, guardianship, as well as voting and holding public office.[176]

Both WI and UFWO clubs also busied themselves with countless cultural and intellectual pursuits. Concerts, sing-alongs, and readings were usual fare. As well, members discussed political trends and current events, held debates on the status of women, and the state of the farm home and family, and studied literature, art, and history.[177] WI branches, for example, long before initiating their Tweedsmuir Histories in the 1940s, invited members to research and record the formative years of their WI club and its surrounding area. Local UFWOs were encouraged to do the same.[178]

Both WI and United Farm women also valued the social benefits of their clubs. They routinely held euchre parties, picnics, teas, lunches, oyster suppers, and strawberry socials.[179] The lofty ideals of Griesbach and the UFO held little appeal for the Smith Falls UFWO who in February of 1922 "organized as a social club having nothing in common with head quarters [sic] at Toronto."[180] Within these local clubs, "sisterhood was the predictable outgrowth of such regular collaboration in sociability."[181]

The similarity of local WI and UFWO clubs had various ramifications. First, it left many UFWO women confused about why they organized. They wondered, " 'what shall we do at our Club meetings?' " and confessed that they organized "without really knowing what we organized for."[182] Second, the similarity made establishing new UFWO clubs difficult in areas where WI branches already existed, and presented the possibility that once these clubs were created, they would be subsumed by the more powerful WI. Indeed, those UFWO groups that survived well after 1923 did so largely in areas lacking WI branches.[183]

Nevertheless, where WI and UFWO clubs did co-exist, their similarities seemed to engender not the rivalry encouraged by the UFWO executive, but a "very great harmony" between them.[184] The Norton WI, for example, passed a motion in 1934 to lend their chairs to a nearby UFWO branch, which presumably had a shortage for well-attended events; the UFWO branch in turn proposed to loan their chairs to the Institute. In 1942, that same UFWO contributed ten dollars to the mobile kitchen project initiated by the WI. The Norton

Branch moved "that a vote of thanks be sent to U.F.W.O." for donating the money.[185] One United Farm woman reproached those cohorts who harboured hostility toward the WI, arguing that "we can no more build our organization by pulling down another than you can build one church by pulling down another. There is lots of work for all to do, so let us cooperate."[186] A Sun Sisters' reader asked WI critic Diana "not to rub it into the W.I. too hard," for "in a way, the Institute is really the 'Mother' of the U.F.W.O."[187]

One reason why local WI and UFWO clubs were so alike (and so often congenial) was that they had a shared membership. Many UFWO members had once belonged to the WI (such as president Brodie) or participated in both organizations concurrently.[188] One such woman was Mrs George Laidlaw who had been an active member of the Wilton Grove WI since its inception in 1909, and held several positions (including president and district director) in the subsequent ten years. When the Wilton Grove WI unofficially disbanded in 1919 (not to resume until 1929), Mrs Laidlaw became active in the Wilton Grove UFWO, bringing flowers to ill members and hosting club meetings.[189]

The most notable UFWO member to participate simultaneously in the WI was MP Agnes Macphail. Born and raised on a farm in Grey County, Macphail possessed a "sincere love for the ... farm people, and especially the farm women, and was well-acquainted with their burdensome lot.[190] Although she was never a card-carrying member of the WI, the politically savvy Macphail never hesitated to address their conventions and branch meetings.[191] In the fall of 1932, for example, she spoke in London at the WI's Western Ontario Convention, which she found "an enriching experience." In October of 1939, she attended a meeting of a Walkerton area WI, where she "made a most earnest and inspiring address of particular interest to women." In a 1936 speech, when Macphail declared that women "have a genius for organization," she pointed to the fact that the WI outlasted the male Farmers' Institutes.[192]

Macphail's involvement in the UFWO, which began in 1919, grew out of her early alliance with the United Farm movement, and intensified with her nomination by the UFO as a candidate for Southeast Grey in the federal election of 1921. As an articulate and charismatic representative of UFO interests, and then as Canada's first woman MP, she was something of a dignitary in UFWO circles: by 1921, she had been appointed to the organization's provincial executive, and was also director of its North York section.[193] For her part, Macphail promoted the cause of the UFWO. She contributed assorted articles to the Sun Sisters' page in the *Farmers' Sun*, and used other agricultural journals such as the *Farmer's Advocate* to expound the group's platform.[194]

Macphail deemed the provincial UFWO as better for farm women than the WI,[195] but her bias spoke more to her loyalty to the UFO than to her strict adherence to equity feminism. Nevertheless, Macphail asserted the equity feminism of the provincial auxiliary. Echoing the sentiments of Griesbach and others, Macphail often denounced, for example, the female separatism and focus of women's clubs. She insisted that "women must get equal place for their section of the political organization, or else have one organization for men and women. The latter is preferable." She referenced fascist countries to illustrate that "where [one's] sex is being stressed woman has ceased to be a person." She argued, moreover, that women should not limit themselves to female-centred causes: "'women fighting for women is an old-fashioned feminism – they must fight for humanity."[196] Having once scorned dedication to "the science and practise of domestic economy," Macphail, possibly alluding to the WI, facetiously remarked that "women are good organizers, so good that they often keep organizations about nothing running for years."[197]

Macphail also championed the social feminist cause, however, espousing, like the WI, notions of female specificity and domesticity, and endorsing women's public "housekeeping" role. She "stressed the importance of women's clubs,"[198] for example, declaring that "thoughtful women do not wish to see their sex imitate man," and its "aping of man's methods in getting work done."[199] Macphail insisted that if "women are to make a lasting contribution they must express their own woman's attitude and thought."[200] In a speech entitled "The Power of Women," she emphasized that "women must be women when they enter actively into government. … Let … we [sic] be true to our own womanly ways in public life and the whole will be enriched."[201] She also admired women's "good housekeeping instinct," explaining that "honest and decent politics is only national housekeeping anyway," and that "women will make good national housekeepers."[202] Macphail biographer Terry Crowley notes that "in feminizing the political message, she made her most original contribution."[203]

Macphail's adherence to the allegedly conservative precepts of social feminism, however contradictory to her more historically appreciated equity stance,[204] is profoundly significant given that she pioneered women's role in federal politics, was widely perceived to hold "ultra-progressive political views,"[205] and resisted traditional societal dictates for women, in particular, to marry and have children. That Macphail's espousals of social feminism were compatible with her unconventional life and life choices speaks to the radical possibilities of social feminism and to the progressivism of the women's groups which embraced it.

By the mid 1920s, the provincial UFWO had largely met its demise. Barely surviving the collapse of the Drury government in 1923, and victim to the infighting and political inexperience of the UFO, as well as to a shrinking farm population,[206] the organization had lost many of its initial leaders, and witnessed a plethora of local clubs folding. While the UFWO proudly reported a membership of 7,000 women in 1921, by 1926 it was a scant 2,312.[207] Although some women remained active in the cause through to the 1950s, the UFWO officially disbanded in 1943, with the United Farm movement following closely behind in 1944.[208] The WI, meanwhile, continued to be immensely popular: by 1940, it claimed 40,300 members.[209]

During the inter-war years, the female separatism and women-centred experiences promoted by the WI through home economics and social reform appealed little to the UFWO leadership, which sought integration with UFO men. For the WI, "community housekeeping," along with a continued commitment to homemaking, facilitated countless progressive, social, economic, and legislative reforms, which addressed the health and safety of rural Ontario, and which made central the lives, experiences, and values of women. These projects cultivated in members skills in fundraising, lobbying, and leadership, and were augmented by activities important to women's cultural, intellectual, and social development. The UFWO leadership, particularly Emma Griesbach, expressed disdain for the social feminist mandate of the WI, but this sentiment was largely absent from the local UFWO clubs where women emulated the homemaking and reform activities of WI branches.[210] Clearly, the social feminist concerns of the majority members diverged from the equity feminist vision of leaders such as Griesbach. This divide was so profound in the UFWO that even after 1922, when social feminist priorities were more fully addressed provincially, recovery was too late: the limited popularity of the movement had come and gone, and the WI was there to pick up the slack. That the UFWO failed was not due to the conservatism of farm women who were drawn to the WI, but to its commitment to equity feminism which invited the detrimental repudiation by UFO men, and undermined the self-sufficiency and values of rural women.

6 "Face the Future. Treasure the Past": Farm Women, Changing Times, and Social Feminism in the 1950s and 1960s

Directing their energies to the war effort in the early 1940s, farm wives in the WI were as secure as ever in the value of their homemaking contributions "to home and country"; however, in the 1950s and 60s, unprecedented change in rural Ontario, as well as a fledgling equity feminist movement, challenged the conventions of farm women and the WI, causing increasing confusion over their post-war roles. Yet, in the face of these challenges, farm women remained steadfast to social feminist values, as did the WI, which cleverly used what it saw as some detrimental trends to both "modernize" the Institute program and reinforce its original tenets. Indeed, the social feminist character of Ontario farm women would not be compromised before 1970.

During the war, farm wives were tirelessly dedicated to war work, and were lauded for their efforts. In a 1941 article entitled "Guns or Butter," for example, A.H. Martin of the Ontario Department of Agriculture declared that "no class of women have less time and have contributed more in materials and work for the comfort and relief of suffering among the fighting forces and war victims than have farm women. ... Farm women have proven themselves equal to every emergency."[1] WI provincial president Emma Duke echoed this sentiment in her "salute" to WI women in particular when she affirmed that while they "'are not wearing the uniform of the Navy, the Army or the Air Force,'" Institute members "'are truly 'Soldiers of the King.'"[2] Flattering comments such as these no doubt accomplished their goal: to reinforce for farm women the value of their labour, and to induce them to toil further.

Within the WI, farm women contributed to the war effort in a variety of ways, all of which capitalized on their domestic proficiency. Most notably, they prepared and packaged clothes and foodstuffs for troops and civilians overseas. The WI cooperated with organizations such as the Red Cross, the Navy League, and the Salvation Army to send blankets, knitted socks, maple sugar, and homemade jam. In fact, by 1944, Ontario WI women had contributed 826 blankets, 383,719 knitted items, 410 pounds of maple sugar, and over 830,500 pounds of Britain-bound jam. By war's end, they had raised $736,865 in funds, of which over $110,000 went to the British War Victims' Funds, the United Nations' Relief Funds, and War Savings Certificates and Bonds.[3]

As food producers on the farm, WI women were reminded of the need for food for soldiers and civilians alike. " 'The army fights on its stomach,' " women were told, and "hungry civilians lack in courage and fortitude."[4] Thus food, asserted Emma Duke, "is the greatest weapon. No factory can turn out milk for cheese; no war plant can produce eggs for dehydration; no machinery or plant can raise hogs which will reach our soldiers in the form of bacon." Only women of the farm "can claim the credit or satisfaction which is that of the women who are able to make this contribution."[5] While food production and conservation were "not as glamorous as driving an army truck," they made the farm woman "a leader in winning the War."[6] Farm women reported that due to the exigencies of war, they kept more hens, milked more cows, cared for more pigs, and assisted in traditionally male field work ·alongside the men.[7] J.A. Carroll of the Ontario Department of Agriculture stated in a 1943 article entitled "The Agricultural Battle" that women who had never before worked the fields were driving tractors, steering horses, and pitching hay. He used the article to "grasp this opportunity of expressing appreciation and congratulations" to them.[8] Likewise, Duke, in her tribute to farm women's contribution to food production, instructed them, like honourable frontline soldiers, to "stand at attention and take the salute."[9]

To aid them in this food production work, farm women were expected to enlist the help of their adult daughters, many of whom were otherwise engaged in city jobs.[10] Not only would the farm labour of these daughters leave their urban positions free for men refused by the military (men whom the WI insisted "are very apt to be discouraged and need our help and understanding"), it would "on the Home-Front Production Line" furnish help that these farm daughters were especially trained to offer.[11] The WI offered assistance to daughters who undertook home vegetable gardens, facilitated their membership in the Girls' Garden Brigades, and awarded "Certificates of Merit" to worthy Brigade recruits.[12] In 1943, wi leader Miss Florence Eadie paid tribute to farm daughters everywhere: "we know the splendid job you are doing in helping make food fight. From early morning until late at night we see you in the field, in the barn, in the garden, in the house, making a magnificent contribution to one of Canada's most important wartime jobs. We know that serving on the home farm is hard work. ... We know it calls for sacrifice. ... Nevertheless we believe you are happy in the doing, knowing that you are helping with the battle of food production."[13] But this opportunity for patriotism might have been cold comfort for those daughters who left their independent, remunerated city work only to find themselves back at home performing unpaid labour. For many of these young women, patriotic enthusiasm would have been more readily achieved alongside the advantages of urban life.

The wi's praise of daughters who remained on or returned to the family farm reflected not only a desire for their labour, but a compulsion to preserve home and family in the midst of national upheaval. "Perhaps the time is opportune," the wi instructed its women at the start of the war, "to cultivate home life to a greater extent."[14] Institute magazine *Home and Country* observed in the winter of 1940–41 that "to keep alive in our community the spirit of freedom[,] tolerance, and understanding is no small ... task. As homemakers we know that this spirit begins in the home. Canadians need the strength of body and mind which can be developed best in good homes. Let us resolve to make our homes more than ever 'the bulwarks of the nation.'"[15] With farm daughters at home during the war, many farm women no doubt felt a greater sense of family cohesion, a condition, believed the wi, necessary for a strong, united country.

For the wartime wi, increased emphasis on the home necessarily meant greater consideration of home economics. In articles such as "Home Economics Aids in War Time" and "Home Economics for Total Victory," the wi continued to assert its importance throughout World War ii, having learned from the First World War not to forsake its *raison d'être*.[16] The time and energy-saving techniques of home economics, after all, expedited the output of Allied care packages, and the increased production of the nation's food. More generally, home economics facilitated the efficiency of homemaking, which, according to Mrs G.W. Keys, the wi provincial convenor of home economics, "is the biggest basic industry in the country, employs the greatest number of men and women, handles the greatest amount of money and allows more working hours than any other industry." Thus, it was "vital to the task of winning the war, securing the peace, and building a new world."[17] By 1946, the secretary of the Wilton Grove WI could report that "home economics is a subject much in the lime light just now."[18]

For the wartime WI, home economics was, as always, crucial to the elevated status and job satisfaction of farm wives, and to the general welfare and educational advancement of farm daughters. Announcing to farm wives in 1941 that "Home Economics Challenges Women," the WI emphasized that, far from being mundane, "keeping the family well fed and the household budget within bounds requires a great deal of thought on the part of the homemaker."[19] With home economics, asserted Mrs G.W. Keys, "there are no 'common tasks,'" making "the profession of homemaker ... the ... most important occupation there is."[20] For farm daughters, the provincial WI established rural Homemaking Clubs for girls. It organized groups, trained and furnished local leaders, and encouraged and enlisted rural girls to join.[21] North Wentworth WIs, "realizing the importance of manual training and domestic science for rural schools," requested that in the post-war curriculum "these subjects be given consideration." They also resolved that "a recommendation be forwarded to the Ontario Educational Association asking that these subjects be stressed in the Normal School curriculum as essentials rather than specials." The Wolfe Island club in the Kingston area resolved that "a Home Economics course suitable for rural girls" be part of the curriculum at the Kemptville Agricultural School near Ottawa, and that "credits be given to lead to higher training." The Derry West WI, outside of Brampton, insisted that the Ontario government create a course in "Household and immediate Science, ... available to girls with a definite ideal toward the improvement of rural home and community life."[22] With the WI reaffirming the relevance of home economics, farm women during the war seemed justifiably proud of their increased food and clothes production. Moreover, they were confident that "the war [had] made [them] realize more and more the importance of the fundamental values of home life."[23]

In the new and ever-changing post-war era, however, farm women and the WI were not so certain of their role and place. They were compelled to make the transition from wartime to peacetime, but were unable to fall back on their seemingly dated pre-war ways. And though farm women of the late 1940s and 50s might have attempted to modernize these methods, in the 1960s they were still made to feel that they were not keeping up: rural sociologist Dr Helen Abell blatantly told a meeting of farm wives in 1961, for instance, that their "traditional ways of doing things will not be adequate for the future."[24]

Critical trends were altering the rural landscape. Hydro-electricity, for example, which had been slowly winding its way through rural Ontario since the 1920s, was becoming almost commonplace after the war. While just under 59,000 farms had hydro in 1940, by 1960, the figure had more than doubled to almost 141,000.[25] In a 1959 study by Dr Abell of 352 Ontario farm homes, 91 per cent had electricity in both the house and barn, while an additional 8 per cent had electricity exclusively in the house.[26] The popularity of the automobile also rose dramatically after the war. While 60 per cent of rural homes claimed a car in 1941, by 1961 the percentage had risen to 82.[27] In Dr Abell's study, 88 per cent possessed one car or more.[28]

Most significantly, between 1951 and 1971, when the total population of Ontario increased, the farm population decreased.[29] While the Ontario population rose from 4.6 million to 7.7 million, the farming population fell by almost half – from 678,000 in 1951 to 363,000 in 1971. This drop was partly attributable to the astonishing 60 per cent of farm sons and 80 per cent of farm daughters who were leaving the family farm.[30] While the farm population was shrinking, however, diversity burgeoned: white Anglo-Protestant men and women from long-settled Ontario farm families were increasingly joined by European immigrants and by migrants from urban areas.[31]

Concurrent with this decrease in the farming population was the consistent decline in the number of farms. In 1951, there were close to 160,000 farms in Ontario. By 1971, their number had fallen to about 100,000. Product demand dictated, however, that the size of those remaining increase. In 1941, the average farm size in Ontario was about 130 acres; by 1971, it was about 170 acres, although farms of several hundred and even several thousand acres were not uncommon.[32]

The nature of crops and farming also changed. The small-scale labour-intensive, mixed-crop farms pervasive in pre-war years began to be subsumed by large-scale, capital-intensive, highly mechanized, specialized enterprises after the war. Although the family farm continued as the backbone of Ontario agriculture, corporations were increasingly supplanting the farm family as large-scale farm owners and food producers.

A response to farm labour shortages and increased acreage during the war, farm mechanization proved the most palpable expression of farm modernization in the mid twentieth century.[33] In 1941, for example, there were just under 36,000 tractors on Ontario farms; only ten years later, this number had tripled to 105,000, and would continue to climb.[34] While a farmer in 1941 was able to produce enough crop for himself and nine others, with greater mechanization by 1962, he was able to produce enough to feed himself plus twenty-five more.[35] Farm mechanization after the war reduced the need for now available hired labour until 1961 when increasingly sophisticated machinery necessitated the on-farm attention of skilled technicians.[36] In that year, Ontario farms alone claimed one-quarter of the total value of farm machinery in Canada.[37]

Myrtleville, the Good family farm near Brantford, exemplified many of these post-war changes in agriculture. In 1945, "a tractor came, then tractors," and by 1960 the last work horse had been discharged. Myrtleville's sprawling fruit orchards were gone, and the farm had become a large-scale, specialized enterprise.[38] Like most Ontario farms after 1945, Myrtleville had experienced the transition from farming as "a 'way of life' to farming as a business."[39] Such transformation did not go unnoticed by the executive of the provincial WI who referred to the "critical time" of the post-war period as "days when living conditions for people everywhere are changing at a speed never known before" in "a world which travels so swiftly."[40]

These changes had an immeasurable impact on farm women's lives. To be sure, hydro and the labour-saving devices that it inspired eased women's domestic work. When the Hillier home acquired hydro-electricity, indoor plumbing, and modern appliances between 1932 and 1940, for example, farm wife Ethel Hillier judged them as "just about the best thing since sliced bread."[41] Some observers defined "the modern farm home" as one "where switches control everything but the children";[42] according to Abell's 1959 study, 85 per cent of homemakers owned an electric or gas stove, 95 per cent owned an electric or gas refrigerator, and a full 98 per cent enjoyed a power washing machine.[43] The tractor and other agricultural technologies also relieved women's work, as they reduced the need not only for farmhands, whom farm wives and daughters were obliged to look after, but for a labour pool staffed by a legion of children.[44]

Some argue that by alleviating the physicality of farm labour, mechanization also facilitated "a more fluid sexual division of labour" on the farm, and, by suggestion, a greater equality between the sexes.[45] But given the likelihood that women performed traditional male work to a greater extent than men performed traditional female work, this change might simply have meant that women's days were consumed by more labour, or, at the very least, were not spared of less.

Others more convincingly point out that increased mechanization made for a more rigid sexual division of labour – that the larger, more mechanized the farm, the more likely that women were barred from the farming itself (although they were not devoting less time to farm chores).[46] This correlation is premised on the fact that large machinery and "complex" technologies have always been perceived as sacred male ground: "agricultural technology, the mechanism by which the enterprise increases the efficiency of its production and captures a larger share of profits, represents the man's sphere of influence in the farm enterprise."[47] With farm technology a male preserve, women's farm labour, such as poultry production (like cheese and butter production decades before), which "lends itself to industrialized production forms," was increasingly appropriated by men, removing women from the only work that they had directly performed for profit and, aside from housework, over which they had governed conditions and assumed some control.[48]

With the mechanized mass production of commercial foods and other goods, moreover, farm women became consumers who were to educate themselves for this new role. As early as 1947, it was reported that "some farm families buy all their butter, bread and eggs, even milk. Where this is so, the farm wife becomes a finance manager" who "has to learn how to budget so the money that comes in when the crop is sold won't be all spent by Christmas."[49] As WI home economist and *Home and Country* editor Ethel Chapman reflected in a 1957 speech, " 'the farm woman's main job in the farm economy is to get the best values she can from her consumer dollar and that isn't easy.' "[50] Aiding women in becoming savvy consumers were the Canadian Association of Consumers, formed by women's organizations in 1947, and Guelph's Macdonald Institute, which by 1970 had changed its name, revealingly, to the College of Family and Consumer Studies.[51]

While consumerism greatly reduced laborious domestic food and clothing production, some women lamented that "food processing and mechanical appliances have taken over much of the work of our hands"[52] – the same work which they found the most creative and pleasurable. Moreover, consumer goods saved women time only in that they had more of it for additional cleaning and child care, standards of which had been steadily rising with increasingly sophisticated domestic technology.[53] Those farm women who sought paid employment in the post-war years did so not because consumer goods such as farm machinery, household appliances, prepared foods, and ready-made clothing afforded them extra time to pursue work away from home, but in order to supplement their husbands' incomes, in part so that they could afford to help purchase these goods.[54]

Farm wives' increasing off-farm employment was a new development in post-war Ontario. Indeed, while off-farm income, earned by men or women, comprised 14 per cent of total family income in 1941, by 1971, the proportion was 60 to 70 per cent.[55] One observer noted in

1958 that "up until a few years ago rural women did not face the problem of working outside the home, but today many of our rural women have returned to teaching school, working in the stores and offices in the nearby towns."[56] In the farm families under study by Abell in 1959, fifty-one farm wives (14 per cent) earned an income, and forty-two of these women (82 per cent) performed non-farm work. Of these, twenty-six, well over half, worked away from the home, fourteen (53 per cent) as part-time workers, and twelve (46 per cent) as full-time workers. These women were employed in traditionally female jobs, and, consistent with the observation above, were most often teachers, or in clerical, office, and sales work.[57] In reflecting upon the implications of her findings, Abell noted in 1964 that "these are indeed family farms where husband and wife adjust their labour and abilities to maintain their homes in their familiar rural environment despite changing economic and social conditions."[58]

Along with the changes in rural Ontario, most notably the decline in women's productive agricultural and domestic work, the urban-centred second-wave women's movement presented a challenge to the role and priorities of farm women. In Canada, this movement dates back to 1960 with the creation of the national peace organization, Voice of Women, and culminated in these formative years with the Royal Commission on the Status of Women, which submitted in 1970 its 167 recommendations for the betterment of Canadian women's lives. Many of the ideas popularized by the feminist organizations and activists of the 1960s, however, had been debated in Canada throughout the 1950s.[59] This was especially true with regard to the ideas of American Betty Friedan, whose commanding 1963 book *The Feminine Mystique* enjoyed an eager readership in Canada, but whose themes, which spoke to women's disillusionment with homemaking, had already been addressed by others and been part of the public discourse here for years.[60] Indeed, *Chatelaine* editor Doris Anderson rejected excerpts of *The Feminine Mystique* in the early 1960s because the magazine had already published articles on this topic.[61] Even a male editor of a Canadian farm publication had asked as early as 1958, "is it possible that womankind is assailed by some kind of inferiority complex ... and, convinced that woman's work is something less than man's, is determined to change? Plenty of indication is available, in our records, to prove that this attitude is something new."[62]

Friedan found that white, educated, middle-class homemakers felt depressed, trapped, lonely, and bored, defeated by an insidious problem "that has no name"; suburban homemaking, which held the promise of female fulfilment, proved stifling and mundane. These homemakers drew both exaggerated praise and contempt from psychology and medical experts in particular, who, according to Friedan, venerated women as housewives and mothers, while deriding them as incompetent neurotics desperate for male, professional guidance. These attitudes left women feeling all that more inadequate, devalued, and blameworthy. One way for women to alleviate this condition, suggested the equity feminist Friedan, was for housewives to escape the domestic drudgery and isolation of the home in favour of careers in the public realm where men had historically garnered their status, respect, and success. Paid employment, not amateur community work which simply busied wives and inhibited their growth, would facilitate the full expression of women's professionalism, intelligence, ambition, and self-worth. Friedan's "problem that has no name" became "a foundation stone of contemporary feminist thought," and introduced equity feminism to an entire generation of women.[63] Many read *The Feminine Mystique* "as a prophecy," and were "shocked … into self-consciousness."[64] For them, the book was the bible of the second-wave movement.

As many feminists have since pointed out, however, *The Feminine Mystique* addressed a very narrow group of women. Their lives and "problem" bore little resemblance to those of single, poor, and/or minority working women, who could only dream about the malaise of being at home.[65] Likewise, *The Feminine Mystique* spoke little to the experience of farm wives, who had always performed non-domestic work on the farm. For most of these women, paid work away from home was simply not feasible. The very survival of the family farm still rested on the full-time (and unpaid) domestic and agricultural labour that women performed at home. Farm wives had no choice but to make this work paramount, while their non-domestic duties, which by urban equity feminist standards were liberating in their maleness, hardly proved more emancipating than housework.[66] Moreover, off-farm work would not relieve farm wives of their housekeeping and child care duties, and with so many young women leaving the land, securing the help of a "hired girl" (a strategy that Friedan had in mind for urban wives) was no longer a viable option. For most farm women – already overburdened – off-farm labour would have exploited them further, not liberated them. In any case, a doctrine which degraded home economics and women's homemaking work, which urged women to conform to male standards of work and success, and which dismissed women's volunteer community service could not have endeared itself to farm women or the WI who had long held dear the social feminist tenets of female domesticity, specificity, and "public housekeeping." Accordingly, farm women would "not play an active role in the Women's Liberation Movement of the 60's."[67] But the popularity of *The Feminine Mystique* and the growing equity feminist movement certainly had farm women, and the WI, reflecting upon their already tenuous roles.

With all of the structural changes in rural Ontario later combined with the second-wave equity feminist movement, it is little wonder that so much uncertainty surrounded farm women and the WI in the post-war period and into the 1960s. In 1948, a *Home and Country* article entitled "Women in our Society To-day" affirmed that there was "current confusion in the attitude towards women," especially "as to what woman's role is and should be." For more than a year, the article stated, "the magazines have bristled or blossomed ... with articles on the 'woman question.' "[68] Indeed, at a 1945 meeting of the Wilton Grove WI, Mrs Jensen "spoke on the subject attracting so much attention at the present time. Woman's Place in the Post War Era."[69] Farm women internalized "this terrific confusion," feeling "unsure of themselves as individuals and uncertain of woman's destiny."[70] Within the clubs of the WI, farm women asked "How Can Women Meet the Challenge of These Times?," and debated whether "modern women are more help to their husbands than their grandmothers [were to their husbands]," and if "the women of today are happier than those of fifty years ago."[71] In this climate of doubt, a speaker at the Wilton Grove club in 1952 was compelled to assure members that "to be a homemaker and a farmer's wife is a life worthwhile."[72]

The uncertain status of farm women was revealed by studies which investigated their work and lives. The academic study supervised by Dr Helen C. Abell in 1959, and referred to earlier in this chapter, was entitled *Special Study of Ontario Farm Homes and Homemakers* and sponsored by the Federal Department of Agriculture and the Ontario Department of Agriculture.[73] The purpose of Abell's study was "to understand what is involved in achieving the best in rural living for farm homemakers and their families," in order that "extension programmes and services for young people, homemakers and farm operators may be governed accordingly."[74] Data for the study was collected by the "professionally trained home economics extension worker," twenty-four of whom visited farm homes to administer, in a three-hour interview, a twenty-nine page questionnaire to 352 farm women across Ontario.[75] The 1959 study spawned nine reports, the last of which was published in 1964. They addressed a variety of issues, including labour-saving equipment, food and nutrition, homemaking training, health and health services, and off-farm employment.[76]

Ontario Farm Radio Forum, an innovative adult education program, also deliberated the "woman question." Farm Radio Forum, which lasted from 1941 to 1965, was a half-hour national CBC radio show conceived by the Canadian Federation of Agriculture, the Canadian Association for Adult Education, and the CBC.[77] Airing on Monday evenings between November and March, Farm Forum discussed and/or dramatized a different agricultural topic each week, and distributed corresponding question books and answer sheets to neighbourhood Farm Forum groups across the country. Each of these groups, comprised of ten to thirty farm women and men (usually about the same number of each[78]), together listened to the broadcast, discussed the questions, recorded their collective answers, and submitted them to provincial Farm Forum headquarters. There, staff tabulated the data and published the results each week "to form a type of nation-wide opinion and reaction poll."[79] As part of the national program, Ontario Farm Radio Forum devoted seven out of several hundred broadcasts to the questionable status of farm women: "The Farmer Takes a Wife" (10 November 1947); "Boy Meets Girl" (1 November 1948); "Farm Women in Public Life" (10 November 1952); "Partners All: Farm Wives as Working Partners" (9 November 1953); "Ladies and Gentlemen" (10 March 1958); "Equality for Women" (15 December 1958); and "Women in Their Place" (25 November 1963). While most of the other Farm Forum broadcasts dealt directly with agricultural concerns such as soil quality, crop prices, and tariffs, topics of particular interest to the male farmer, it was revealing of women's ambiguous status that the female-centred subjects, albeit relatively few, were even discussed at all.

These Farm Forum polls, while intended to be objective, posed shamelessly biased questions. The "Equality for Women" broadcast in 1958, for example, without specifically defining "equality," asked women if they would "accept full equality with men – including their responsibilities." It also asked women if they were "willing to sacrifice" their "privileges as a woman" to achieve equality with men.[80] In a rare appearance by women in the Farm Forum literature, Dr Margaret McCready, principal of Macdonald Institute, illuminated some of the weaknesses of these questions. Of the first query, she asserted that "it is not 'equal rights' with men to dig ditches, mine coal and fight wars, that women seek, but intelligent cooperation from men in all their worthwhile endeavours, including the unpaid but honoured job of homemaking." Unlike those who formulated the Farm Forum poll, McCready understood that sexual equality was not contingent upon sexual sameness, with women conforming to male standards and norms. Significantly, she believed that farm women, too, understood and endorsed this social feminist doctrine. Of the second question, McCready doubted "whether the 'privileges as a woman' ... affect more than the most celebrated women to whom the world pays court and homage," and added that "even such women may pay heavily for such homage."[81] As implied by her reference above to women's "unpaid" domestic work, McCready questioned the Farm Forum assumption that society privileged women, and inferred that even for those revered few, (male) chivalry on women's behalf necessarily came at a price.

The Farm Radio Forum recognized the strain that these contentious issues about women's status could evoke between the sexes, and thereby acknowledged the differing self-interests of women and men. The guide for the broadcast "The Farmer Takes a Wife" recommended that "women and men meet separately at first, then come together to compare conclusions for joint discussion."[82] Some groups took this advice when discussing "Farm Women in Public Life," but those that did not, such as the Phillipsburg Forum in Waterloo County, "found this ... a very difficult topic for discussion" because "a topic of this sort is difficult to discuss in a mixed [sex] group as it leads to arguments instead of a good discussion."[83] The Islay Forum in Victoria County recorded that "this meeting was like a debating team 5 women Versus 5 men."[84] When the women of the Cuboss Alpo Forum in Bruce County revealed that for husbands to improve conditions on the farm, women had to "just keep nagging away," their husbands in the group insisted that this approach could work to the contrary.[85] Despite such tension (or perhaps because of it) these Farm Forum topics which directly addressed the female experience captured the interest of the women participants, who sometimes, as the men occasionally complained, "did most of the talking," and "talked too much together."[86]

Farm Forum answers for "The Farmer Takes a Wife" program reflected the confusion of both women and men with regard to the status of farm women. The Denfield Forum in Middlesex County, for instance, proved misinformed when it assumed that "a woman has joint ownership [of the farm] when she married a farmer"; the Sunnybrook Forum in Wellington County was evasive when it referred to the possibility of a farm woman's allowance as "a very ticklish question"; the men of the Crumlin Forum in Middlesex County seemed dismissive or unaware when they noted that "none of the ladies gave any complaints so we take it that they are all satisfied"; a forum in Bruce County was contradictory when it attributed women's absence from forum meetings to "long hours of farmwork," and then asserted that to better their lot "women should enter more organizations." Another Bruce County forum thought a wife "should have a little pin money," and then stated with some inconsistency that "husband and wife should be partners in handling the money."[87] Perhaps the most profound indication of confusion among Farm Forums, however, was when a group responding to the "Equality for Women" broadcast confessed that "we are not sure what equality is."[88]

As the role of farm women began to assume ambiguity, crisis loomed for an anxious WI. While membership numbers dramatically rose right after the war, they did not meet Institute projections, and in the 1950s began a largely irreversible slide.[89] In the spring of 1946, the Ontario WI claimed 35,000 members, and hopes were high that it could enlist 50,000 members by its 1947 golden jubilee.[90] As part of a recruitment campaign, WI superintendent Anna Lewis travelled to conventions province-wide, and offered awards to those districts and clubs able to enlist the most members and garner the greatest attendance.[91] Lewis was particularly interested in attracting "the young matron" – newly married homemakers whom the WI needed for their youthful energy and zeal. She recommended that clubs appeal to young wives by providing child care at meetings, by electing young women to executive positions, by scheduling a "bride's meeting" (where members could wear their wedding gowns), and by arranging paid-up memberships for war brides.[92] Provincial officer Mrs J.E. Houck suggested a different approach. She wanted WI members, who were, according to her, largely rural women of means, to invite tenant farm women and the country wives of urban workers to join the WI. In fact, accurately sensing that the dropping Institute membership was attributable in part to the shrinking rural population generally, Houck asserted that not just country women, but "'any woman who was interested in things rural, should be welcome in our organization.'"[93] By the winter of 1947–48, the group's half-century mark, WI membership had risen dramatically to 38,600, but failed to meet the hopeful goal of "50,000 members for our 50th Anniversary."[94]

In 1950, although membership reached an unprecedented high of 47,250, it fell short of the revised Institute wish for "Fifty Thousand Members by 1950," and thereafter began its decline.[95] By 1956, the secretary of the Federated Women's Institutes of Ontario (FWIO) admitted to feeling "very much like the Bird of ill-omen" when she had to report a drop in membership for the second year in a row.[96] In certain regions, it was not unusual for clubs to acknowledge "fearing the necessity of disbanding due to dwindling membership." As early as the winter of 1944–45, Institute branches had been asking the FWIO for information on proper procedure for dissolving clubs and disposing of funds.[97] In 1956, the WI executive conceded that "it might be advisable to set up a committee to find the cause of this falling off in membership."[98]

While Mrs J.E. Houck supposed that many local branches exerted little or no effort to recruit new members, the provincial wi blamed its lagging membership in the 1950s and 60s on other factors.[99] First, the wi pointed to the group's overwhelmingly aging membership. Many wi women had been affiliated with the organization since its early years, and by the post-war period were at least middle-aged.[100] Indeed, program topics of some wi clubs began to reflect this older membership: the Brougham Institute at Pickering, for example, officially debated whether "'active middle-age surpasses youth in the joys of life,'" resolving, of course, that it did; the Cayuga, Haldimand wi conducted a debate entitled "Life Begins at Forty," which also culminated in an affirmative victory; and the Cornwall Centre wi in Stormont County held its "annual Grandmother's meeting," which had for its "roll call," "'Why I admire Elderly Ladies.'"[101] Despite this optimistic approach to vitality in old age, however, older members, according to Ethel Chapman, did "not feel equal to" the "strenuous" fundraising required by Institute projects. One branch reported that in lieu of hosting a social to raise funds for a scholarship, members were donating two dollars each to avoid undue work.[102]

Occupied with business concerns, members were dissatisfied that there was little time for sociability and programming, and partly for this reason, claimed Chapman, "'old members are dropping out and it is impossible to attract new ones.'"[103] They complained about the wi's rigorous fundraising efforts, and called for more social clubs. In sociability, Institute women found "comradeship," an opportunity for which they "resisted any suggestion," either by eager wi activists or by outside observers, "that 'a cup of tea' is a waste of time."[104] In 1956, the FWIO president announced that there would be no provincial fundraising initiatives that year, a respite that Ethel Chapman compared to the farmer's fallow field: "could we make this a summer fallow year? Just as a farmer sometimes rests his land from heavy cropping and tills back into it the vegetation it needs to nourish the soil, could we give ourselves a rest from the business that drives us and turn our attention to enriching our Institute life?" With a view to social feminist values, Chapman concluded that the reprieve would mean "good programs with the members studying and discussing together things vital to women ... homemaking and family relationships and how to make the community a better, happier place."[105]

The wi maintained that the emphasis on home economics would sustain the older membership, yet older women, who no longer had small children to care for, felt that they had outgrown the need for information on homemaking.[106] Reflecting on the declining membership,

Chapman conceded that their disinterest was understandable. Older members of the WI, in addition to craving sociability, placed a premium on learning and culture. Chapman herself supported these interests, and, in the fashion of a geriatrics professional, proposed that the WI meet the intellectual needs of its elderly members: "if we believe in the mental therapy of 'continuous learning,' an Institute, whatever the age of its members, is doing something worth while if it stimulates our thinking in a discussion, sets us reading a good book, shows us films on Canadian art, gets us to listen to good radio programs and discard the others. For we have it on good authority that keeping our minds active is one of the best ways of warding off senility."[107] Notwithstanding Chapman's plea, Institute clubs generally persisted with home economics activities.

Interestingly, the WI journal *Home and Country* never overtly attributed the organization's shrinking membership to the dying off of its predominantly elderly members which was, in fact, a major cause.[108] The provincial executive, however, was undoubtedly aware of this trend. In the mid 1940s, the organization began memoriam columns in *Home and Country* which eulogized early members. In the winter of 1954, for example, it paid homage to Dr Helen MacMurchy, who, before her death at age ninety-three, was a "staunch ally" of the WI. It also honoured Miss Gertrude Gray, who between 1903 and 1945 had variously been a WI speaker, demonstrator, and nutrition supervisor; "to see Miss Gray give a cooking demonstration," reflected the tribute, "was to see the work of a skilled craftswoman and artist."[109]

By the early 1960s, Ethel Chapman also blamed the off-farm employment and busy lives of young rural women for the WI's languishing membership: "most of our young women are working during the day and some of them already belong to more clubs than they have time for."[110] By 1966, disclosures in various annual branch reports suggested that because "there are so many organizations in the community, and so many 'working' women with little spare time for meetings, ... the Institute is having a hard time to carry on."[111] According to the reports, however, local clubs made every effort to attract young women. To Chapman's dismay, one anxious club even considered plans for a bowling league, a recruitment scheme which deviated from Institute programming, and which highlighted an activity associated with working-class men.[112]

Certainly, for younger women, some of the WI rhetoric and programs must have seemed antiquated, although the WI's longstanding agenda was not a major cause at this time of declining membership.[113] Nevertheless, the WI itself considered on the occasion of its sixty-fifth anniversary in 1962 "whether the plans made by our founders sixty-five years ago are outdated." The organization in fact acknowledged in 1963 that with its focus historically on "good home-making" there were those who believed that it had "outgrown the main purpose for which it was founded."[114]

This recognition, however, did not prevent the post-war WI from paying tribute to the past. In anticipation of its golden jubilee, the WI launched its Tweedsmuir History project in 1945. At the suggestion of Lady Tweedsmuir, widow of Canada's former governor-general, clubs compiled the history of their own communities, profiling area founders, institutions, and landmarks, and sharing the story of their own growth and development. By the mid 1950s, 989 clubs were undertaking Tweedsmuir histories.[115] At the fiftieth anniversary cele-bration in Guelph, Institute history literally took centre stage as an elaborate "historical pageant" entitled "Let There Be Light" drama-tized the epic story of the WI.[116] Canada's centennial celebrations in 1967 also afforded WI clubs an opportunity to honour the past, and "momentarily forget the rapid changes that were transforming rural women's lives."[117] Special occasions aside, WI members themselves remained ever appreciative of female pioneers such as Nellie Mc-Clung and Adelaide Hoodless, and ever mindful of the debt "we owe to the women who have gone before us."[118]

The WI's reverence for the past did at times prove self-defeating. Although the Institute boasted, perhaps naively, that "many of the topics considered vital fifty years ago still have a large place in Women's Institute activities today," its continued support of "Sab-bath observance," for example (even with the supposed ban on sec-tarian issues), seemed undeniably fusty in the increasingly secular society of the post-war era.[119] In addition, as clubs after 1945 voiced the same complaints about the WI as those articulated after 1918, it seemed that little had been done by Institute leaders to better organi-zational policy in the intervening years. Provincial officer Mrs J.E. Houck conceded in 1949 that "if we are adult now and we ought to be at fifty-two years of age, it is well for us, at times to assess our work and recognize and try to correct our faults."[120] According to mem-bers, they included, as they had for twenty years, an overemphasis on fundraising and business.[121]

But despite all of the confusion and scrutiny which was by now surrounding farm women and the WI, both held true to their belief in the social feminist precepts of female specificity, domesticity, and public service. Responding to the "Equality for Women" broadcast of the Ontario Farm Radio Forum in 1958, farm women in the greatest number of groups, 80 out of 151, reported that they would not "ac-cept full equality with men" if it meant adopting male obligations and duties.[122] In the same vein, women in the greatest number of groups, 72 out of 151, declared that they were not willing "to sacrifice" privileges of womanhood for the sake of equality with men.[123] The women of the Brookdale Forum in Hastings County understood, in fact, that "if we have to sacrifice anything there could be no equality."[124] Indeed, in responding to a question about what "inequalities" had "bothered" them most, women asserted that they deserved equality by virtue of their womanhood, not in spite of it, and felt that "privileges as a woman," if they did in fact exist, should be more forthcoming.[125] Indeed, as wives who contributed female-specific labour to the farm enterprise, women in the greatest number of forums, 48 out of 151, reported that women "should have marriage partnership in law and equal property rights."[126]

When asked in the "Woman in Their Place" broadcast of 1968 if women were "interested in entering occupations outside the home," forums gave replies that hardly resembled equity feminist rhetoric. The second largest group, thirty-two out of eighty-nine, did remark that "a number of the women in our community work outside the home,"; yet they worked not as an expression of women's rights, but for "extra income and to provide luxuries."[127] The largest number of groups, thirty-seven out of eighty-nine, responded that "the majority of women in our group haven't the time or interest in working outside the home."[128] The farm women of the Roseville Forum in Waterloo County maintained that with all of the extra jobs to be done for the enterprise "many of us consider ourselves to have part-time jobs on the farm."[129] When somewhat accusingly asked "what would be the effects of women spending much of their married lives outside the home," groups were overwhelmingly negative in their perceptions of women's off-farm work. They most often cited in social feminist style that "there would be a loss as far as the home atmosphere is concerned."[130]

Farm Forum revealed, however, that farm women's aversion to off-farm employment did not preclude a role for women in public life, a pursuit which ultimately benefitted the home. When asked whether "women have a special contribution to bring to public affairs," all of the 270 groups under study responded in no uncertain terms that they did. All of these groups also agreed that "a woman who is active in community work can do a better homemaking job than one who has no interest outside of her home."[131]

Like farm women generally, the post-war WI remained loyal to its long-held notions of social feminism, but the organization tempered its obvious reverence for the past with an appreciation for the dictates of modern times. As such, it sought to be current and progressive by contemporary standards. Past president of the Federated Women's Institutes of Canada (FWIC) Mrs Cameron Dow proclaimed in 1947 that "'we honour the work of the pioneers, but we cannot stand still ... we must move forward.'" Mrs J.E. Houck declared in a 1949 issue of *Home and Country* that "in a world ... where new discoveries and ideas are so important, rural women can not [*sic*] afford to neglect the chances they may have to keep up with a modern age." Ethel Chapman reiterated this point in 1969 when she insisted that "education in the skills of homemaking is as important today as it ever was; but programs must relate to present conditions."[132]

That Chapman still had to promote this idea twenty years after Houck, however, was symptomatic of the double message articulated by the WI. While Chapman boasted in 1962, for example, that "the Women's Institutes have an up-to-the-minute program for their sixty-fifth anniversary year," she also announced that "it's all within the framework of the Constitution laid down sixty-five years ago." Chapman lauded "the imagination and wisdom" of WI women who, while "adapting and reshaping" Institute goals "to meet the needs of changing times," had "kept the original plans always in mind."[133] While the WI promised on its fiftieth anniversary to "'Face the Future,'" it also pledged to "'Treasure the Past.'"[134]

Thus, although contemporary agricultural and women's issues, so pertinent to the lives of farm women, could not go unnoticed by the WI, they were certainly not trends that the group could wholeheartedly embrace. These matters, deemed the WI, and particularly *Home and Country* editor Ethel Chapman,[135] undermined its original values. Cleverly, however, the WI was able to use varied and timely issues, including second-wave feminism, consumerism, working women, sexually integrated WIs, the study of family, the glorification of the professional, the bureaucratic approach to reform, and international concerns, to modernize its long-established agenda, while simultaneously manipulating them to reinforce its early mandated social feminist goals.

The modernity of the WI, for example, was evident in its *Home and Country* magazine, which referenced Betty Friedan, but which had featured the similar ideas of Irene McBride as early as 1948.[136] McBride described aspects then of what Friedan later termed "the problem that has no name," and wrote of the precarious status of the post-war domesticated woman: "as wife and mother a woman lives in a world whose values, goals and rewards are largely intangible, and in our materialistic society she is apt to feel inferior because of this, especially if she tries to measure herself and her achievements in terms of the world outside the home."[137] For Friedan, liberation for women waited for them in the male public sphere where they could acquire the status and worth that men had. McBride, too, had recognized that "woman herself has other needs besides those satisfied in her role as wife and mother."[138]

With the burgeoning equity feminist movement of the 1950s and 60s, the WI took the opportunity to boast about the inroads that Institute women were making in traditional male public arenas; these proud achievements, however, were chiefly in the social feminist context of public service. Provincial president Mrs J.R. Futcher, for example, was one of the first two women in 1950 appointed to the Royal Winter Fair Board; the president of the Southampton WI in Bruce County was the first woman to be elected to the Southampton Town Council; and Simcoe Centre WI member Mrs Marjorie Hamilton was the first woman mayor of Barrie, as well as one of the first woman mayors in Ontario. Mrs Hamilton, who was "'practically raised in the Women's Institute,'" maintained, like other WI women who became notable figures, that "'an Institute background must be an excellent preparation for public life.'"[139] For wives, public life, according to the WI, was indeed a distinctly female avenue for women's self-fulfilment. This point was underscored in the Farm Forum broadcast "Farm Women in Public Life," in which Mrs Futcher, in her interview on the CBC, referred not to their paid employment or personal political ambition, but precisely to their "public service." Futcher believed that "it is a woman's duty to get out of the kitchen and off the farm and have a share in community projects for the protection of her children."[140] As well, propounded the WI, women in public life need not to conform to the behaviours and traits of men. As McBride observed in *Home and Country*, "as a group, women are more realistic, more concrete, practical-minded, less aggressive, more alert to human relationships and find it easier to be concerned with detail. Would not all these characteristics be of inestimable value in conducting the affairs of the world?"[141]

These laudable female attributes, asserted McBride and others, should deter the unhappy suburban homemaker with no paid job from measuring herself according to male standards of public success. McBride proposed that the homemaker should understand that "the values she is concerned with are fully as important, if not more so, than those of the outside world."[142] Twenty years later, new *Home and Country* editor Maryn Pardy, in her article "Adelaide Hoodless Said," echoed McBride's social feminist sentiment: "many women who claim no vocation other than the job of providing a well kept home for their families have a tendency to apologize for being engaged only, in this apparently simple occupation. But is it so simple? ... No woman ... should feel the need to apologize for being engaged in such an imposing list of duties. No woman who takes seriously her duties as a wife or mother should feel that she is not fulfilling the potential abilities in herself when she lists herself as a housewife."[143] Chapman, like McBride and Pardy, desired to "give the business of homemaking the dignity it deserves," and resented those "Betty Friedans who would pour it down the drain completely because they think an interest in the home is just a woman's escape from competition with men in the world outside." For Chapman, Friedan's popular book was worthy of attention, but its viewpoint ultimately generated "more heat than light."[144]

Longstanding women's groups such as the WI helped link feminism's first-wave movement at the turn of the century and the second-wave movement of the 1960s, but the WI "did not grow successfully into second-wave feminism."[145] It is true that the FWIC was one of many women's organizations, social feminist groups among them, that lobbied the government to establish the Royal Commission on the Status of Women (RCSW) in 1967, and in 1971 was on the initial steering committee for the National Action Committee on the Status of Women, but shortly after its initial burst of activism, the FWIC dissociated from the second-wave movement, buttressing the claim that the WI was "a relatively intact relic of first-wave feminism."[146] While the FWIC's 1967 submission to the RCSW included revolutionary recommendations consistent with the contemporary women's liberation movement – widespread availability of abortion and birth control, compulsory alimony and child support payments, and better access to daycare – it also called for more secondary school home economics courses, a recommendation that the new movement of the late 1960s surely would have perceived as old-fashioned.[147] Nevertheless, although second-wave feminism proved distasteful to the WI, its treatment of the issue kept the group current, and served as a platform, ironically enough, to reinforce its cherished social feminist perspective.

Institute attention to consumerism functioned in the same way. Because consumerism helped modernize home economics, it infused the WI with a new purpose: to instruct homemakers in the skill of purchasing consumer goods.[148] Ethel Chapman insisted that "the new foods and textiles and appliances coming on the market, the high pressure selling of these times, constantly bring new problems to the homemaker," and thus "today the farm women like everyone else needs consumer education."[149] As early as 1945, the WI transformed its "old dressmaking courses" into modern "clothing classes with considerable training in Buymanship," and aligned itself with the Canadian Association of Consumers, which arranged a special group membership for local wi clubs.[150] The wi also convinced farm women of the importance of their new job as consumers. In a *Home and Country* article entitled "Buying is Your Business," farm women were told that "consumer buying is Canada's largest business, and women control and direct it."[151] wi provincial convenor Mrs Wilmer Keys declared to members that "we homemakers are the real economists of the nation," noting that, collectively, Canadian wives assumed the greatest role in income disbursement.[152]

Consistent with social feminist values, the wi also acknowledged, however, that consumerism, consumption, and the commodification of women's traditional labour were undercutting the role of the farm woman as homemaker and mother. In 1957, Ethel Chapman asked regretfully "in an age when gadgets seem to count for more than graciousness, how can we preserve or create the intangibles that give a character and sweetness to family living?"[153] A year later she asked "does modern homemaking offer scope for the mind and the heart and the skills of the most gifted women? Or could a robot take over, with the help of the delicatessen, the baby sitter, the teacher, the librarian, the clubs and scouts and brownies and all the extra-curricular clubs that take so much responsibility for the social processing of the high school youngster?"[154] To restore value and priority to women's traditional work, the wi hoped to assist women in reviving their talent and appreciation of "creative homemaking." Chapman maintained that "creative homemaking is one of the biggest jobs of these times," and insisted that if wi clubs made it a part of their programs, women would take up the cause.[155]

The wi's focus on women's domestic life allowed the group to recognize that the shift to consumerism, consumption, and commodification that altered women's household labour did not necessarily afford women added leisure.[156] Chapman observed that "making a home may be more complicated now than it has ever been," and suggested that this job of becoming a well-versed consumer, of buying new-fangled foods, and of caring for costly machinery made heavy demands on a woman's time.[157] Given that women largely performed their labour without the assistance of servants and grown daughters, and increasingly combined this work with paid employment, the situation for most women might have been "more work for mother."[158]

"The timely question of the Working Mother," however contrary she ran to the Institute model of womanhood, was also addressed by the wi.[159] Consistent with Chapman's view that the organization wanted to "do some thinking on the popular controversy," the Castlemore branch in Peel County, for example, held a debate about whether or not "a career and marriage can be combined success-fully."[160] As the topic was contentious for women, Chapman instructed WI members to approach their discussions with caution. She believed that "because every Institute is likely to have members who feel keenly on one side or the other it is better to avoid direct debate," and not "set ourselves up as judges of one another."[161]

Although the WI made an effort to treat the issue fairly, in reality the organization did not approve of working wives and mothers, who would inevitably neglect family and domestic responsibilities. Outgoing WI president Mrs Duke herself reported with some remorse that even her volunteer position "had required well over one hundred days from home." When WI superintendent Anna Lewis married in 1955, she avoided this dilemma by immediately abdicating her ten-year post.[162] In an article entitled "A Thought for the Family," Chapman reflected on the trend of the working mother by expressing regret that she "doesn't stay at home watching the road any more. A considerable part of the time she's on it, usually in good cause, but not always. ... Perhaps we should not be surprised at a recent indictment from a Church that 'children are suffering from the lack of the experience of mother love.'"[163] That Chapman later admonished members not to judge those women who worked seems ironic. Clearly, she herself laid blame on the absent mother.

While the WI objected to the idea of working wives and mothers, it also sympathized with their efforts to manage both household and job and, in keeping with its social feminist platform, offered support to these women through home economics and reform efforts.[164] Indeed, for the WI, the modern, ill-prepared, pressed-for-time, working mother afforded a new target membership for home economics instruction. For her, more than for full-time homemakers, training in housekeeping and child care was vital, as she had not the time "for trial and error methods that are common to beginning house-wives."[165] Even if she delegated her housework to a maid, the working mother required knowledge of domestic skills in order to guide the housekeeper effectively.[166] It was the responsibility of the WI, then, to "consider how the mother who works outside her home can plan things so that her family do [sic] not suffer because of it."[167] The WI's reform efforts included both legislative and interpersonal lobby-ing. In 1951, the WI called on the government to legislate "'equal pay for equal work'" between women and men in order to better women's economic status as family wage earners, and also urged the husbands of women who worked outside of the home to contribute more fully to domestic life – a "new pattern ... which seems to best meet the needs of both men and women and the needs of society to-day."[168]

Indeed, the "new pattern" in the post-war years of gender-integrated participation in both the public and private spheres inspired the wi to reflect carefully upon this trend with regard to its own organization. Even prior to war's end, wi provincial convenor Mrs T.D. Cowan suggested that clubs debate or discuss " 'ways in which this war is leading men and women to work more closely together to solve social and economic problems,' "[169] and such rhetoric moved the wi to contemplate the increased involvement of men in its programs. After all, the *Toronto Star* reported that at one New York high school "boys are flocking" to the home economics course.[170] In a 1956 editorial entitled "Programmes for Men, Too," Ethel Chapman noted that the province's Home Economics Extension Service, which oversaw the wi, was considering the possibility of co-educational courses. Chapman claimed that some boys and the rare man had been "asking to be admitted to our craft classes."[171] In 1947, the Port Colborne wi, near Welland, actually "introduced the new custom of accepting men as associate members."[172]

Chapman, in her social feminist take on mixed-sex groups, attempted to make them palatable for members of the separatist wi. Certainly, its separatist tradition necessarily suggested that the involvement of men would prove disadvantageous to women, a view which was highlighted by Irene McBride when she stated in *Home and Country* in 1948 that women proved apathetic in mixed-sex groups.[173] Chapman, however, focused on cooperation within, and the preservation of, the traditional nuclear family structure. She emphasized that in integrating the sexes, a husband and wife would study and learn together, and would share an interest in family life. Significantly, Chapman also underscored in her discussion the distinctiveness of women's labour by referring to men's domestic work in masculine terms, which included "home planning," "remodelling," and "household engineering." As well, Chapman suggested that the presence of men at meetings could serve to benefit women in important ways: "men may not pay much attention to a woman's story of the weird things that can develop in settling an estate without a will, while they – the men – would be very much impressed if they heard the same facts from a man with knowledge of and experience in settling estates. ... So, when an Institute is having a speaker on a topic like Wills, shouldn't they have it at an open meeting where men can hear it too?"[174] Unfortunately, the cooperation that

Chapman encouraged here was undermined by her belief that men regarded women as having no credibility.

Ironically, Chapman's emphasis on family welfare, a seemingly outdated approach, actually reflected a popular trend in the 1950s and 60s to examine the family and family relations. Because the family was facing new challenges and stresses, all branches of professionals at this time, according to Chapman, were investigating the specific causes and effects of family dysfunction.[175] Macdonald Institute's name change to the College of Family and Consumer Studies was one response to this new emphasis on the family. The College's revised name and curricula in 1970 signalled the decade's educational eclipse of home economics by family studies, whose interdisciplinary emphasis on family living over the pragmatic, "how to" (albeit scientific) approach to clothing and food, was generally regarded by educators as more academic and socially relevant.[176] This increasing threat of the new "family studies" to home economics made Chapman understandably defensive about the WI's role as an early expert in the study of domestic life. After all, the WI, long before contemporary society's concern for the family, had focused on the home, and while it never specifically addressed the new "psychology of family living,"[177] it had done far more than promote sewing and cookery. Institutes had always emphasized the health, welfare, and restorative powers of the family: "take the home out of the Institute program and you'll still have some sort of organization," explained Chapman, "but it won't be a Women's Institute."[178] She lamented in 1966 "the irony" in the fact that the WI, which had long ago popularized the study of family life, "had fallen by the wayside" in the new push to investigate the family.[179]

Nevertheless, given that in the 1950s and 60s, family studies, according to the WI, was "one of the top-ranking studies for progressive organizations,"[180] it, too, took up this modern field, but examined it within the context of the group's beloved home economics. The WI recognized that although it had always "used vision and common sense" to address issues of home and the family, "perhaps there has never been more need for this vision and resourcefulness as there is today."[181] Chapman urged the WI to "Study the Family, Too," and "To Learn About Family Living," for with so many harmful influences on family life, "human relations [is] about the most important thing in a woman's education."[182] The WI, however, never approached the topical study of the family as a field of cutting-edge (male) social science. Early on, in fact, the "psychology of family living" was conceptualized as "the newest thing in home economics."[183] "The field of home economics gets broader and broader," Chapman observed in 1956, and the WI has "a unique opportunity to move with this trend, taking thought for the interests and the welfare of the whole family."[184] That the Home Economics Service in its quest to be "modern" secured a psychologist, not a home economist, to instruct WI courses in "psychology for the homemaker" might have contributed in 1956 to their low enrolment and subsequent cancellation, and to the departure of the extension service psychologist.[185] Certainly WI members would have been more receptive to the familiar discourse of home economics. Even when family studies began posing a real threat to home economics at the close of the 1960s, Chapman defended its worth by echoing the sentiments of home economics advocate Adelaide Hoodless. Chapman theorized that "some homes of the future might be happier, ... some forms of delinquency might be prevented, if every child in the public school years, boys as well as girls, could have some home economics training in human relations."[186] Studying the family, implied Chapman, did not have to mean family studies.

Notwithstanding its suspicion of social science practitioners, the WI, like the rest of society, glorified "the professional," but perceived the modern home economist as no less credible. Chapman wrote of up-to-date WI clubs that invited "authorities to acquaint ... people with new trends in education," and that held "child study discussions" led by educational, religious, social service, and mental health professionals whose formal education and training produced an unchallenged expertise.[187] The WI, however, had also boasted of its own home economics professionals since at least 1949. The provincial WI relayed that year that "a new forward step was taken" in 1934 when Miss Bess McDermand, "a qualified Home Economist," became the first woman superintendent of the provincial WI. It was proud to report that ever since that time "a university graduate in the field of Home Economics has held this position." McDermand was followed by Mary A. Clarke, who had graduated in home economics from the University of Toronto, received an M.A. from Columbia University, and taught at Macdonald Institute in Guelph. Her successor, Anna Lewis, was also a home economics graduate from the University of Toronto who did graduate work at Columbia. Before overseeing the WI, she worked as a hospital dietician and as a home economics instructor. Lewis's replacement, Helen McKercher, graduated from Macdonald College in 1930, after which time she received a Master's Degree in Home Economics and Extension [Education] at Cornell University. She was later appointed chief of Home Economics Service in the federal Department of Fisheries.[188]

Despite such accomplishments, however, home economists rarely seemed to reap the esteem accorded other health and social service professionals.[189] Ethel Chapman admitted in 1967 that "the profession of home economics has its detractors here and there. There are educationists who would relegate it to technical schools or limit it to food science, taking away the humanities concerned with human thought and human relations."[190] Almost certainly she was referring to emerging family studies educators, many of whom had in fact been teachers in home economics,[191] but whose relatively elevated status as social science educators corresponded with their new affiliation to a male-defined field rather than to a women-centred discipline. Chapman must have been only too happy to reprint in *Home and Country* a statement from the Canadian Welfare Council that affirmed the need for home economists, and that aligned them with other professionals: " 'social welfare is becoming a business under responsible management with a sharp eye on the results of its investments. What is the good of new low-cost housing if the families who move in have no idea how to keep house? What is the good of job training for a youth if he and his young wife are clueless consumers? What is the good of all the clinics, camps and clubs if boys and girls are badly fed at home? Nobody sees more clearly than the home economist that poor nutrition means poor health and poor job performance whether the job is at the plant or at home or school. This is why Home Economists are needed, out in the community on the health and welfare team along with doctors, nurses, town planners, social workers and the rest.' " The council concluded its declaration by affirming the importance of training professional home economists in significant numbers.[192]

The WI itself continued to work on community reform, but the group assumed, like many modern organizations in the 1950s and 60s, a more official, impersonal, bureaucratic approach to implementing change, a strategy which the WI capitalized on in order to benefit its members and facilitate their social feminist work. The once informal, independent, and grassroots approach of local WI branches was forced to bureaucratize in order to survive among, and cooperate with, competing services and groups; the result was that the relative autonomy and agency of these clubs were forever compromised. Nevertheless, this approach emancipated overworked members by now presuming shared institutional and government involvement in social reform. Ethel Chapman reflected in 1963 on this new procedure: "there was a time when Institutes made things hard for themselves by doing work and raising money for projects that should have been the responsibility of the whole community. For instance, they bought equipment for schools that should have been provided by the school board and paid for out of everyone's taxes. Now the Institute asks the board to do what needs to be done; and perhaps the board likes it better this way too."[193] Clearly, decades of laborious reform work and fundraising had convinced exhausted members that female influence need no longer mean self-sacrifice. Indeed, their understanding that all community institutions and groups were obligated to contribute to the betterment of society had always been a social feminist truism. This more modern and efficient approach to change also facilitated the more effective execution of Institute projects by engaging the resources of a variety of services and groups. In doing so, the WI was able to continue working in support of its favourite causes, undertakings that were remarkably similar to those first social feminist efforts established after World War I. WI branches in the 1950s and 60s were still "organizing community social events, providing … playground equipment for schools; recognizing the births of babies with a gift …; sending cards, flowers or fruit to the sick and shut in; assisting victims of … misfortune; contributing to the building of halls, hospitals and community centres; taking an active interest in Children's Shelters and Homes for the Aged; promoting and assisting libraries; getting the people of the district to come to chest X-ray surveys; sponsoring baby clinics; subscribing funds to an endless number of causes."[194] No doubt these local reform efforts continued to appeal to long-time Institute members who had grown adept at this work, and who still believed in its merit.

While the post-war WI is often accused of conservatively turning inward to community, home, and family, it actually adopted an expanded, international world view. As Chapman reported in 1962, "after two world wars, Institute women began to see that their community had broadened to take in the whole world." They recognized that "the world is now one neighbourhood and that loss of peace and freedom in one part of the world means also loss of freedom everywhere in the world." The WI president insisted in 1954 that "it now behooves us … to broaden our horizons and view the world at large with the intimacy we once applied to our own communities."[195] The WI subscribed to what it deemed the "present trend" among organizations of entertaining international concerns and practicing reform work worldwide.[196]

Chapman reported that some in the WI opposed this new trend, but she also indicated that the WI generally perceived its international reform work as conforming to the character of its pre-war social feminist efforts. Opponents of the global approach to reform feared that

clubs "were going beyond their depth in the study of world problems" – problems which were "too big for us."[197] They also might
have worried that this expanded outlook would distract members
from their more pertinent local concerns. It was at the local level,
many believed, where the WI made its greatest impact; once on the
world stage, the organization could be inviting a diminishing influence. Yet, in an article revealingly entitled "New Trends and Old Traditions," it appeared that the WI essentially saw its post-war work as
"all in keeping with the original pattern," and viewed its modern
international character simply as "accept[ing] wider areas of social
responsibility."[198] As such, WI leaders affirmed the international influence of women by using the language of social feminism. The provincial WI president, for example, asserted that "the world's women
can lead the way to universal peace. ... Let us consider ourselves
moulders of the fate of humanity." WI superintendent Anna Lewis insisted that Institute women were obligated as mothers " 'to exert an
influence in the world community.' "[199] Their international reform
work included sponsoring children in war-torn and underdeveloped
countries, providing a tractor for war widows in a village in Greece,
sending sewing machines to war widows in Korea, and furnishing
equipment for training facilities in Ceylon.[200] The reformist impulse
shared by Ontario's rural women and those in foreign lands did not
go unnoticed by Lewis, who in the spirit of social feminism declared
that " 'when country women of the world work together for the common good we can determine the direction of human history. Neither
guns, nor gold, nor governments can contribute as much as, working
together, we can do.' "[201]

The effort by farm women during World War II reinforced their
confidence in their role and work, but with war's end this sense of security was undermined by the changes that pervaded rural Ontario
for the next twenty and more years. These changes included dramatic
demographic, agricultural, and technological shifts, which redefined
the work and responsibilities of farm women, as well as the advent of
the second-wave equity feminist movement, which condemned or ignored the experiences that shaped their lives. Doubt and confusion
about the role of farm women gave rise to studies which examined
their place, and to self-scrutiny by the lagging WI. But through it all,
both farm women and the WI adhered to social feminist values. Indeed, the WI was able to use what it deemed some undesirable trends
to simultaneously "modernize" its agenda and promote social feminist goals. Only after 1970 did a host of independent and activist farm
women's organizations collectively emerge with grassroots initiatives
designed to accommodate the principles of equity feminism.

7 "A new breed of farm women is developing": The Decline of Social Feminism after 1970

The argument that Ontario farm women between 1900 and 1970 were social feminist is further supported by a profound shift in the feminist discourse of rural women who, after 1970, participated in a new tide of farm women's activism that swept over rural Ontario. The formation of a new farm women's movement was inevitable after decades of dramatic change, which in the 1970s and 80s culminated in devastating farm bankruptcies and foreclosures, more off-farm work than ever before for struggling farm women and men, and widespread personal stress and depression.[1] This activism was also precipitated by an established feminist movement after 1970 which revitalized "farm-women's consciousness of women's issues."[2] The new farm women's movement, while in some ways similar to the WI, rejected the WI's seemingly conservative ways, and espoused an equity feminist doctrine that held profound appeal for young, rural Ontario women of the 1970s and 80s.

The issue of marital property law was at the centre of farm women's new burst of activism. The matter captured their attention after Alberta farm woman Irene Murdoch, a wife of twenty-five years, and an unpaid farm and domestic worker since 1958 on her husband's 480-acre ranch, left her abusive marriage in 1968, and sued her husband for half ownership of the "family farm." Five years later in 1973, the Supreme Court of Canada rejected Murdoch's claim, a ruling premised on the Married Women's Property Act, which specified that only direct monetary contributions by the wife to the purchase and maintenance of property entitled her to a legal share of it. Murdoch's long-time contribution of labour to the farm, reasoned the court, was simply a manifestation of her wifely duties.[3] The injustice of the Murdoch case "rallied Canadian women (and some men) to their most publicized crusade since suffrage."[4]

In Ontario, farm women formed a host of new groups to address their rural concerns. They included Women for the Survival of Agriculture (or Women in Support of Agriculture) (WSA), Concerned Farm Women (CFW), and the Ontario Farm Women's Network (OFWN).[5] Unlike the Women's Institutes and the United Farm Women of Ontario, these organizations were autonomous, grassroots, single-issue groups with no government or partisan affiliations.[6] Out of these groups, observed Molly McGhee, in her 1984 government-sponsored study *Women in Rural Life – The Changing Scene*, "a new breed of farm women is developing."[7] These zealous young women, she discovered, were eager to transform their image from dutiful farmers' wives to farmers in their own right, an identity, they believed, to which their womanhood was not immediately relevant.[8] Ironically, it was this effort to downplay the tradition of female specificity among farm women that prompted them, in part, to form single-sex groups. These women were aware that men's farm groups had virtually ignored the issue of women's status on the farm.

As political scientists demonstrate, however, even with the emergence of this vigorous new campaign, social feminism persisted among farm women in rural Ontario in the 1970s and 80s[9]. Even leaders of the new farm women's movement offered rhetoric consistent with social feminism, and which resembled that of older farm women's groups.[10] Indeed, many members of the new farm women's organizations were already members of the WI.[11]

Certainly, then, the divide asserted by some scholars and farm women activists between the "old" farm women's movement, as embodied by the traditional WI, and the new farm women's groups, can be overstated.[12] It belies the fact that the WI was, as Agnes Bongers declared in 1985, the "grandmother of today's farm women's movement."[13] As Institute executives themselves pointed out, the WI had long cultivated in farm women the very skills necessary to pioneer the new movement.[14] Indeed, the disparity between the WI and the new farm women's activism has been exaggerated to the detriment of the WI. The proposed differences undermine the progressivism of the Women's Institutes, and the extent to which all of these groups were similar. The WI, for example, had for decades criticized the marital property law denounced by Murdoch and the new farm women's groups.

Despite the influence of the WI on the modern farm women's movement, however, and the viewpoints that they shared, the new organizations, akin to the UFWO of the past, censured the WI.[15] They characterized it as a polite social club, ignorant or uncaring of the economic crisis and policy issues that were crucial to the lives of younger farm families; as consumed with bureaucracy, procedure, and fundraising that inhibited flexibility and innovation among its members; as perpetuating traditional notions about farm women's homemaking role – stereotypes which precluded their activist, political role; and as an organization whose agenda was not really agrarian at all.[16]

It was partly in opposition to the WI that the new farm women's organizations of the 1970s and 80s embraced equity feminist principles, most notably gender integration. In fact, Ontario farm associations urged farm women to see themselves generally as " 'farmers first and women second.' "[17] The McGhee study revealed that many women were "emphatically opposed to the segregation of the sexes," and "disapproved of special programs for women, once commonplace at the farm meetings." Farm women, she found, were anxious to participate in agricultural programs alongside their husbands.[18] McGhee observed that women were "no longer willing to be *relegated* to an upstairs room or basement to watch a cooking demonstration or fashion show while their husbands are learning about changes in tax legislation, vomitoxin, or embryo transplants" (emphasis mine).[19] Accordingly, "little need was seen for the traditional home economics courses" as offered by the WI.[20] McGhee found that, unless same-sex organizations assisted in job placement or career education, "young working women elected not to join them."[21] Clearly, the traditional emphasis by farm women on female specificity and separatism and on women-centred rituals and domesticity was losing its appeal in favour of "modern" equity feminist principles of sexual sameness and integration.

The exclusively female CFW, for example, had as its plan to function in an "ancillary role with male-dominated rural groups."[22] Like the equity feminist UFWO, the group maintained that "economic woes must be resolved before attention to gender-related concerns was possible."[23] Accordingly, members sought to promote the notion of a cohesive farming class, referring to themselves not as "farm women," but more generically as "farmers."[24] Although the new farm women's groups prized their autonomy, they remained "open to co-operative politicking with their male counterparts," while "choosing to work outside ... single-sex affiliations such as the Women's Institutes."[25]

Unlike the WI, the new farm women's organizations challenged the traditional sexual division of labour both on and off the farm, and sought "to improve women's skills and knowledge in fields normally reserved for men."[26] For farm women in the first half of the twentieth century, evading "exploitive" male farm labour (field and livestock work) was an expression of female specificity, and of resistance to women's excessive work. For farm women in the 1970s and 80s, however, "male" farm labour spoke to female "autonomy and self-assertion, expressed in terms that they understood as feminist."[27] Shared feminist leanings could be found most commonly among younger women who performed the quintessential male farm job of tending large livestock.[28]

The new farm women's movement introduced a vital and popular equity feminism into rural Ontario, and signalled a shift among women that ended an era. By 1990, after almost a century of unquestioned support, the province had terminated its fixed funding of the WI.[29] Like the new farm women's groups, which had long been vying for government dollars, the WI was reduced to applying for government grants. The special status of the WI was lost to the commanding influence of the new farm women's organizations, as well as to tightening state coffers.[30]

Between 1900 and 1970, farm women demonstrated an allegiance to social feminism, which emphasized the specificity of women's values and experiences that were shaped by domestic and agricultural life, the informal and organized separatism of women, and women's moral influence over the male public sphere. Early in the century, wives and daughters recognized that while the family farm required the full dedication of both women and men, the sexes held differing, often conflicting priorities and self-interests. Farm women protested their mistreatment and devaluation by husbands and fathers, who denied them greater ease of work and financial reward. They, in turn, sought self-determination and self-betterment, and implemented a variety of strategies to achieve these goals. While economically bound to the patriarchal family and the male-owned farm enterprise, and at risk of upsetting their position in both, farm women bravely called attention to their distinctive plight as farm wives, daughters, and workers.

The home economics movement afforded farm women a more formal avenue of social feminist expression. Home economics, a women-centred field of study, appealed to farm women who had nurtured a tradition of female kinship and ritual. Home economics sought to elevate the status, value, efficiency, and safety of women's paid and unpaid domestic work, and to provide for women progressive education and careers. It critiqued the male-formulated knowledge of conventional disciplines that ignored the particular needs of women, and it respected the work that most of them as housewives would ultimately perform. Female-centred education and careers meant that women did not have to compete with men for university spots and white-collar jobs, positions for which men would have almost certainly been chosen. The movement, with Adelaide Hoodless at its helm, inspired the creation of Macdonald Institute in 1903, which for modern farm daughters held the promise of personal and professional advancement. Home economics also spawned the formation of the WI in 1897, which offered farm wives household instruction and provided women with greater opportunity to bond with one another in an exclusively female space. The organized female separatism of the WI was a bold initiative within a male-defined rural culture centred on the "partnership" between husband and wife, and on the connection between propertied fathers and inheriting sons.

In the post-World War I ferment of the politicization of Ontario farmers and the struggle for suffrage, the feminism of some farm women sought expression in the equity feminist UFWO. It was critical of the homemaking focus of the WI, which by this time, in fact, also trained women in fundraising, government lobbying, and social reform in order to infuse female values into the male public sphere. These efforts were particularly related to issues of justice for women under the law. By assuming a role in public political life, farm women sought to abrade public/private distinctions which had for so long restricted women's influence over societal change. The UFWO never enjoyed the popularity of the WI, and it contributed to its own early demise by depending on acceptance from and integration with the unreceptive men of the UFO. Local branches of the UFWO were more successful than their provincial parent only because, like the WI, they emphasized domestic concerns. The "progressive" UFWO also resembled the WI in its social reform efforts, in its social and intellectual pursuits, and in its membership lists, a fact which undermines the notion of a conservative and impassive Institute.

Homefront efforts during World War II reinforced for farm women and the WI a sense of certainty and self-worth, but dramatic changes in 1950s and 60s rural Ontario and the advent of the second-wave equity feminist movement put the traditional role of farm wives into question. Studies such as those conducted by Dr Helen Abell and Ontario Farm Radio Forum attempted to assess women's function on the farm, and to illuminate their perceptions of farm life. For the WI, the post-war era was a time of self-scrutiny. With its numbers declining after 1950, the WI reflected on the pertinence of its program to modern society. In the face of change, doubt, and confusion, however, farm women and the WI remained true to the values of social feminism. Indeed, the WI adapted to modern times by addressing and adhering to many contemporary trends of the post-war era, and used these trends not as a justification to abandon their principles but as a vehicle by which to assert them. It was not until 1970 that the influence of social feminism abated with the advent of the new equity feminist farm women's movement.

That Ontario farm women between 1900 and 1970 found expression in social feminism should really come as little surprise. Their combined patriarchal home and workplace, which both undervalued and relied upon their domestic and agricultural labour, heightened at once a sense of female distinctiveness, oppression, and power, all necessary ingredients for a feminist sensibility. The family enterprise also undermined restrictive notions of separate private and public spheres, a condition which facilitated farm women's public service and social reform. Farm women, then, made likely reformers. In asserting a distinctively female world view, they challenged the privileges and priorities of men, as well as the ambition of those women who sought to emulate male standards. Certainly, the social feminism of farm women within the androcentric culture of rural Ontario did not preclude their progressivism – it served to promote it.

Notes

CHAPTER ONE

1 Rankin, "Beyond the Kitchen and the Cornfield" and "The Politicization of Ontario Farm Women."
2 Carbert, "Agrarian Feminism" and *Agrarian Feminism*; Brandt and Black, "'Il en faut un peu.'"
3 See, for example, Haley, "Getting Our Act Together," 172. When Haley explains that a particular farm women's group "has been a forerunner for

feminism in rural Canada since 1975," she precludes the possibility that a "forerunner for feminism" could have existed before 1975.

4 Historians have addressed issues of feminism only with regard to notable women connected with rural Ontario, specifically Adelaide Hoodless and Agnes Macphail. See, for example, Crowley, "Madonnas Before Magdalenes" and *Agnes Macphail*; Stamp, "Adelaide Hoodless"; and MacDonald, *Adelaide Hoodless*.

5 Kechnie, "The United Farm Women of Ontario." Historians who have recently examined the lives of American farm women have also resisted the feminist label. They variously argue for the strength, agency, and empowerment strategies of American farm women within the family, community, and organizational setting, but largely sidestep the question of their feminism. See, for example, Osterud, *Bonds of Community*; Neth, *Preserving the Family Farm*; and Holt, *Linoleum, Better Babies, and the Modern Farm Woman*.

6 Ambrose, "Problems in Doing Rural Women's History," 22, 9.

7 Cook, "Measuring Feminist Consciousness," 72–3.

8 Black, *Social Feminism*, 10. As farm women never called themselves "feminists," I avoid naming them as such. Instead, I refer to them as "feminist," emphasizing, like Black, women's propensity for feminism over their self-identification as feminists (the same holds true for the notion of separatism). In the United States, the word feminism first appeared in 1910, and was popularly used beginning about 1913. In Canada, this trend likely occurred several years later. For more on the origins of the word, see Cott, *The Grounding of Modern Feminism*, 13–16.

9 Halpern, "Beyond the Dell," *Matrix*, 7; Rankin, "Beyond the Kitchen and the Cornfield," 2; Rasmussen et al., *A Harvest Yet to Reap*, 43.

10 Fink, "Sidelines and Moral Capital," 55.

11 See, for example, various articles in Haney and Knowles, eds., *Women and Farming*; in Coward and Smith, Jr., eds., *The Family in Rural Society*; and in the *Rural Sociologist* 1 (November 1981). Also see Hundertmark, "Rural Feminism."

12 Merrell et al., "Home Economics, Feminism and the Family," 277–87.

13 Kechnie, "Keeping Things Tidy for Home and Country." My initial research on the Ontario WI led me to this unsatisfying conclusion, although I did emphasize that "to depict the Ontario government as a manipulator of the Women's Institutes, however, is to mask their enduring vitality, for while the province made demands on the Institutes, they, in turn, made demands on the province." See Halpern, " 'Practically Part of the Government.' "

14 The use by women's organizations such as the WI of formal parliamentary procedure at meetings has also been equated with the conservatism of club women. Certainly, their practice of such procedure during a time in

which they did not yet have the vote hardly indicates political compla-
cency, or disinterest in political affairs. See Blair, *The Clubwoman as Feminist*, 117.

15 Strong-Boag, "Pulling in Double Harness," 44–5.

16 "Branch Puts Across 'New Fangled' Ideas," *London Free Press*, "The
Women's Institute 50th Anniversary" (supplement), 16 June 1947, 10, HFP,
UGL, Box 4, File – Photographs etc. 1940–49. Newspaper Clippings, Letters, Publications. Also see Brookes et al., "Religion and the Rural Community."

17 Schull, *Ontario Since 1867*, 181.

18 Bacchi, "Divided Allegiances," 101.

19 See, for example, ibid., 100–4, and Cleverdon, *The Women's Suffrage Movement*, 46–83.

20 Bacchi, "Divided Allegiances," 100–4; Prentice et al., *Canadian Women*,
219–20.

21 Brandt and Black, "'Il en faut un peu,'" 75.

22 Siltanen and Stanworth, "The Politics of Private Woman," 102.

23 Ibid.

24 Vickers, "Feminist Approaches to Women in Politics," 17.

25 Ibid., 20, 23.

26 Black's book *Social Feminism* examines three social feminist organizations
with their roots in the early twentieth century: The Women's Co-operative
Guild (England), L'Union Feminine Civique et Sociale (France), and the
League of Women Voters (United States); Carbert's thesis relies on 117
surveys conducted in Huron and Grey Counties, Ontario, in 1989; quanti-
tative data; and the scholarly literature of "liberal modernization theory,
agrarian politics, and the women's movement," to investigate the politi-
cal/feminist consciousness of contemporary Ontario farm women. See
Black, *Social Feminism*, 107–303, and Carbert, "Agrarian Feminism,"
Abstract and 2.

27 Carbert and I are joined by Linda Ambrose in using Black's social femi-
nism model to examine Ontario farm women. See Ambrose and Kechnie,
"Social Control or Social Feminism," 233. Black and collaborator Gail
Cuthbert Brandt also use the paradigm to examine the farm women of
Quebec and France in "'Il en faut un peu'" and *Feminist Politics on the
Farm*.

28 Carbert, "Agrarian Feminism," 2–3.

29 Black, *Social Feminism*, 1, 67.

30 Ibid., 66.

31 Ibid., 65.

32 Ibid. Given the overlap of family and work life on the farm, farm women
experienced less of a distinction between public and private than did their
urban sisters. This did not preclude farm women's adherence to social

feminism, however, whose concept of the public sphere centred far less on notions of work there than on public and social service.

33 Ibid., 53.

34 Historian Wayne Roberts, for example, refers to the "maternal feminist" facet of the Toronto suffrage movement as "characterized by stifling definitions of motherhood" and "prim moralism," and perceives the "human rights" side of the movement as "inspired by self-fulfillment and equality," attributes "antithetical" to maternal feminist ideology. Accordingly, Roberts asserts that the "conservative" feminism of the maternal movement "severely undercut and negated" the efforts of early suffragists who "sought women's emancipation from social and intellectual oppression." Likewise, Carol Bacchi blames her "social reformers" for the "dilution" and "taming" of the suffrage movement, and claims that once under their leadership, the movement "lost its association with feminist causes." Bacchi maintains that only Canada's early suffragists "can legitimately be called feminists," as they demanded "complete equality of the sexes," and sought to penetrate traditional male occupations. See Roberts, "'Rocking the Cradle for the World,'" 27, 19, 20, and Bacchi, *Liberation Deferred?* 29, 143, 39, 146.

35 See ch. 5, n. 26.

36 Black, *Social Feminism*, 31.

37 Ibid.

38 Ibid., 33.

39 Ibid.

40 Bacchi, *Liberation Deferred?* 148–9.

41 Black, *Social Feminism*, 34.

42 Ibid., 34–5.

43 Bacchi, *Liberation Deferred?* 147.

44 Black, *Social Feminism*, 35.

45 Ibid., 38. See, for example, O'Neill, *Everyone was Brave.*

46 Strong-Boag, "'Ever a Crusader,'" 311, 312.

47 Roberts, "'Rocking the Cradle for the World,'" 18.

48 Black, *Social Feminism*, 25.

49 Ibid., 26.

50 Ibid. As stated previously in this chapter, neither must we limit the term "political" to mean only activities in the public sphere.

51 Ibid.

52 Ibid., 35, 41, 56 n. 1, and Bacchi, *Liberation Deferred?* 25. It is often asserted that equity feminism preceded social feminism, and that social feminism emerged quite late in the suffrage battle in response, according to Black, to "changed attitudes or as concessions to some perceived political necessity." For examples, see Kraditor, *The Ideas of the Woman Suffrage Movement*, chapter 3; O'Neill, *Everyone was Brave*, 34; and Roberts, "'Rocking

the Cradle for the World,' " 26–7. Black, however, argues that although the 1848 Seneca Falls Declaration of Sentiments, the first official suffrage document, was modelled after the Declaration of Independence, and was therefore"the preeminent example of equity feminism,"it should not be overlooked that"the accompanying resolutions included large and significant doses of social feminism, as did the assembly's debates."See Black, *Social Feminism*, 35.

53 Ibid., 41; Prentice et al., *Canadian Women*, 190.

54 Bacchi, *Liberation Deferred?* 12; Black, *Social Feminism*, 41, 20.

55 Lemons, *The Woman Citizen*, viii.

56 Kaledin, *Mothers and More*, i, ii.

57 Black, *Social Feminism*, 67.

58 Ibid., 67, 54, 57.

59 Blair, *The Clubwoman as Feminist*, 71.

60 Baxter, "Preface," xii. Although by urban standards exclusively female clubs were largely considered unnecessary and outdated with the triumph of suffrage, today it is radical feminists who most often advocate the existence of women-only organizations. See Black, *Social Feminism*, 68.

61 Black, *Social Feminism*, 29, 67.

62 Ibid., 105, 4, 73.

63 Ibid., 53.

64 Ibid., 61.

65 Ibid., 3.

66 Ibid., 53.

67 Roberts, " 'Rocking the Cradle for the World,' " 19.

68 Black, *Social Feminism*, 3.

69 Ibid., 53, 24. That the rejection of dependency by social feminists meant their repudiation of one of the most profound traits associated with women is an irony not lost on Black.

70 Sheehan, " 'Teasippers or Crusaders?' " 22–5; Cott, "What's in a Name?" 825.

71 Phillips, review of *Social Feminism*, 158.

72 Cott, "What's in a Name?" 820.

73 Ibid., 820–1.

74 Carbert, "Agrarian Feminism," 3.

75 Ibid., 2.

76 Ibid., Abstract.

77 Ibid., 3, 4.

78 Ibid., 4.

79 Ibid.

80 Ibid., 6.

81 Ibid.

82 Neth, *Preserving the Family Farm*, 18. Mutuality, affirms Nancy Grey
    Osterud, was an "empowerment strategy" for farm wives – "a collective
    response to gender inequality." See *Bonds of Community*, 275, 276.
83 Carbert, "Agrarian Feminism," 6.
84 Ibid. As an example, Carbert cites Elbert, "The Challenge of Research on
    Farm Women."
85 Zwarun, "Farm Wives 10 Years After Irene Murdoch," 178.
86 Dymond, *The Laws of Ontario*, 32.
87 Dranoff, *Women in Canadian Law*, 48; Chambers, *Married Women and Prop-
    erty Law*, 179.
88 Dawson, "Politics, Woman and the Boon She Will Crave," 2234.
89 Boivin, "Farm Women," 67; Cebotarev, "From Domesticity to the Public
    Sphere," 209.
90 The adult farm daughter was also disadvantaged by the system of
    household commodity production, and by the patriarch of family and
    farm. As will be discussed in chapter 3, the daughter on the farm was
    often subjected to unpaid domestic and agricultural work, to a scanty in-
    heritance, and to lost educational and job opportunities. While the
    concept of agrarian feminism generally references the situation of farm
    wives, it also has acute meaning for farm daughters.
91 Carbert, "Agrarian Feminism," 3.
92 Fink, *Agrarian Women*, xv.
93 Ibid., 10.
94 Ibid., 28, 128, 10.
95 Ibid., 10.
96 Carbert, "Agrarian Feminism," 112.
97 Strong-Boag, "Pulling in Double Harness," 32.
98 Ibid., 33.
99 Ibid.
100 Just how many Ontario farm women between 1900 and 1970 were femi-
    nist, and more specifically social feminist, will always be a matter of spec-
    ulation. Unfortunately, farm women did not articulate or document their
    feminism in any quantifiable way. Moreover, they might have moved in
    and out of feminism throughout their lives, asserting it and abandoning it
    as they deemed necessary. The sizable membership of the social feminist
    WI, however, although not an accurate measure, certainly suggests that a
    substantial number of farm women were indeed social feminist.

CHAPTER TWO

1 Carbert, "Agrarian Feminism," 103.
2 Marshall, *Half Century of Farming in Dufferin*, 49. See also Dahms,
   "Ontario's Rural Communities," 331.

3 Marshall, *Half Century of Farming in Dufferin*, 49.
4 Leckie, "Female Farm Operators," 3.
5 The notion that Ontario rural life began its decline with the advent of the twentieth century is supported by Fuller, "The Development of Farm Life," 7, 10, 11; Dahms, "Ontario's Rural Communities," 330; and Reaman, *A History of Agriculture*, 170. The major developments in rural Ontario post-World War II are surveyed in chapter 6. In census records prior to 1951, "rural" was defined as those areas outside incorporated cities, towns, and villages – irrespective of their size. Beginning in 1951, the census defined "rural" according to "the aggregate size of population rather than provincial legal status." Cities, towns, and villages with a population exceeding 1,000, whether incorporated or not, were classified as "urban" – remaining areas were demarcated "rural." See Canada, Dominion Bureau of Statistics, *Census of Canada 1951*, 1:15.
6 Densmore, *Seasons of Change*, 64; Reaman, *A History of Agriculture*, 58.
7 Ladell and Ladell, *A Farm in the Family*, 120; Densmore, *Seasons of Change*, 64. By 1941, the number of tractors had reached almost 36,000. See Fuller, "The Development of Farm Life," 20, table 1.3.
8 Ladell and Ladell, *A Farm in the Family*, 130; Densmore, *Seasons of Change*, 64.
9 Densmore, *Seasons of Change*, 64. The threshing machine also revolutionized farming at this time, as did the combine (combination reaping and threshing machine). See 69, and Ladell and Ladell, *A Farm in the Family*, 120.
10 Davies, "Ontario and the Automobile," 302.
11 Ibid., 331, 334, 336.
12 Ibid., 308, 305, 311, 312, 316, 324.
13 Reaman, *A History of Agriculture*, 256.
14 Fuller, "The Development of Farm Life," 21, table 1.5.
15 Ibid.
16 Densmore, *Seasons of Change*, 9, 81.
17 Fuller, "The Development of Farm Life," 6; Densmore, *Seasons of Change*, 81.
18 Fuller, "The Development of Farm Life," 17, figure 1.3.
19 Ibid.
20 Ibid., 14. The 1931 census defined "farm" as a parcel of land – owned, rented, or managed – the size of one acre or more which in 1930 yielded agricultural products valued at at least fifty dollars or which in 1931 produced crop or afforded pasturing. "Farm population" referred to all people residing on farms, including those engaged in non-farming labour but excluding those farm workers and their families who did not reside on farms. See Canada, Dominion Bureau of Statistics, *Seventh Census of Canada, 1931*, 8:xxv, and 1:331.

21 Ibid., 15, table 1.1.
22 Brown and Cook, *Canada 1896–1921*, 2. Even by 1911, Ontario's urban population of about 1,328,400 only outnumbered its rural population of about 1,198,800 by a marginal 129,600. See Canada, Dominion Bureau of Statistics, *Census of Canada* 1951, table 13: Population by Sex, for Provinces and Territories, Rural and Urban 1871–1951. This disparity was close to the half-million mark by 1921, and the one million mark by 1941.
23 Marshall, *Half Century of Farming in Dufferin*, 3.
24 Lawr, "The Development of Ontario Farming," 239.
25 Kohl, "Image and Behaviour," 91–2; Coward and Smith, Jr., "Introduction," 1, 3.
26 Bettmann, *The Good Old Days*, 45.
27 Brandt and Black, " 'Il en faut un peu,' " 75.
28 Kohl, "Image and Behaviour," 101.
29 The historical neglect of farm women was brought to my attention about fifteen years ago while researching an undergraduate history paper on white tenant farm women in the American South, and then while researching my Master's thesis. The thesis examines the Woman's Land Army of America, a women's organization that recruited urban, female college students to perform agricultural work during the farm labour shortage of World War I. See Halpern, " 'Our Mother Earth Has Called Us.' "
30 Jensen, *With These Hands*, xvi–xx.
31 See, for example, Ethel Hillier (MacDonald) Diaries (unpublished).
32 Marshall, *Half Century of Farming in Dufferin*, 8.
33 Kechnie, "Keeping Things Tidy," 141–2. As Kechnie points out, one must consider to what extent the voices of these privileged women reflected those of the larger WI membership.
34 Mrs Erland Lee, in Walker et al., *Fifty Years of Achievement*, 6, QU.
35 Ontario Department of Agriculture, *Report of the Women's Institutes of the Province of Ontario*, 1917, 46–7, QU.
36 Kechnie, "Keeping Things Tidy," 26.
37 Mitchinson, "Early Women's Organizations," 80.
38 See chapter 5.
39 Todd, "The Work of Women's Institutes in Canada," 16; Mrs Erland Lee, in Walker et al., *Fifty Years of Achievement*, 6, QU.
40 Ontario Department of Agriculture, *Report of the Women's Institutes of the Province of Ontario*, 1922, 26, QU.
41 Terry Crowley points out that women's pages in the agricultural press catered to "middling farmers" of British and Irish background, who comprised most of the rural population. Minorities, including Germans, Mennonites, and blacks, "were seldom mentioned." Natives, he notes, despite some participation in farming, "were considered outside the farm sector." See Crowley, "Experience and Representation," 240–1.

42 For historical information on farm women in northern Ontario, see Kechnie, "The Women's Institutes in Northern Ontario," 263–74.

43 Rosenfeld, *Farm Women*, 39. Also see Boivin, "Farm Women," 52.

44 Rosenfeld, *Farm Women*, 39.

45 The nuclear family arrangement at the heart of the "family farm," which conceptualizes farm women chiefly as "farm wives," has helped ensure that almost no historical attention has been paid to rural heterosexual women who never married, or to rural lesbians who did or did not become wives. Largely invisible to family, friends, and neighbours, lesbians in rural areas have also been neglected by scholars focused on lesbian urban culture. Single and/or gay farm men have suffered from similar scholarly neglect, although unlike women's status, men's status as "farmer" within the community is unaffected by their marital status. This undifferentiated social status can either benefit or further oppress gay men by helping to conceal their sexuality. For a rare consideration of lesbians in rural areas, see Sachs, *Gendered Fields*, 24–5, 134. For recollections by both lesbians and gays who live in rural Canada, see Riordon, *Out Our Way*. Ontario is largely represented in this book by those who reside in the northern part of the province.

46 Cebotarev and Beattie, "Women Strengthening the Farm Community," 255; Leckie, "Female Farm Operators," 26, 79, 87.

47 Osterud, "Land, Identity and Agency," 76–7.

48 The term "farming class" appears regularly in the *Weekly Sun* and the *Farmers' Sun*, and in Saidak, "The Inception of the Home Economics Movement," 135.

49 Johnston, "'A Motley Crowd,'" 237–56. Perhaps only in frontier regions were there fewer socio-economic distinctions, which might help explain why pioneering farm men and women of the Canadian and American West have received far more historical attention than established farm families in the West or anywhere else.

50 Ibid., 238.

51 See, for example, ibid., 237–56. In 1901, 85 per cent of Ontario farm land was owned, as opposed to rented or partly owned, by the farm operator. See Fuller, "The Development of Farm Life," 18.

52 Rankin, "Beyond the Kitchen," 20; Garkovich and Bokemeier, "Agricultural Mechanization," 222; Rosenfeld, *Farm Women*, 28.

53 For a discussion on geography in this regard, see Ambrose, "Problems in Doing Rural Women's History," 18, 20.

54 Fink, "Sidelines and Moral Capital," 55.

55 Cebotarev and Beattie, "Women Strengthening the Farm Community," 256.

56 Of course, not all of these chores were characteristic of farm women's work throughout the period under study.

57 Fink, "Sidelines and Moral Capital," 55–6.
58 This labour, along with other efforts to cultivate the bonds of extended family, may be referred to as "kin keeping." See McCannell and Herringer, "Changing Terms of Endearment," 65.
59 Garkovich and Bokemeier, "Agricultural Mechanization," 212.
60 Sachs, *The Invisible Farmers*, 109.
61 Ibid., 82.

CHAPTER THREE

1 Strong-Boag, "Discovering the Home," 40. Tension often characterized the relationship between farm wife and farmhand. She resented the extra household work that he generated, and he disliked (and often spurned) taking orders from a woman. Farmhands were not unknown to sexually assault farm wives and daughters, particularly when farm owners were away in town. See Dubinsky, *Improper Advances*, 58.
2 "Is Marriage a Failure?" *Farmer's Advocate* 47 (14 November 1912): 1983.
3 Neth, *Preserving the Family Farm*, 27.
4 Vanek, "Work, Leisure, and Family Roles," 428.
5 Campbell, *From Chalk Dust to Hayseed*, 113.
6 Buchanan, "The Woman on the Farm," 448; Dawson, "The Woman on the Farm," 406–7; Adelaide Hoodless, "The Relation of Domestic Science to the Agricultural Population," December 1896, 5, HFP, UGL, Box 1, File – Addresses and Reports. See also "Barbara Wylie to Organize Boycott of the Dominion," *Moose Jaw Evening Times*, 18 June 1913, in Rasmussen et al., *A Harvest Yet to Reap*, 22.
7 Dawson, "The Woman on the Farm," 406–7.
8 Latzer, *Myrtleville*, 253, 268; Halpern, "Beyond the Dell," (SA)*FIRE WORKS*, 38.
9 Selina Horst (b. 1921). Horst Interview, tape 1, side 2, OHT 658, KPL.
10 Dorothy Franklin, in Grayson and Bliss, *The Wretched of Canada*, 119.
11 "Farmers' Wives and Insanity," *Farmer's Advocate* 40 (4 May 1905): 656. The United States Department of Agriculture circulated a bulletin in 1912 whose object was to counter the notion that farm women were prone to insanity. Turn-of-the-century Alabamians believed that only men could go insane from overwork – a clear symptom of "excessive masculinity." See Sachs, *The Invisible Farmers*, 23, and Hughs, "The Madness of Separate Spheres," 56, 60.
12 "Farmers' Wives and Insanity," *Farmer's Advocate* 40 (4 May 1905): 656.
13 Ibid.
14 Ibid.
15 McIntosh, "Lo! The Poor Farmer's Wife," *Canadian Countryman*, 2, UGL. McIntosh adds that "here we have no record of the bushels of potatoes

she peeled, the meat she roasted and fried and boiled, the gallons of tea she steeped, and the seven or eight hundred plates of porridge which she must have served for breakfast." As the article did not appear on the women's page of the journal, McIntosh could have been a man.

16 Mrs W.E. Hopkins, *Farm and Dairy* (14 November 1912): 18, in Young, "The Countryside on the Defensive," 40.

17 MacDougall, *Rural Life in Canada*, 128; McDiarmid, "Should Farm Women Go On Strike?" 1136. American farm women were no less agitated, as exemplified by a series of six articles in *Harper's Bazaar* entitled "The Revolt of the Farmer's Wife!" See Martha and Robert Bruère.

18 Cebotarev, "From Domesticity to the Public Sphere," 200.

19 Strong-Boag, "Pulling in Double Harness," 33. The significance of farm journals (and their women's pages) cannot be overestimated with respect to numbers. In 1917, eight Ontario farm journals (in addition to Montreal's highly popular *Family Herald and Weekly Star*) had an Ontario circulation of approximately 224,848 (except for the *Farmer's Advocate*, this figure includes the small circulation numbers for outside Ontario). Given that the *Canadian Newspaper Directory* of 1918 estimated 223,260 farms in Ontario, circulation figures "reveal a wide acceptance of these journals by rural readers." Three of the most popular Ontario journals, *The Farmer's Advocate, Canadian Countryman*, and *Farm and Dairy*, are heavily represented in this chapter. See Talman, "Reading Habits of the 1917 Ontario Farmer," 68, 70, 86, 66. My utilization of the agricultural press as a source in this chapter, however, as well as in the chapters which follow, is selective rather than exhaustive, and thus does not incorporate social science methods of content analysis.

20 Stephen, "Appeal to the Reader," 21.

21 "A Sidelight on a Self-made Man," *Farm and Dairy* Third Annual Special Magazine Household Number (5 October 1911): 8.

22 McDiarmid, "Should Farm Women Go On Strike?" 1136.

23 Chapman, "Machinery For Women," 54.

24 Neth, "Building the Base," 355; Fink, *Agrarian Women*, 62–3. As Carolyn Sachs points out, "interdependence does not necessarily equal equity." See Elbert, "The Farmer Takes a Wife," 174.

25 Neth, *Preserving the Family Farm*, 26.

26 Bruère, "War on Drudgery" (November 1912), 539, 580. American reformers Martha Bruère, a home economist, and her husband, Robert, an economist, disparaged frugality and promoted consumerism and consumption. See Marsh, "Suburban Men," 117.

27 Young, "The Countryside on the Defensive," 74–5.

28 Densmore, *Seasons of Change*, 123.

29 Elaine Bitz (b. 1928), interview by author.

30 "Feminism on the Farm," *Farmer's Magazine* (17 November 1921): 9.

31 Chapman, "Machinery For Women," 55. Similar comparisons were made in the United States: "Laundry machinery is to the farmer's wife what the self-binder and the thresher are to her husband, with the important difference that it saves her time and muscle and the spine of her back fifty-two weeks in the year instead of a few days at harvesting season. What then, shall be said of the farmer who buys for himself the self-stacking, self-sacking, self-weighing thresher while he lets his wife wash, as it were, with a flail?" See Bruère, "War on Drudgery" (November 1912), 539, 550.

32 Chapman, "Machinery For Women," 55; John Ewing Marshall also makes this point, conceding that farm women complained "with some justification." See Marshall, *Half Century of Farming in Dufferin*, 16.

33 "Feminism on the Farm," *Farmers Magazine* (17 November 1921): 9, and Chapman, "Machinery For Women," 55; Knowles, " 'It's Our Turn Now,' " 314; "Feminism on the Farm," 9. With some contempt for the farmer's viewpoint, Ethel Chapman facetiously supposed that homemaking was to be "something that woman does unaided by the genius of her natural domestic instincts." See Chapman, "Machinery For Women," 24.

34 Chapman, "Machinery For Women," 55.

35 Bruère, "War on Drudgery" (November 1912), 550; Cragg, *Father on the Farm*, 27; Elaine Bitz, interview.

36 Cragg, *Father on the Farm*, 29.

37 Ibid.

38 Sachs, *The Invisible Farmers*, xii.

39 Cragg, *Father on the Farm*, 10.

40 Bass, "The Woman on the Farm," 560–1. This is evidenced by the special household issue of *Farm and Dairy* which profiled several female-run enterprises. See, for example, Jull, "Ready Money," 3; and "A Successful Poultry Woman," *Farm and Dairy* Third Annual Special Magazine Household Number (5 October 1911): 12.

41 "Farming for Women," *New York Times*, 13 April 1919, sec. 3, 3, in Halpern, " 'Our Mother Earth Has Called Us,' " 102. See also Cragg, *Father on the Farm*, 10.

42 Anne Higginson Spicer, "Training at Libertyville, Illinois," *Farmerette* 1 (January 1919): 2, National Agricultural Library, us. Department of Agriculture, in Halpern, " 'Our Mother Earth Has Called Us,' " 102; Jull, "Ready Money," 3; "Farming for Women," *New York Times*, 13 April 1919, sec. 3, 3, in Halpern " 'Our Mother Earth Has Called Us,' " 102. Kenneth Cragg recalled that his mother "claimed hens had to be fussed over." See Cragg, *Father on the Farm*, 46.

43 Jull, "Ready Money," 3.

44 "A Successful Poultry Woman," *Farm and Dairy* Third Annual Special Magazine Household Number (5 October 1911): 12; (Dr) Annie L. Backus,

Farm and Dairy, Third Annual Special Magazine Household Number (5 October 1911): 16. As Marjorie Griffen Cohen chronicles, farm women's traditional role as cheese and butter producers before the mid nineteenth century declined as cheese factories and creameries assumed all aspects of dairy production. By 1900, cheese production by farm women had essentially ended, and, although their household butter production continued, the advent of large-scale, mechanized dairy farms, and the existence of expanding markets, all but excluded women from dairying by the 1930s. See Cohen, *Women's Work.*

45 Ladd, "The Farmer's Wife as a Partner," *Canadian Countryman,* 6, UGL.
46 Dawson, "The Woman on the Farm," 405.
47 Crowley, *Agnes Macphail,* 7.
48 Dawson, "The Woman on the Farm," 405.
49 Uncle Peter, "Partners in the Business," *Farm and Dairy* Third Annual Special Magazine Household Number (5 October 1911): 21.
50 "Feminism on the Farm," *Farmer's Magazine* (17 November 1921): 9.
51 "Keeping Boarders with Pure Bred Jersey Cows," *Farm and Dairy* (8 October 1914): 4.
52 "What is a Woman's Work on the Farm?[:] A Discussion of this Oft Times Burning Question by Members of *Farm and Dairy*'s Home Club," *Farm and Dairy* (8 October 1914): 7.
53 Jensen, *With These Hands,* 32. This tradition did not hold true for Eastern European, African, and indigenous North American women, for example, who customarily performed field work.
54 Ibid.; Sachs, *The Invisible Farmers,* 19, 3. As Sachs argues, this point is especially salient with reference to the Plantation South where white slave owners used black women as field labourers, a fact which clearly reveals the racial discrepancies inherent in the expectations surrounding women's work (25).
55 Yates, "Agriculture for Women," 183.
56 Sister Evelyn, "No Sympathy for Men," *Weekly Sun,* 29 May 1918, 6.
57 Elizabeth Davis, in Anderson, *Remembering the Farm,* 252.
58 Elaine Bitz, interview; Sachs, *The Invisible Farmers,* 28.
59 John Cairns, in Anderson, *Remembering the Farm,* 94.
60 Bass, "The Woman on the Farm," 560. For a similar viewpoint, see Dream, "The True Homemaker Defined," *Farm and Dairy* (8 October 1914): 7, 10.
61 Yates, "Agriculture for Women," 183.
62 A Worshipper, "The Farmer's Wife," *Farmer's Advocate* 44 (17 June 1909): 1000.
63 Sachs, *The Invisible Farmers,* 13.
64 Breese, "The Woman Upon the Farm," 495. Mrs Breese is described as a farmer's wife who "is well acquainted with the life she describes" (494).
65 Dot, "Let Us Give and Take, But –," *Farm and Dairy* (8 October 1914): 7.

66 MacMurchy, *The Woman – Bless Her*, 143, 91.

67 Sachs, *The Invisible Farmers*, 13.

68 A Worshipper, "The Farmer's Wife," *Farmer's Advocate* 44 (17 June 1909): 1000.

69 Householder, "Farm Women and Outdoor Work," *Farmer's Advocate* 53 (7 March 1918): 370.

70 Sachs, *The Invisible Farmers*, xi.

71 See, for example, A Worshipper, "The Farmer's Wife," *Farmer's Advocate* 44 (17 June 1919): 1000.

72 Atkeson, "Women in Farm Life and Rural Economy," 188. Atkeson insightfully pointed out that although the farm woman "was not allowed to ride the disc-harrow, or the reaper in the fields, no one objected to her working long hours over a steaming washtub, or cleaning the chicken house, or handling the deadly heavy cans of milk in the dairy, although this was a part of the heaviest work done on the farm."

73 "Cooperation in the Home," *Farm and Dairy* Third Annual Special Magazine Household Number (5 October 1911): 15.

74 "A Woman's Duty," *Farm and Dairy* (8 October 1914): 10. Also see n. 73 above.

75 McCutcheon, "The Single Woman in the Country," 5.

76 Because men's labour was not organized according to a weekly routine, a husband could often not distinguish the daily differences in a woman's work week. The diaries of men acknowledge women's work only "when it affected their own." See Neth, *Preserving the Family Farm*, 27.

77 Another Hired Man, "Life History of a Farm Woman," *Farm and Dairy* Third Annual Special Magazine Household Number (5 October 1911): 21.

78 "The Greatest Women in History," *Farm and Dairy* Third Annual Special Magazine Household Number (5 October 1911): 14.

79 Ethel Hillier (MacDonald) Diaries (unpublished), 26 March 1923. Ethel Hillier, 1891–1984. Ethel makes no mention in her diary of which side won.

80 Cragg, *Father on the Farm*, 45, 167.

81 Densmore, *Seasons of Change*, 133.

82 Dream, "The True Homemaker Defined," *Farm and Dairy* (8 October 1914): 10.

83 "Is Marriage a Failure?" *Farmer's Advocate* 47 (14 November 1912): 1983.

84 "A Woman's Duty," *Farm and Dairy* (8 October 1914): 10.

85 Roxie Hostetler (b. 1889). Hostetler Interview, tape 2, OHT 132, KPL.

86 Hillier Diaries (unpublished). See, for example, 10 August 1921, 20 June 1923, 5 October 1923. Appreciation for the farm daughter's workload should have inhibited one man from advising that "girls should learn to do housework instead of sitting on rocking chairs and reading trashy novels from morning to night." See Amey, *Farm Life As It Should Be*, 13.

87 Elaine Bitz, interview.

88 Ibid. In 1928, at the age of thirty-seven, Ethel gave birth to her only child, Elaine (Bitz).

89 Nephew Frank, "Would You Marry a Farmer?" *Farm and Dairy* (8 October 1914): 7. Ethel Hillier married farmer Thomas MacDonald in July of 1926. They moved to a farm six miles from her parents' home in Plympton Township (Elaine Bitz, interview by author). Between 1900 and 1950, the percentage of Ontario farm daughters who married farmers fell from 92 to 77. See Cebotarev, "From Domesticity to the Public Sphere," 209.

90 Marie Henderson, in Anderson, *Remembering the Farm*, 58. Also see Johnston, *Before the Age of Miracles*, 77, for an account of a five-year-old farm girl who suffered asthma attacks when she was denied the opportunity to perform barn work with her father. When her parents eventually sanctioned her trips to the barn, the asthma disappeared.

91 Beatrice Snyder (b. 1908). Snyder Interview, tape 2, side 1, OHT 105, KPL. Male butchering jobs included preparing the tools and equipment, and killing the animals; female jobs included cleaning the casings, cutting the fat, and making the lard.

92 Ibid., and tape 1, side 2, OHT 104, KPL.

93 Snyder Interview, tape 2, side 1, OHT 105, KPL.

94 One must wonder whether doctors would have attributed Beatrice's stroke to hard labour if she had been strenuously performing traditional women's work. It is revealing that women's excessive "male work" attacked the body (a comment on the superior physicality of men), and women's excessive "female work" attacked the mind (a comment on the deficient connection between the frail female body and the unstable female mind).

95 Snyder Interview, tape 2, side 1, OHT 105, KPL.

96 Jean Lozier (b. 1920). Lozier, "This is My Story," 2 (unpublished memoir).

97 Snyder Interview, tape 2, side 1, OHT 105, KPL.

98 Ferguson, "Should Daughters Be Compensated," 6.

99 Pringle, "What Girls Need Most," *Canadian Countryman*, 14, UGL. Pringle was born on a farm "in a long-settled district of Ontario," and as a young adult lived in Selby, Ontario. This article was one of several winning letter in a contest to address the question "What Girls Need Most in a Rural Community."

100 McCutcheon, "The Single Woman in the Country," 5. The insistence by adult farm sons and daughters that they should be paid for their work on the family farm was a new development in early twentieth-century Ontario. Before this time, they understood their labour as a debt owed to their parents for shelter, food, and clothing. See Parr, "Hired Men," 97. According to McCutcheon and others, however, the claim of sons to compensation was proving far more successful than the claim of daughters.

101 Pringle, "What Girls Need Most," *Canadian Countryman*, 14, UGL.
102 Brown, "What Girls Need Most in a Rural Community," *Canadian Countryman*, 14, UGL. This article was a winning letter in a contest to address this question.
103 Ferguson, "Should Daughters Be Compensated," 6.
104 Ibid.; Brown, "What Girls Need Most," *Canadian Countryman*, 14, UGL.
105 Hillier Diaries (unpublished), last pages of 1924 diary. In 1924, Ethel, who kept meticulous records of her business transactions, sold, for example, 1,156 pounds of butter and 1,126 dozen eggs. It is unclear whether she kept the money that she earned.
106 Ferguson, "Should Daughters Be Compensated," 6, and Brown, "What Girls Need Most," *Canadian Countryman*, 14, UGL.
107 "Floy," "The Stay-at-Home Daughter," *Farmer's Advocate* 65 (25 December 1930): 1883.
108 McCutcheon, "The Single Woman in the Country," 5.
109 Black, "A Plea for Farmers' Daughters," *Canadian Countryman*, 11, UGL. For general information about women, children, and the law, see Dymond, *The Laws of Ontario*.
110 A Farmer's Daughter, "Independence For the Daughters," *Farmer's Advocate* 43 (23 January 1908): 129.
111 Dawson, "The Woman on the Farm," 405–6.
112 Black, "A Plea for Farmers' Daughters," *Canadian Countryman*, 11, UGL.
113 A Farmer's Daughter, "Independence For the Daughters," *Farmer's Advocate* 43 (23 January 1908): 129.
114 Ibid. Legal scholar Michelle Boivin confirms that the disparity in inheritance between farm daughters and sons is a deeply entrenched rural tradition, but in 1986 she incorrectly asserted that young women were only beginning to dispute this convention. Clearly, they have been contesting it at least since the start of the century. See Boivin, "Farm Women," 67.
115 Cebotarev, "From Domesticity to the Public Sphere," 208; Sachs, *The Invisible Farmers*, 29–30. Decisions about farming equipment and crops were usually made by the man alone, while decisions about the household were usually made by the woman alone. Those decisions surrounding the purchase of machinery for the home, however, were jointly made by husband and wife, which is suggestive of either her influence, or his control, over the conditions of her labour.
116 Marjorie Jean Pentland, in Anderson, *Remembering the Farm*, 7. Of course, the legal status and economic privilege of farm men as property owners of the family farm meant that wives were never "the boss" in any real sense.
117 Cragg, *Father on the Farm*, 29, 30.
118 Beattie, *A Season Past*, 71, 72.

119 Sachs, *The Invisible Farmers*, 30; Rosenfeld, *Farm Women*, 25.

120 Johnston, *Before the Age of Miracles*, 75.

121 Mrs Stewart Nolan, in Grayson and Bliss, *The Wretched of Canada*, 153. Bennett sent five dollars.

122 A Farmer's Daughter, "Independence For the Daughters," *Farmer's Advocate* 43 (23 January 1908): 129.

123 Hillier Diaries (unpublished), 11 March 1921.

124 Cragg, *Father on the Farm*, 131.

125 *Bavin vs Bavin* (1896) *Ontario Reports*, 27:575–7, in Breault, "Educating Women About the Law," 35.

126 Fink, *Agrarian Women*, 81. Fink points to, among other things, the popularity of the temperance movement among farm women as evidence of the pervasive alcohol problem among farm men. Sources of stress for farmers included fatigue, routine, overwork, precarious weather conditions, lack of money, and/or conflict with sons. See Rosenblatt and Anderson, "Interaction in Farm Families," 159, 152.

127 Aitken, *Never a Day So Bright*, 206. Aitken (b. 1891) grew up in Beeton, Simcoe County, where her father ran the general store which was patronized by the surrounding farming community.

128 Ibid., 205.

129 MacMurchy, *The Woman – Bless Her*, 104; Beattie, *A Season Past*, 114, and *A Walk Through Yesterday*, 283.

130 Kinnear, " 'Do You Want Your Daughter to Marry a Farmer?' " 43. Notwithstanding the lack of effective birth control measures, parents knew that children in large numbers would prove an asset to the labour-intensive family farm as future fieldhands and domestic help.

131 Marshall, *Half Century of Farming in Dufferin*, 163.

132 Beattie, *A Season Past*, 16.

133 Snyder Interview, tape 1, side 1, OHT 104, KPL.

134 Beattie, *A Walk Through Yesterday*, 25.

135 Beattie, *A Season Past*, 16.

136 Johnston, *Before the Age of Miracles*, 156. Not until 1969 was the Canadian Criminal Code amended to allow for abortion under the condition that a medical doctor performed the procedure with the approval of a hospital abortion committee. The committee had to find that the continued pregnancy of a woman " 'would or would be likely to endanger her life or health.' " See Dranoff, *Women in Canadian Law*, 41.

137 Beattie, *A Season Past*, 16.

138 When that very evening fire struck the home in which her children were alone, Mrs Howe "dropped to her knees. 'Lord, don't let it happen to them,' she cried. 'I told you I didn't want so many ... I'm sorry ... don't punish me.' " Months later, she gave birth to her thirteenth child – a girl. Ibid., 21.

139 Johnston, *Before the Age of Miracles*, 157.
140 Ibid.
141 Ibid., 156.
142 Ibid., 158.
143 Ibid., 158, 157.
144 Not until 1950 did the maternal mortality rate decrease from 1 death per every 1,000 live births. In 1920, it reached a high of 6.75 deaths per 1,000 live births, although until the 1940s maternal deaths among rural women, who generally did not have their babies in hospitals, were lower than for urban women. See Oppenheimer, "Childbirth in Ontario," 36, 55.
145 Latzer, *Myrtleville*, 242, 259.
146 Johnston, *Before the Age of Miracles*, 39; Beattie, *A Season Past*, 54.
147 Johnston, *Before the Age of Miracles*, 113.
148 Beattie, *A Walk Through Yesterday*, 27.
149 Hostetler Interview, tape 2, OHT 132, KPL. Roxie married at age twenty-three.
150 Brookes and Wilson, " 'Working Away' From the Farm," 282.
151 S.H. Hopkins, "Rural Depopulation in Ontario," honours thesis, Ontario Agricultural College, 1914, 26, in ibid., 283; Bachelor, *Farmer's Advocate* (5 October 1905): 1614, in Young, "The Countryside on the Defensive," 31.
152 Leslie, "Domestic Service in Canada," 76; Barber, "Help for Farm Homes," 3. Domestic service in the country differed from service in urban homes. The work was far more demanding and the pay far lower on the farm, but the relationship between farm mistress and servant was friendlier, owing perhaps to the isolation of the wife and/or to her desperate need for household help. The relatively elevated status that the hired girl enjoyed on the farm held less true, however, for the thousands of British Barnardo girls who took up rural domestic posts in abusive Canadian homes; indeed, the neighbour's daughter might have been just as vulnerable to sexual assault at the hands of her male employer. See Leslie, "Domestic Service in Canada," 76, 88; Parr, *Labouring Children*; Dubinsky, *Improper Advances*, 52–3.
153 Pringle, "What Girls Need Most," *Canadian Countryman*, 14 UGL. See also Brookes and Wilson, " 'Working Away' From the Farm."
154 Brookes and Wilson, " 'Working Away' From the Farm," 282. Domestic service in the city would prove particularly disappointing for farm girls. See Amey, *Farm Life As It Should Be*, 37–41.
155 Beattie, *A Walk Through Yesterday*, 198, 153.
156 Ferguson, "What Education," 17.
157 Corkery, "What Girls Need Most in a Rural Community," *Canadian Countryman*, 21, UGL. This article was a winning letter in a contest to address this question.

158 Beattie, *A Walk Through Yesterday,* 153.
159 Latzer, *Myrtleville,* 176.
160 Anne Henry (b. 1889). Henry Interview, OHP, UGL.
161 Latzer, *Myrtleville,* 294.
162 Beattie, *A Walk Through Yesterday,* 155.
163 Lucinda Allendorf (b. 1889). Allendorf Interview, tape 1, side 2, OHT 084, KPL.
164 Women journalists in the agricultural press urged farm daughters to become agricultural professionals and independently own their own farms. But arguments based on the liberating male character of farm ownership, and on the opportunity to elude traditionally female careers would not have impressed most farm daughters who, in addition to wanting to leave farm life behind, and eventually marry, were not inclined toward male jobs. Moreover, the systemic barriers that impeded farm ownership by women no doubt seemed insurmountable. Accordingly, by 1971, female farm owners in Ontario numbered 3,910, only 4.3 per cent of the province's farm operators. For arguments made by women journalists for female agriculturalists, see "Women in Agriculture," *Farmer's Advocate* 60 (6 August 1925): 1118; Emilia Houlton, "Gardening as a Profession," 4; Graham and Hemming, "Women in Agriculture," 468–9; Yates, "Agriculture for Women," 185. For statistical information, see Leckie, "Female Farm Operators," 86, table 3–1. Leckie points out that the census did not allow for the tabulation of farm operators by sex until the 1970s. See 26, 79, 87.
165 Campbell, *From Chalk Dust to Hayseed,* 22; Latzer, *Myrtleville,* 176.
166 Scott, *The Conditions of Female Labour in Ontario,* 224. By about 1900, the income of a teacher in the city was sometimes triple that of a rural teacher. In 1901, the average salary for male rural teachers in Ontario was $359; for female rural teachers, it was $262 – a disparity of $97. By 1928, this gap had increased to $134, with men earning $743 and women earning $609. See Graham, "Schoolmarms and Early Teaching in Ontario," 192 and 194, table 4. Elgin Thompson, in Anderson, *Remembering the Farm,* describes how "when a schoolteacher came into the area, about five or six young men immediately set their caps for her, and the one that got her was usually considered pretty lucky" (64).
167 Latzer, *Myrtleville,* 243, 248, 258.
168 Edward Amey reproached young women like Louise when he asserted that "farmers' daughters should not be … afraid to soil their hands when they possess pianos or organs." See Amey, *Farm Life As It Should Be,* 12.
169 Louise Ritz (b. 1895). Ritz Interview, tape 1, side 1, OHT 400, and tape 2, side 1 and tape 2, side 2, OHT 401, KPL.
170 Edwards, "Compilation," 152.

171 Janet McPherson (b. 1911). McPherson Interview, OHP, UGL.

172 Henry Interview, OHP, UGL.

173 Latzer, *Myrtleville*, 266, 255, 275.

174 "Farm Interests for Girls," *Farm and Dairy* Third Annual Special Magazine Household Number (5 October 1911): 15.

175 "Bookkeeping for Papa," *Farm and Dairy* Third Annual Special Magazine Household Number (5 October 1911): 15.

176 Emma Johnston (b. circa 1900). Johnston Interview, OHP, UGL. This particular comment by Emma reflects neither the differing conditions and job descriptions of urban and rural domestic labour, nor the fact that domestic labour by a farm daughter at home, unlike urban domestic service, was an unpaid position. In both rural and urban settings, however, domestic labour was gruelling and generally undervalued.

CHAPTER FOUR

1 Pedersen, " 'The Scientific Training of Mothers,' " 179; Sachs, *The Invisible Farmers*, 56; Saidak, "The Inception of the Home Economics Movement," 123; Costantakos, "The Home Economics Idea," 185. Home economics was the term assigned to the discipline at the post-secondary level, and was also used as the umbrella term for the field, which was known as domestic economy in grade schools and domestic science in high schools. See Saidak, "The Inception of the Home Economics Movement," 121. I use the terms home economics and domestic science interchangeably.

2 Pedersen, " 'The Scientific Training of Mothers,' " 179; Saidak, "The Inception of the Home Economics Movement," 8.

3 Saidak, "The Inception of the Home Economics Movement," 126.

4 Ibid., 122. Canada's first women chemists, including Edith Curzon, Clara Cynthia Benson, and Katherine T. Lyman, like many American female chemists, became pioneer home economists. Some of these women turned to home economics because of their restricted career opportunities within the traditional, male-dominated, science disciplines; others simply recognized that science was as complex and revolutionary in its applications to the home as it was within the confines of the laboratory.

5 Saidak, "The Inception of the Home Economics Movement," 123. It should not be surprising that many of Canada's early women doctors, such as Elizabeth Smith Shortt, were proponents of domestic science. See 73.

6 Saidak, "The Inception of the Home Economics Movement," 123–5; Judy Annette Jax, "A Comparative Analysis of the Meaning of Home Economics: The 1899–1908 Lake Placid Conference and 'Home Economics: A Definition,' " doctoral dissertation, University of Minnesota, 1981, 153,

in Saidak, "The Inception of the Home Economics Movement," 125. Art was also deemed worthy of study, as the emphasis on sciences did not preclude the importance of aesthetics which was seen as integral to moral, mental, and physical health. See 123, 125.

7 Saidak, "The Inception of the Home Economics Movement," 122. Saidak quotes Ellen H. Richards, "Ten Years of the Lake Placid Conference on Home Economics: Its History and Aims," *Proceedings* 1908, 21, 22.

8 Robert Clarke, *Ellen Swallow* (Chicago: Follett Publishing Company 1973), 79, in Merrell et al., "Home Economics, Feminism and the Family," 271.

9 Saidak, "The Inception of the Home Economics Movement," 122.

10 Dale Spender, ed., *Men's Studies Modified: The Impact of Feminism on the Academic Disciplines* (New York: Pergamon Press 1981), 3, in Thompson, "Home Economics," 320. It is no wonder that as a discipline derived from a female perspective, home economics has suffered from "the general devaluation of things female and female-related." See Costantakos, "The Home Economics Idea," 193.

11 Thompson, "Home Economics," 319; Saidak, "The Inception of the Home Economics Movement," 122.

12 Saidak, "The Inception of the Home Economics Movement," 120, 127.

13 Hayden, *The Grand Domestic Revolution*, 3; Merrell et al., "Home Economics, Feminism and the Family," 271, 265, 268, 286, 284. Barbara Bovy indicates that the home economics movement initiated the change of the "passive term 'housewife' to the more active, gender-inclusive term 'homemaker.'" See her essay, "Feminist Research," 293.

14 Saidak, "The Inception of the Home Economics Movement," 119–20, 126, 133–4, 141, 136, 137, 127, 130, 131, 138, 140, 135. By 1902, after much debate, home economics was generally understood by its proponents to mean "'the study of the laws, conditions, principles and ideals which are concerned on the one hand with man's immediate physical environment and on the other hand with his nature as a social being, and is the study especially of the relation between those two factors.'" Home economics, they asserted, was also "'something to connect and bind together into a consistent whole the pieces of knowledge at present unrelated.'" See Keturah Baldwin, *The AHEA Saga* (Washington, DC: American Home Economics Association 1949), 15, 16, in Saidak, "The Inception of the Home Economics Movement," 126.

15 Merrell et al., "Home Economics, Feminism and the Family," 266; Thompson, "Home Economics," 321.

16 Merrell et al., "Home Economics, Feminism and the Family," 265, and Thompson, "Home Economics," 321; Merrell et al., "Home Economics, Feminism and the Family," 266, and Saidak, "The Inception of the Home Economics Movement," 163. "Family" was defined as a husband, a wife, and their children, but in the last two decades or so home economists

have come to define "family" in a variety of ways. See Saidak, "The Inception of the Home Economics Movement," 66.

17 Merrell et al., "Home Economics, Feminism and the Family," 275; Bovy, "Feminist Research," 295.

18 Thompson, "Home Economics," 327.

19 Crowley, "Madonnas Before Magdalenes," 523; Ambrose, *For Home and Country*, 18; and Crowley, "Adelaide Hoodless' Vision." Hoodless was later criticized by her more educated contemporaries in the home economics movement for her lack of formal academic and scientific training. See Saidak, "The Inception of the Home Economics Movement," 76; MacDonald, *Adelaide Hoodless*, 88; and Crowley, "Adelaide Hoodless' Vision."

20 Ambrose, *For Home and Country*, 17.

21 Crowley, "Madonnas Before Magdalenes," 523–4.

22 Ibid., 527, 533.

23 HFP, Box 2, "Modern Ideas on Education"; Speech in Milwaukee, 1910, both in Crowley, "Madonnas Before Magdalenes," 533.

24 Crowley, "Madonnas Before Magdalenes," 525–8.

25 Ibid., 528; MacDonald, *Adelaide Hoodless*, 92.

26 Saidak, "The Inception of the Home Economics Movement," 130.

27 Crowley, "Madonnas Before Magdalenes," 531.

28 Adelaide Hoodless, "Domestic Science," *Women Workers of Canada, 1902*, in Stamp, "Teaching Girls," 25.

29 HFP, Box 3, "It Was Charming Talk," 1898; "Manual Training for Girls," 1894; Box 2, "The Social and Ethical Value of Home Economics"; Adelaide Hoodless, "Home Economics," Dominion Educational Association, *Proceedings 1907*, 195–6, all in Crowley, "Madonnas Before Magdalenes," 535.

30 Crowley, "Madonnas Before Magdalenes," 533.

31 Mary E. Whelan, "A Woman of Vision: Mrs. Adelaide Hoodless," 28 January 1952, HFP, UGL, Box 2, WI Scrapbook – Hamilton Area, A. Hoodless Material; John Weaver, "Home Fires Burning," *Hamilton Report*, Special Issue, 1990, 14–18, HFP, UGL, Box 4, File – Newspaper Clippings, Undated Articles.

32 See Stamp's "Adelaide Hoodless, Champion"; Cheryl MacDonald, "Adelaide Hoodless: Our First Feminist?" *Hamilton Spectator*, 29 February 1980, Hoodless Scrapbook, HPL.

33 Bassett, *The Parlour Rebellion*, 164.

34 Stoddart and Strong-Boag, "'… And Things Were Going Wrong,'" 43.

35 "Domestic Science Taught," 1898, HFP, UGL, Box 3, File – Newspaper Clippings, 1898.

36 Cheryl MacDonald, "The Education of Mothers," *Horizon Canada* 2 (August 1985): 573, HFP, UGL, Box 1, File – Addresses and Reports; Saidak, "The Inception of the Home Economics Movement," 65.

37 Adelaide Hoodless, Newspaper clipping, HFP, UGL, Box 3, File – Newspaper Clippings 1900; [Guelph?] *Herald*, 15 March 1910, HFP, UGL, Family Scrapbook.

38 Ibid.

39 Adelaide Hoodless, Newspaper clipping, HFP, UGL, Box 3, File – Newspaper Clippings 1900.

40 HFP, Box 2, "New Methods in Education," in Crowley, "Madonnas Before Magdalenes," 532.

41 "Adelaide Hunter Hoodless," *Herald*, 28 February 1910, HFP, UGL, Family Scrapbook.

42 Saidak, "The Inception of the Home Economics Movement," 158.

43 Ibid. Today's women's studies courses espouse this view that experience as well as intellect must inform theory.

44 MacDonald, *Adelaide Hoodless*, 136–7.

45 Adelaide Hoodless, "Domestic Science," lecture to Public School Board Members and Trustees, April 1908, St Catharines, HFP, UGL, Box 3, File – Newspaper Clippings 1908.

46 Archives of Ontario, Education Department Records, Adelaide Hoodless to Richard Harcourt, 15 July 1901, in Stamp, "Adelaide Hoodless, Champion," 219.

47 Hunter, "Compilation," 145.

48 MacDonald, *Adelaide Hoodless*, 146, 137.

49 Archives of Ontario, Adelaide Hoodless to Richard Harcourt, 22 April 1904, in ibid., 146.

50 Saidak, "The Inception of the Home Economics Movement," 164.

51 Adelaide Hoodless, "The Relation of Domestic Science to the Agricultural Population," December 1896, 4–5, HFP, UGL, Box 1, File – Addresses and Reports.

52 Newspaper clipping, 1897, HFP, UGL, Box 3, File – Newspaper Clippings 1897. 1918 marked the first year that women were accepted into the degree program in agriculture at the OAC. A short course in "practical farming" for women was also offered. See Ross, *The College on the Hill*, 89.

53 Newspaper clipping, 1897, HFP, UGL, Box 3, File – Newspaper Clippings 1897. Hoodless's son, in fact, attended the OAC. See letter from Adelaide Hoodless to Sir William Macdonald, 8 March 1901, HFP, in MacDonald, *Adelaide Hoodless*, 118.

54 Walker et al., *Fifty Years of Achievement*, 3–4, QU.

55 Newspaper clipping, 1897, HFP, UGL, Box 3, File – Newspaper Clippings 1897.

56 Neth, "Building the Base," 339, Kohl, "The Making of a Community," 185, and Osterud, *Bonds of Community*, 11; Langford and Keating, "Social Isolation and Alberta Farm Women," 48.

57 Ambrose, " 'What Are the Good of Those Meetings Anyway?' " 7.

58 Neth, "Building the Base," 341. These ties among women, however, did
    not preclude women's full interaction with men. As the husbands, fa-
    thers, sons, neighbours, and friends of farm women, men were a part of
    the family, work, and social fabric of their lives. See, for example, Anna
    Burkholder Diaries, MDHM; Hillier Diaries (unpublished); and Osterud,
    Bonds of Community. This chapter and chapter 4, however, will show that
    Osterud, although referring to nineteenth-century New York State, may
    be overstating her case when she claims that "rural women did not create
    a separate subculture around their gender-specific experiences" (89).

59 See, for example, Marie Henderson, in Anderson, Remembering the Farm,
    108, and Horst Interview, tape 1, side 1, OHT 658, KPL. For some overbur-
    dened farm women, however, even going to church and related activities
    was not always possible. Jessie Beattie noted that "because [our house-
    hold] was such a large one, including workmen with hardy appetites,
    Mother and my sisters took turns staying at home to prepare dinner." See
    Beattie, Along the Road, 146. Trenton-area farm woman Vera Hood, who
    sent her children off to church but stopped attending herself, declared
    that "you don't get no Sundays off on the farm." Vera May Hood
    (b. 1921), interview by Melanie Clare.

60 Bass, "The Woman on the Farm," 561.

61 Cragg, Father on the Farm, 131. Cragg noted that for men, this distraction
    came in the form of alcohol, men's groups, and local politics.

62 Conroy, 300 Years of Canadian Quilts, 79–80.

63 Ibid., 86.

64 Bass, "The Woman on the Farm," 561.

65 See Tebbutt, Women's Talk?

66 Campbell, From Chalk Dust to Hayseed, 23. Not all young women were so
    reverent, however: Galt farm daughter Jessie Beattie recollected that at
    one particular bee, a young woman named Sophia "had got down on the
    floor and shown the other ladies how to play leap frog." See Beattie, A
    Walk Through Yesterday, 54.

67 Campbell, From Chalk Dust to Hayseed, 23. Like the bees, quilts themselves
    helped seal generational bonds among female family and friends. Older
    women routinely bestowed quilts to new wives and mothers as expressions
    of affection. Jessie Beattie recollected that when the family's orphaned
    "hired girl" Lulu planned to marry, "Mother was active in preparing for
    Lulu's [wedding] and the quilting which might have stopped with autumn
    went on through the fall season until Christmas. ... Her large blue eyes
    were tearful with appreciation as she looked upon the donations to her
    dowry and to her wardrobe." See Beattie, A Season Past, 146–7.

68 Aitken, Never a Day So Bright, 103, 107. Kate Aitken (1891–1971), a re-
    nowned home economist, was a radio broadcaster, columnist, and writer,
    and was an active member of the Federated Women's Institutes of

Canada. See Canada, Minister of Supply and Services, *Women's Archives Guide*, 9–10.

69 Aitken, *Never a Day So Bright*, 107. For a description of one woman's preparation and menu for threshing meals, see 107–8. Also see Neth, *Preserving the Family Farm*, 154–6.

70 Hillier Diaries (unpublished), 14 July 1926.

71 Ibid.; ibid., 18, 19, 20, July 1926.

72 Anderson, *Remembering the Farm*, xiii. Anderson wryly notes that this tendency to visit was "sometimes overdone. Some farm wives were glad when winter came, for then they wouldn't look out the window and see more damn friends coming down the lane in their buggies." Also see Vanek, "Work, Leisure, and Family Roles," 428.

73 Beattie, *A Season Past*, 100.

74 Latzer, *Myrtleville*, 200, 253.

75 Ladell and Ladell, *Inheritance*, 99.

76 Vera Dahmer (b. 1902). Dahmer Interview, tape 1, side 2, OHT 205, KPL. Selina Horst remembered that her mother enjoyed Sunday visits from family, and herself "was a great visitor." Horst Interview, tape 1, side 1, OHT 658, KPL.

77 Beattie, *A Season Past*, 66.

78 Latzer, *Myrtleville*, 197.

79 Beattie, *A Walk Through Yesterday*, 54.

80 Conroy, *300 Years of Canadian Quilts*, 80.

81 Ladell and Ladell, *Inheritance*, 96–7.

82 Osterud, *Bonds of Community*, 221.

83 Beattie, *Along the Road*, 159.

84 Campbell, *From Chalk Dust to Hayseed*, 22, 39. In 1918, when Campbell was twenty-one years old, she married a farmer, and lived the next twenty-one years on a farm, raising five children (116).

85 Cragg, *Father on the Farm*, 83. Cragg noted that "father didn't take the matter seriously enough to suit mother."

86 Beattie, *A Walk Through Yesterday*, 159, 167–9, 175–6.

87 Latzer, *Myrtleville*, 257, 250.

88 Ritz Interview, tape 1, side 2, OHT 400, KPL. Her devotion to her sisters, however, did not preclude Louise from reflecting that "I signed my life away you might say." In 1943, with the death of Louise's parents, her sister with polio entered a nursing home in Cobourg.

89 Vera May Hood, interview by Melanie Clare, tape 1, side 1; Hood Interview, in Melanie Clare, "Sacrifice, Reward and Equality," 11.

90 Beattie, *A Season Past*, 14.

91 Latzer, *Myrtleville*, 267.

92 Beattie, *A Walk Through Yesterday*, 150, 151. Despite their desire for Jean to stay on the farm, Jessie and Lil encouraged her chance at travel: "all were

agreed that Jean must be permitted this opportunity to take part in a way of life unfamiliar to us, a farming family. … Without a sign of jealousy or fear on becoming a substitute, as well as carrying her own responsibilities, my sister Lil shared in the preparations for Jean's exciting adventure."

93 Elaine Bitz, interview.

94 Saidak, "The Inception of the Home Economics Movement," 135.

95 Maddock, "Why Women's Institutes," 385.

96 Pedersen, " 'The Scientific Training of Mothers,' " 184; Adelaide Hoodless, "A New Education for Women," *Farmer's Advocate*, 15 December 1902, in Stamp, "Teaching Girls," 33.

97 Saidak, "The Inception of the Home Economics Movement," 135.

98 Ibid.

99 See ibid., 122, 79, 89.

100 Ibid., 122.

101 Ibid., 132.

102 Reaman, *A History of Agriculture*, 222.

103 Ross, *The College on the Hill*, 75. The Kemptville Agricultural School, near Ottawa, opened in 1920 as a more practical alternative to the academically oriented OAC, and by 1922 it too offered domestic science courses for farm daughters. See Dutchak, *College With a Purpose*, 9, 24, 46.

104 Those in "Household Science" comprised 504 out of 2,558 Canadian undergraduate women. See Robin S. Harris, *A History of Higher Education in Canada, 1663–1960* (Toronto: University of Toronto Press 1976), "Enrolment in Canadian Universities 1911–1912," table 628, 629, in Saidak, "The Inception of the Home Economics Movement," 98.

105 Crowley, "Madonnas Before Magdalenes," 524.

106 Saidak, "The Inception of the Home Economics Movement," 97. Pedersen contends that "probably the greatest single success of the domestic science promoters was their creation of a new career option for educated, young, middle-class women seeking a profession." See Pedersen, " 'The Scientific Training of Mothers,' " 194.

107 Saidak, "The Inception of the Home Economics Movement," 97.

108 Crowley, "Madonnas Before Magdalenes," 525.

109 Ibid., 525; Archives of Ontario, RG 2, P2, Box 60, xix–37, Regulations of the Education Department with Respect to the Study of Domestic Science in Public Schools, 29 January 1897, in Crowley, "Madonnas Before Magdalenes," 525.

110 Stamp, "Adelaide Hoodless, Champion," 221. Hoodless married a Conservative, but was herself a staunch Liberal. Her political affiliation would both help and hinder her later career. See Crowley, "Madonnas Before Magdalenes," 523, and Stamp, "Adelaide Hoodless, Champion," 221.

111 Crowley, "Madonnas Before Magdalenes," 525–6. An article which eu-
     logized Hoodless in 1910 noted that "had she received the support that
     such a cause [domestic science] was worthy of, this city [Hamilton]
     would to-day, in all probability, have been the home of the greatest in-
     stitution in Canada for the promotion of that science. In spite of the
     sometimes coldness and sometimes open opposition of those from
     whom she should have received the strongest support, she worked per-
     sistently and saw success crown her efforts, although her loved home
     city did not benefit to the extent she had planned." See "Devoted Noble
     Life to the Cause of Women," 28 February 1910, Hoodless Scrapbook,
     HPL.
112 MacDonald, *Adelaide Hoodless*, 90; "Manual Training for Girls," 1894,
     HFP, UGL, Box 3, File – Newspaper Clippings 1894.
113 "Manual Training," 1894, HFP, UGL, Box 3, File – Newspaper Clippings
     1894; Terry Crowley, "WI Founder Instrumental in Education," *Globe and
     Mail*, 31 March 1987, review of *Adelaide Hoodless: Domestic Crusader* by
     Cheryl MacDonald, HFP, UGL, Box 3, File – Newspaper Clippings 1893.
114 Sachs, *The Invisible Farmers*, 58.
115 Dorothy Drew, "Instruction in Domestic Science – Mrs. Hoodless Com-
     ing to Give Lectures," HFP, UGL, Box 3, File – Newspaper Clippings
     1898.
116 Crowley, "Madonnas Before Magdalenes," 526–7.
117 Ibid., 536.
118 Ibid., 537. Domestic science courses included "Physics, Chemistry,
     Dietetics, Food Economics." Domestic Art courses included "Costume
     Designing, Millinary, Dressmaking." See Hunter, "Compilation," 145.
119 Crowley, "Madonnas Before Magdalenes," 537, 536. Referring to this ar-
     ticle, Saidak defends Hoodless by saying that "the class snobbery for
     which Hoodless has been noted, was at least partially the consequence
     of a commonly held fear that without the highest standards, including
     pupils and teachers of 'the better class,' the acceptance and continuation
     of home economics would be jeopardized." See Saidak, "The Inception
     of the Home Economics Movement," 129.
120 Crowley, "Madonnas Before Magdalenes," 537.
121 MacDonald, *Adelaide Hoodless*, 118; Crowley, "Madonnas Before
     Magdalenes," 538–9.
122 Crowley, "Madonnas Before Magdalenes," 538. Hoodless's son, as noted
     earlier, had attended the OAC.
123 James Mills, "The Need of Instruction in Domestic Economy and Some
     Suggestions as to Where it Should be Taught," *NCWC Report* 1899, 197, in
     Saidak, "The Inception of the Home Economics Movement," 27.
124 Crowley, "Madonnas Before Magdalenes," 538.
125 Ferguson, "Giving the Girls a Chance," 35, 36.

126 *Women Workers*, 1899, 196–200, in Crowley, "Madonnas Before Magdalenes," 538.

127 Crowley, "Madonnas Before Magdalenes," 539; James Robertson had also been the Canadian Agriculture and Dairying Commissioner. See Ontario, Lieutenant-Governor, *Report of the Commission of Inquiry*, 22; HFP, UGL, Box 3, "Formal Opening of Macdonald Institute," 1904, and University of Guelph, Archival Collections, Rei Mac A0055, William Macdonald to James Mills, 25 February 1901, both in Crowley, "Madonnas Before Magdalenes," 539.

128 HFP, UGL, Box 1, James Mills to Adelaide Hoodless, 9 March 1900, in Crowley, "Madonnas Before Magdalenes," 539.

129 Crowley, "Madonnas Before Magdalenes," 539.

130 Watson attended several Lake Placid Conferences, the annual New York meeting (1899–1908) of home economists worldwide, and was elected a vice-president of the American Home Economics Association (AHEA). Saidak refers to Watson and University of Toronto professor Anna Louisa Laird as having had "the primary responsibility for establishing the academic standards for Canada's first home economists." See Saidak, "The Inception of the Home Economics Movement," 94.

131 Crowley, "Madonnas Before Magdalenes," 540, 541.

132 Letter from Adelaide Hoodless to Sir William Macdonald, 8 March 1901, HFP, UGL, Box 1, File – Correspondence 1876–1909.

133 That Hoodless did not refer to farm daughters as teachers, and that Macdonald Institute offered a specific non-teaching program for farm daughters did not preclude their possible enrolment in teacher-training. It does indicate, however, the agenda of Macdonald Institute, as referenced by the remarks made by Hoodless, to keep farm daughters on the land, and better trained for their future role as farm wives.

134 Ontario Agricultural College, *Annual Report* 1901, vii, in Ross, *The College on the Hill*, 54; HFP, UGL, Box 1, James Robertson to James Mills, 16 December and 12 November 1901, in Crowley, "Madonnas Before Magdalenes," 541.

135 Ross, *The College on the Hill*, 42, 57. The dairying courses had been open to women since 1893. The sincere but condescending Professor of Dairying had declared that year that the women " 'have made excellent students, have become proficient butter-makers, and no longer attribute inferiority of product to luck, witches, or the position of the moon, but can give scientific and common sense reason for each defect in flavour, grain, or colour.' " See Ontario Agricultural College, *Annual Report* 1893, 133, in Ross, *The College on the Hill*, 42. As late as 1919, however, a presumably male author in the *Farmers' Sun* reasoned that women, even to a greater extent than men, excelled at dairying not because of scientific instruction, but because "milk's first customer is the baby," and before

them as they work is "the vision of countless baby faces." See "The Dairy Woman," *Farmers' Sun* 29 (1 October 1919): 7.

136 Reaman, *A History of Agriculture*, 97; "A Farm Home," 28 March 1908, 101, HFP, UGL, Box 3, File – Newspaper Clippings 1908. Students of the one-year Homemaker Course studied assorted domestic science subjects, in addition to physics, chemistry, and biology. See MacDonald, *Adelaide Hoodless*, 141.

137 "Farm Daughters and Macdonald Institute," *Farmer's Advocate* 62 (19 May 1927): 806.

138 Beattie, *A Walk Through Yesterday*, 53, 198.

139 Latzer, *Myrtleville*, 239.

140 Halpern, "Beyond the Dell," *Matrix*, 9.

141 Brown, "What Girls Need Most," *Canadian Countryman*, 20, UGL.

142 Happy Picnicker, "The Greatest Thing," *Farmers' Sun*, 24 July 1920, 6.

143 By 1921, the Departments of Nature Study and Manual Training had been all but phased out. See Ross, *The College on the Hill*, 75; Macdonald Institute promoted this modern image of itself in articles such as "The Educated Woman – A Macdonald Conception," *O.A.C. Review* 23 (February 1911): 275–7, and "The Progress of Domestic Science," *O.A.C. Review* 20 (May 1908): 466–7.

144 Ferguson, "What Education," 17.

145 "Farm Daughters and Macdonald Institute," *Farmer's Advocate* 62 (19 May 1927): 806.

146 Junia, "Independence for Farm Daughters," *Farmer's Advocate*, 65 (25 December 1930): 1883.

147 "Farm Daughters and Macdonald Institute," *Farmer's Advocate* 62 (19 May 1927): 806. Only five years after it opened in 1903, Macdonald Institute could boast of a yearly enrolment of "about 260 girls and women." Approximately 110 of them lived in the campus women's residence, Macdonald Hall. See "A Farm Home," 28 March 1908, 101, HFP, UGL, Box 3, File – Newspaper Clippings 1908.

148 Ross, *The College on the Hill*, 105. This disparity was attributable not only to the popularity of Macdonald Institute, but to the suspicion of agricultural schools by sceptical farmers, whose sons, if college material, had the option of training for a vocation more lucrative than farming (105).

149 Beattie, *A Walk Through Yesterday*, 154.

150 Beattie, "Working for Skirts," 4, Lillian A. Beattie Papers, UGL. Lillian reported that after much persuasion, her father "then saw the light and wanted me to accept the loan with no promise to repay." In the second year of her program, Lillian participated in an academic debate entitled " 'Resolved that women contributed more to the world's advancement than men.' " She and her debating partner Ethel Chapman, the future activist on behalf of farm women, home economics, and the WI, took the

affirmative, and proved victorious with the decision of a male judge. Upon completion of her program in 1913, Lillian took a course at Toronto General Hospital and became a hospital and prison dietician (21, 42, 43).

151 6 September 1911, WI Minute Books, Wilton Grove, UWO.

152 Beattie, *A Walk Through Yesterday*, 194. Jean designed the house to be equipped with what she knew to be the most modern water, heating, and lighting systems.

153 Pringle, "What Girls Need Most," *Canadian Countryman*, 14, UGL.

154 In 1908, the cost of one year at Macdonald Institute, including fees and board, was estimated at slightly below $200. A three-month short course plus expenses was estimated at $60. See "A Farm Home," 28 March 1908, HFP, UGL, Box 3, File – Newspaper Clippings 1908.

155 Letter from W.A. Mackintosh, Vice-Principal and Dean, Queen's University, Faculty of Arts to Director of Home Economics, 28 June 1948, MIR, Associate Director, UGL. Also see letter from J. Rutherford, Deputy Minister of Education to Dorothy M. Lindsley, 24 August 1948, MIR, Associate Director, UGL; "Macdonald Institute, Department of Home Economics, Ontario Agricultural College – Application for Admission: One Year Course"; Correspondence between Miss Dorothy M. Lindsley and Miss Agnes Turnball, 13, 16 August 1948; Reference Letter from Irving W. McNaughton to Director of Home Economics, Macdonald Hall, Guelph, 1948, all in MIR, Associate Director.

156 MacDonald, *Adelaide Hoodless*, 141. After 1948, those in the new four-year degree program were expected to be proficient in grade 13 math and science, although the school did prove somewhat flexible if applicants were of a mature age, were university educated, and/or had prior teaching experience. See correspondence, for example, between Margaret Elaine Wilson, whose father was an Agricultural Representative, and Dorothy Lindsley, and correspondence regarding Miss Florence E. Elford, 15 July 1947, 21 June 1948, 27 July 1948, MIR, Associate Director, UGL. In 1948, the first year that the four-year degree program in home economics was offered, twenty-five women were enrolled in the program. In 1949, this number more than doubled to fifty-six. Canada's first four-year degree program in home economics was offered by the University of Toronto in 1902. The University of Manitoba and McGill University were the next to claim degree programs in 1918. See Ross, *The College on the Hill*, 128; Saidak, "The Inception of the Home Economics Movement," 66.

157 "Farm Daughters and Macdonald Institute," *Farmer's Advocate* 62 (19 May 1927): 806.

158 All students attended lectures in "Plain Cookery, Laundry, Care of the House, Foods, Sanitation, Home Nursing, English." Half the students

took classes in "Undergarments, Millinery," while the other half learned "Shirtwaist, Embroidery." See Watson, "The New Venture," 2052.

159 "Farm Daughters and Macdonald Institute," *Farmer's Advocate* 62 (19 May 1927): 806.

160 Letter from Miss Jessie M. Lambden, Instructor in Foods and Nutrition to Miss Lucy McMechan, 3 July 1946, MIR, Associate Director, UGL. Preference was also given to women who served during World War II in the military – likely as nurses and secretaries.

161 Saidak, "The Inception of the Home Economics Movement," 135.

162 Walker et al., *Fifty Years of Achievement*, 8, QU; Ross, *The College on the Hill*, 72.

163 Letter from Mrs F.M. Carpenter, President of the Woman's Institute of Saltfleet to Sir William Macdonald, 11 January 1902, Minute Book, WI of Saltfleet, vol. 2, 30, NA.

164 Walker et al., *Fifty Years of Achievement*, 3–4, QU. Following the official formation of the WI, Adelaide Hoodless had little to do with the workings of the organization. See MacDonald, *Adelaide Hoodless*, 76.

165 MacMurchy, *The Woman – Bless Her*, 118–19.

166 Minute Book, WI of Saltfleet, vol. 1, 2, NA. The Constitution of the WI was drafted by interested women, in addition to Erland Lee and politicians F.M. Carpenter and E.D. Smith (the founder of the Winona jam company which bears his name). Smith's sister was Elizabeth Smith Shortt, one of the first women doctors in Canada (see n. 5 above), and his wife was the first president of the Saltfleet WI. See Nash, *The First Women's Institute in the World*, 4, QU. For detailed information concerning Dr Elizabeth Smith Shortt and the Smith family, see the Elizabeth Smith Shortt Collection, UW.

167 Minute Book, WI of Saltfleet, vol. 1, 3–4, NA. The WI Constitution also outlined the movement's involved executive hierarchy. Leadership within each branch consisted at the very least of an elected president, vice-president, secretary, and treasurer. See 5–6. Executive officers also sat at the district level, and, by 1919, at the provincial level as well.

168 Minute Book, WI of Saltfleet, vol. 1, 14, 26, 29, 80, NA.

169 4 March 1909, 6 May 1909, 8 July 1909, 1 June 1910, in WI Minute Books, Wilton Grove, UWO; 1 February 1911, in WI Minute Books, Wilton Grove: the topic of labour-saving devices for women might have been selected because farm husbands, who had the purchasing power for such devices, were also in attendance at this particular meeting; 6 December 1911, in WI Minute Books, Wilton Grove; 3 April 1912, in WI Minute Books, Wilton Grove. Diana Pedersen cautions her readers against undermining the value of domestic science concerns: "a knowledge of the 'dangers of dust' was critical at a time when dust could harbour the 'white plague' of tuberculosis, and improper feeding techniques during

these years resulted in the needless deaths of thousands of infants." See Pedersen, " 'The Scientific Training of Mothers,' " 193. In the same vein, Patricia J. Thompson asserts in her article that "categorizing 'everyday knowledge' as trivial, ephemeral, banal, or transitory masks its revolutionary potential, i.e., its power to transform the everyday lives of everyday people." See Thompson, "Home Economics," 322.

170 16 December 1897, Minute Book, WI of Saltfleet, vol. 1, 29, NA; 27 April 1899, Minute Book, WI of Saltfleet, vol. 1, 60.

171 6 January 1910, 7 April 1910, 4 December 1912, 7 August 1912, 5 August 1914, in WI Minute Books, Wilton Grove, UWO.

172 George Creelman, "The Formation of The Women's Institutes," *Report of the Superintendent of Farmers' Institutes of the Province of Ontario* 1900, Toronto, 1901, 3–4, in Terry Crowley, "The Origins of Continuing Education for Women: The Ontario Women's Institutes," *Canadian Woman's Studies* 7 (Fall 1986): 80; Joseph Schull, *Ontario Since 1867* (Toronto: McClelland and Stewart 1978), 176; and *Ontario Department of Agriculture, Report of the Women's Institutes of the Province of Ontario, 1916*, part 1 (Toronto: 1917), 105, all in Halpern, " 'Practically Part of the Government,' " 4. Some suspected a more political motivation behind government support of the WI. See chapter 5.

173 For an illustration of how modest these grants really were, using figures from 1915–18 issues of the *Report of the Women's Institutes of the Province of Ontario*, see Halpern, " 'Practically Part of the Government,' " 7, 19; Minute Book, WI of Saltfleet, vol. 1, 2, NA; Reaman, *A History of Agriculture*, 76–8.

174 See Halpern, " 'Practically Part of the Government.' " This point is discussed further in chapter 5.

175 Walker et al., *Fifty Years of Achievement*, 17, QU; Mrs Jno. Bray, Kingsmill, in Ontario Department of Agriculture, *Report of the Women's Institutes*, 1917, 50, QU.

176 Letter from Adelaide Hoodless to Sir William Macdonald, 8 March 1901, HFP, UGL, Box 1, File – Correspondence 1876–1909.

177 Ambrose, *For Home and Country*, 26.

178 Ibid., 26, 34. Arguably, their first and third concerns would come true to some extent. Reasons for the additional membership expense are outlined in Hopkins, "The Trend of the Women's Institutes," 251.

179 A 1958 *Maclean's* article on the WI acknowledged that "men have been heckling the WI for sixty one years." Men continue to mock Institute gatherings by dubbing them "stitch and bitch" meetings. See Robert Collins, "The biggest country club in the world," *Maclean's* (5 July 1958): 46, in Carbert, *Agrarian Feminism*, 161.

180 Ambrose, *For Home and Country*, 27–8.

181 Ambrose, " 'The University for Rural Women.' "

182 Walker et al., *Fifty Years of Achievement*, 2, QU; Ontario Department of Agriculture, *Report of the Women's Institutes* 1918, 120, QU. The Institute movement was also spreading across Canada and around the world. From 1919, it was represented nationally by the Federated Women's Institutes of Canada, and from 1933 internationally by the Associated Country Women of the World.

183 The WI Constitution of 1897 proclaimed that "*meetings shall be confined to ladies exclusively.*" See WI of Saltfleet, vol. 1, 5, NA; MacDonald, *Adelaide Hoodless*, 76. In 1947, Mrs E.D. Smith's grown daughter, who sat in on some meetings as a child, recollected such times. See "Tribute to Stoney Creek 1897 Institute, 1947," *Home and Country* 12, no. 4 (1947): 4, HFP, UGL, Box 4, File – Photographs etc., Newspaper Clippings, Letters, Publications 1940–49.

184 R.B.M., "Are Women's Institutes Here to Stay?" *Farmer's Advocate* 39 (22 September 1904): 1273; Chapman, "Mrs. Adelaide Hoodless," 17; and 28 May 1909, 2 October 1912, 13 June 1912, in WI Minute Books, Wilton Grove, UWO.

185 Carbert, "Agrarian Feminism," 111; Ambrose, " 'What Are the Good of Those Meetings Anyway?' " 9. Of course, one could argue that solidarity among WI women also relied upon their shared identity as farm folk, and as common members of a specific locale.

186 27 April 1899, Minute Book, WI of Saltfleet, vol. 1, 60, NA; 16 December 1897, Minute Book, WI of Saltfleet, vol. 1, 29.

187 7 August 1912, 4 February 1914, in WI Minute Books, Wilton Grove, UWO.

188 "In Feminine Focus," *Hamilton Herald*, 10 February 1927, HFP, UGL, Box 3, File – Clippings, etc. 1920s and 1930s.

189 Black, *Social Feminism*, 351.

190 Freedman, "Separatism as Strategy," 13.

191 The childhood home of Adelaide Hoodless in St George was purchased by the WI in 1959 "as a mecca for Women's Institute members the world over." See Rand, *Federated Women's Institutes of Canada*, QU.

CHAPTER FIVE

1 Walker et al., *Fifty Years of Achievement*, 80, QU; "Branchton Women's Institute," in *South Waterloo District Women's Institute*, QU.

2 4 February 1914, 18 January 1916, in WI Minute Books, Wilton Grove, UWO; 11 January 1917, in WI Minute Books, Wilton Grove.

3 4 August 1915, in WI Minute Books, Wilton Grove, UWO; 27 April 1916, in WI Minute Books, Wilton Grove.

4 27 April 1916, in WI Minute Books, Wilton Grove, UWO, and Walker et al., *Fifty Years of Achievement*, 81, QU; 27 April 1916, in WI Minute Books,

Wilton Grove; "Galt Women's Institute," in *South Waterloo District Women's Institute*, QU.

5 Walker et al., *Fifty Years of Achievement*, 80, QU.

6 Ontario Department of Agriculture, *Report of the Women's Institutes*, 1918, 18, QU.

7 Todd, "The Work of Women's Institutes," 15; Mrs Williams of the Wilton Grove WI, for example, reported at a meeting in 1912 of "the success that attended her efforts to get advertisements from the business men of London to pay the cost of getting out the cookbook." See 6 November 1912, in WI Minute Books, Wilton Grove, UWO.

8 *Federated Women's Institutes of Canada* (1977), 5, QU.

9 "History of Wilton Grove Women's Institute and Norton Women's Institute," introductory summary; 8 May 1918; and 5 June 1920, in WI Minute Books, Wilton Grove, UWO. Louise Carbert notes, however, that WI membership country-wide "did not decline after the First World War as drastically as it did in other first-wave women's organizations such as the National Council of Women … or the Woman's Christian Temperance Union." See Carbert, *Agrarian Feminism*, 17.

10 "Galt Women's Institute," in *South Waterloo District Women's Institute*, QU.

11 28 January 1920, in WI Minute Books, Wilton Grove, UWO. The WI performed some social reform work prior to the war, but it was largely limited to issues of health and sanitation in rural schools. See Walker et al., *Fifty Years of Achievement*, 76, QU.

12 The Wilton Grove WI, which unofficially disbanded in 1919, was superseded by the Norton WI in 1922. The branch changed its name back to the Wilton Grove WI in 1945. See "History of Wilton Grove Women's Institute and Norton Women's Institute," introductory summary, in WI Minute Books, Wilton Grove, UWO.

13 19 September 1929, 8 September 1930, in WI Minute Books, Wilton Grove, UWO.

14 Mrs J.K. Kelly, *Home and Country* 3 (Summer 1937): 2.

15 Rutherford, "What the Institute Has Meant," 6.

16 Babb, "A Young Woman's Accomplishments," 7–8.

17 MacMillan, "Training Future Housekeepers," 6.

18 Babb, "A Young Woman's Accomplishments," 7.

19 Critics of the WI and various scholars have asserted this viewpoint, as the chapter will later discuss.

20 "Fall Fair Exhibits Claim Attention of Women's Institutes," *Home and Country* 4 (Winter 1937–38): 2. For an examination of the participation of Alberta women in agricultural fairs, see Jones, " 'From Babies to Buttonholes,' " 26–32.

21 Chapman, "How the Women's Institutes can Cooperate," 18. This article was part of a regular WI column in *Ontario Farmer* which featured "News and Views of Women who Belong to the Great Society."

22 MacMillan, "Training Future Housekeepers," 6.
23 "Special Short Courses Help Girls Find Employment," *Home and Country* 4 (Spring 1938): 1. Courses included "Catering for Tourists," "Marketing of Home Baked Foods," "Rug Making," and "Simple Dressmaking and Remodelling."
24 Row, "Saving Labour in the Home," 3.
25 15 April 1940, in WI Minute Books, Wilton Grove, UWO, and "Standing Committees 1945," *Home and Country* 11 (Spring 1945). Additional standing committees addressed Home Economics, Education, Agriculture and Canadian Industries, Historical Research, Canadianization, Peace Education and International Relationships, Publicity, Resolutions, and, in wartime, War Work; Resolutions presented to the provincial government were first submitted by WI branches, and then sanctioned by delegates at district annual meetings and regional annual conventions before being approved and put forth by the Provincial Board of the Federated Women's Institutes of Ontario. See "Resolutions," *Home and Country* 1 (October 1935): 2.
26 Louise Carbert cites Caroline Andrew when she notes that " 'in pushing for and organizing services and programs designed to improve social conditions, women played an important role in setting the stage for the development of the welfare state.' " Carbert insists that "one can take Andrew's argument further and say that the WI not only set the stage but also operated as a rural arm of the state. In terms of providing services, provincial government bureaucracies could not penetrate the dispersed society that characterized rural Canada, and the WI often filled the administrative gaps." See Caroline Andrew, "Women and the Welfare State," *Canadian Journal of Political Science* 17, no. 4 (1984): 673, in Carbert, *Agrarian Feminism*, 16.
27 Durnin, "Family Relationships Important," 3.
28 Collins, "Our Superintendents Through the Years," 7.
29 The Federated Women's Institutes of Ontario, *Fiftieth Anniversary Celebration*, 8, QU.
30 Powell, "Out of the Past," 1; "Superintendent Visits All Conventions," *Home and Country* 12 (Fall and Winter 1946–47): 2.
31 Durnin, "Family Relationships Important," 3.
32 McDowell, "Greetings From the Provincial President," 2.
33 Mrs W.F. Parsons, *Home and Country* 1 (September 1933): 3; "With the Women's Institutes," *Social Welfare* (1 September 1920): 336. In 1944, the Greensville WI even requested "that instruction in sex education be approved by the Department of Education of the Province of Ontario, and be given in the Public and High Schools of the Province." See Duke, "Resolutions Indicate Interests," 4.
34 "With the Women's Institutes," *Social Welfare* (1 September 1920); 336; Mrs W.F. Parsons, *Home and Country* 1 (September 1933): 3.

35 Mrs W.F. Parsons, *Home and Country* 1 (September 1933): 3; "With the Women's Institutes," *Social Welfare* (1 September 1920): 336.

36 "With the Women's Institutes," *Social Welfare* (1 September 1920): 336; "Preston Women's Institutes," in *South Waterloo District Women's Institute,* QU.

37 Hopkins, "The Trend of the Women's Institutes," 251.

38 "With the Women's Institutes," *Social Welfare* (1 September 1920): 336; Norell, " 'The most humane institution in all the village,' " 38–50. Women's rest rooms were furnished rest stops established by the WI in towns and cities, including those in Ontario, and were designated for fatigued farm women and their children who were shopping for the day away from home. The rest rooms, aside from offering toilet facilities, provided women with a safe and comfortable place to eat lunch, read a magazine, and converse with each other. Norell notes that the establishment of women's rest rooms by the WI often "signalled the victory of local women over indifferent or recalcitrant politicians and merchants" (38).

39 Woltz, "Neighbourliness and Good Cheer," 6; 20 November 1930, in WI Minute Books, Wilton Grove, UWO; "News Flashes From the Branches," *Home and Country* 2 (January 1936): 4; 16 October 1930, and 20 November 1930, in WI Minute Books, Wilton Grove, UWO.

40 "The Women's Institutes Convention," *Social Welfare* (1 January 1922): 73; "Resolutions," *Home and Country* 1 (January 1935): 2; "With the Women's Institutes," *Social Welfare* (1 September 1920): 336.

41 Letter from Mrs W. Buchanan to the women's page of the *Farmer's Advocate* 47 (4 April 1912): 642. In fact, by 1912, even the farmer's wife and daughter, who were propertyless in the eyes of the law, were eligible for election as school trustees; however, as Mrs Buchanan pointed out, an "amusing feature" of this reform was that "these women unless assessed for property in their own right, have no vote themselves, to elect anybody or anything. Consequently, if there are to be women on rural school boards, it will [be] up to the men to elect them unaided. … as the women have not the power to put men in or out of office, there is nothing to influence them [men] to elect women, except the innate chivalry of good men who admit the divine right of women … to be placed in any position for which they are qualified and in which they can best serve the community."

42 "Ontario Women's Institutes Featured at London, Eng., Meeting," Ottawa *Evening Citizen*, 5 November 1929, Ross, "Legislation," 3.

43 Ross, "Legislation," 3, 4.

44 "News Flashes From the Institutes," *Home and Country* 5 (Winter 1938/39): 4; 18 May 1938, in WI Minute Books, Wilton Grove, UWO.

45 Ontario Department of Agriculture, *Report of the Women's Institutes*, 1918, 20, QU.

46 "Are Rural Women Indifferent?" *Farmer's Advocate* 52 (29 March 1917): 527.
47 Although the vote might not have held much attraction for many farm women, there is little evidence to suggest that Ontario farm women actively opposed female suffrage. See Powell, "The Opposition to Woman Suffrage," 13.
48 Abigail Shearer (b. 1896). Shearer Interview, tape 1, side 1, OHT 580, KPL.
49 Ladd, "The Farmer's Wife as a Partner," 6, UGL.
50 Kechnie, "The United Farm Women," 278.
51 Taps, "An Opinion from Wentworth County," *Farmer's Advocate* 47 (4 April 1912): 642.
52 Mrs W. Buchanan, Letter to women's page, *Farmer's Advocate* 47 (4 April 1912): 642.
53 Taps, "An Opinion from Wentworth County," *Farmer's Advocate* 47 (4 April 1912): 642.
54 Dawson, "Politics, Woman, and the Boon," 2233.
55 Mrs W. Buchanan, Letter to women's page, *Farmer's Advocate* 47 (4 April 1912): 642.
56 Taps, "An Opinion from Wentworth County," *Farmer's Advocate* 47 (4 April 1912): 642.
57 "Should Women Have the Suffrage," *Farmer's Advocate* 47 (4 April 1912): 641.
58 Mrs W. Buchanan, Letter to women's page, *Farmer's Advocate* 47 (4 April 1912): 642.
59 "Should Women Have the Suffrage," *Farmer's Advocate* 47 (4 April 1912): 641.
60 Ontario Department of Agriculture, *Report of the Women's Institutes*, 1909, 18, QU.
61 Schull, *Ontario Since 1867*, 181.
62 Ontario Department of Agriculture, *Report of the Women's Institutes*, 1917, 52, QU.
63 Ibid., 1918, 117, QU.
64 7 December 1910, WI Minute Books, Wilton Grove, UWO.
65 Ontario Department of Agriculture, *Report of the Women's Institutes*, 1916, 61, QU. This dictate likely originated with the Farmers' Institute in the early 1890s when Mowat's Liberal government sought to discourage the growing influence of the Patrons of Industry. Thanks to Kerry Badgley for bringing out this point.
66 Ibid., 1918, 27, QU.
67 See chapter 1, 6.
68 Mrs Torrington, in Ontario Department of Agriculture, *Report of the Women's Institutes*, 1917, 80, QU. "Politically" refers here to issues of party politics, but to think politically can also mean to contemplate issues of

access, privilege, power, and strategy. Certainly in this sense, the WI necessarily thought politically.

69 Ontario Department of Agriculture, *Report of the Women's Institutes*, 1918, 116, QU.

70 Dr Annie Backus, in ibid., 1916, 30, 27, QU; Ontario Department of Agriculture, *Report of the Women's Institutes*, 1917, 14, QU. See also McCall, *Women's Institutes*, 10.

71 Ontario Department of Agriculture, *Report of the Women's Institutes*, 1918, 27, QU.

72 The argument goes that the state financed the WI in order to handicap competing women's sections of populist parties, and, in the case of provincial Liberals, to buy women's party allegiance now that women had the vote. See Carbert, *Agrarian Feminism*, 11–12.

73 Certainly, not all aspects and espousals of the UFWO can be classified as equity feminist (in the same way that not all those of the WI can be labelled as social feminist). As discussed in chapter 1, "for both individuals and groups," equity and social feminism often "went hand in hand," with women sensing no contradiction between them (as will be evidenced by Emma Griesbach). See Black, *Social Feminism*, 41. Nevertheless, there is no doubt that the UFWO was predominantly equity feminist, at least in terms of its early rhetoric.

74 This approach embodies expressions of both liberal and socialist feminism, and as such comes under the rubric of equity feminism. See Black, *Social Feminism*, 1.

75 Staples, *The Challenge of Agriculture*, 38.

76 Good, *Farmer Citizen*, 64, 93; Staples, *The Challenge of Agriculture*, 41. These groups included numerous government-funded Farmers' Clubs, The Grange, farm specialty groups, and the rare co-operative. The Ontario Department of Agriculture had established Farmers' Clubs in 1908 (some report the date as 1905), and, like the original Farmers' Institutes and the WI, were forbidden from entertaining political debate at group meetings. See ibid., 40.

77 H.H. Hannam, in Good, *Farmer Citizen*, x. Hannam joined the staff of the UFO in 1928 as educational secretary (238).

78 Staples, *The Challenge of Agriculture*, 43.

79 Ibid., 51, 64, 66.

80 Ibid., 147. Staples and Good concurred that the original intention of the UFO was not to form a political party. As a farm organization, it simply planned to back those independent farmer candidates who held UFO principles. Ibid., 150, and Good, *Farmer Citizen*, 120. See also Crowley, "J.J. Morrison and the Transition in Canadian Farm Movements," 330–56.

81 Staples, *The Challenge of Agriculture*, 142, 143, 145.

82 Ibid., 63, and Crowley, "J.J. Morrison and the Transition in Canadian Farm Movements," 340–1; Good, *Farmer Citizen*, 120. This unexpected victory was owing to the disorder of Ontario's Liberal and Conservative parties, the disproportionate number of rural seats relative to the majority urban population, anger over the conscription issue, and a historical shift which witnessed "agriculture in transition." See Kechnie, "The United Farm Women," 273, and Macleod, "The United Farmer Movement," 201.

83 Kechnie, "The United Farm Women," 273; Laws, "Hints for Meetings," 6.

84 Kechnie, "The United Farm Women," 273. The failure of the UFWO as a political movement was attributable in part to the group's shortcomings outlined later in this chapter; however, as the chapter also later indicates, the failure was inextricably linked, as well, to the fate of the UFO, whose internal disputes and political inexperience helped cause its swift downfall. See 273–4. The rapid decline of the agricultural population also played a part. See Macleod, "The United Farmer Movement," 204.

85 A.S.T., "U.F.O. to Welcome Farm Women Members," *Weekly Sun*, 19 June 1918, 6.

86 Mills, "The U.F.W.O.," 6.

87 A.K., in Diana, "A Peep at My Letters," 6. The eyewitness account of A.K. reveals that some WI members themselves resented what they perceived as government control and Institute submission.

88 "The United Farm Women of Ontario," *Farmers' Sun*, 18 December 1920, 7.

89 Marion J. Macpherson, in Joan, "In Answer to Pollyanna," *Farmers' Sun*, 3 January 1929, 11.

90 Ibid.

91 Letter from A.W. to Diana, "W.I. Not Broad Enough," *Weekly Sun*, 3 July 1918, 6.

92 A.K., in Diana, "A Peep at My Letters," 6.

93 "Mrs Brodie's Holstein Speech," *Weekly Sun*, 12 February 1919, 6.

94 The UFWO, however, did not restrict its membership to farm women either: in 1920, UFWO provincial secretary Meta Laws listed other members of the rural community, including teachers and minister's wives, who qualified to join. They were likely made welcome in order to boost membership numbers, and to increase solidarity within rural communities. See Meta Schooley Laws, *Farmers' Sun*, 21 January 1920, 6.

95 Letter from Muuver to Diana, "Muuver Wears Overalls," *Weekly Sun*, 17 July 1918, 6.

96 Letter from A United Farm Woman to Diana, "W.I. and U.F.W.O.," *Farmers' Sun*, 3 December 1919, 6. The commitment of the WI to farm interests came under question by the UFO as early as 1917 when Institutes were passing resolutions in favour of the manufacturing of oleomargarine, a butter substitute. The UFO accused the WI of undermining the Ontario

dairy industry in favour of urban manufacturers who produced the "counterfeit butter." See "Women's Institutes Being Involved?" *Weekly Sun*, 19 September 1917, 4; "The w.i. and Oleomargarine," *Weekly Sun*, 19 September 1917, 1. Louise Carbert insists, however, that although "wi members were less politically sophisticated than populist radicals, their activities were perhaps no less agricultural." They, too, "were dedicated to preserving the agrarian and rural way of life." See Carbert, *Agrarian Feminism*, 8–9.

97 Letter from District Secretary, Bruce County to Diana, "The Women's Institute," *Farmers' Sun*, 24 December 1919, 6.

98 Haley, "Getting Our Act Together," 170. Margaret Kechnie contends in her dissertation that the early wi "was essentially a movement of small-town women and not farm women," but later states that "the actual ratio of farm women to smalltown women in the Ontario wi is unknown." See Kechnie, "Keeping Things Tidy," 11, 12. I question Kechnie's view that smalltown women comprised the majority of wi membership. Although I, too, can offer no statistical support for my claim, I can point to five compelling facts: the wi was conceived as a farm women's organization by founder Adelaide Hoodless, was originally an auxiliary of the Farmers' Institute, was managed by the Department of Agriculture, was affiliated with the Ontario Agricultural College, and offered programs which catered to the needs of physically and culturally isolated women, and which often addressed agricultural issues. We may never know how many wi members were farm women, but the aforementioned items clearly suggest that the organization was intended for them, and that they more than likely played a significant role in its development. We can assume, however, that the proportion of town women likely increased over the years as the Ontario farm population declined.

99 Copy of letter from Simcoe County Archives to Kerry Badgley, 13 July 1999; death register for Johanna Griesbach, 1913, sca; "Griesbach" [obituary], *Collingwood Enterprise-Messenger*, 28 February 1907, sca. Many thanks to historian and archivist Kerry Badgley for providing me with the biographical information and sources regarding Emma Griesbach and her family.

100 For just under two months, when the editorial was first introduced, Diana was simply known as "Sister." See Sister, "A Page For Women," (7 November 1917), 1.

101 "Foreword," *Weekly Sun*, 10 April 1918, 6. Not until 1919 did Diana's by-line include the name of her rural home "Greybrook Farm." Before this time, she made no reference to her "farm" or she referred to it, perhaps revealingly, as "Greybrook Manor."

102 Letter from Dorothy Wells to Diana, "Thoughts from Idleness," *Farmers' Sun*, 20 August 1919, 6. Diana responded by reassuring her readers that

"I am a farm woman for sure, but I am a (partly) emancipated one. You know my view of the farm woman is that she's a slave. The situation in my case had developed so that one of two alternatives had to be taken – (a) Keep up an everlasting round of drudging tasks, or (b) Cut out a lot of it. I decided to cut a lot of it." Of course, the second alternative was not a possibility for most farm women, whose every contribution to the farm was necessary for its survival; Letter from Sister E [Victoria County] to Diana, "Women's Work on Farms," *Weekly Sun*, 19 March 1919, 6, Letter from United Farmerette to Diana, "Can't Keep Wives From Voting," *Farmers' Sun*, 29 October 1919, 6, and Letter from Happy Picnicker to Diana, "The Greatest Thing," *Farmers' Sun*, 24 July 1920, 6.

103 Staples, *The Challenge of Agriculture*, 60; *Farmers' Sun*, 2 April 1919, 1. In January of 1920, the *Farmers' Sun* began to be published twice instead of once a week.

104 Staples, *The Challenge of Agriculture*, 112.

105 Jean Macleod asserts that the *Sun* "was the most effective contact between the organization and the u.f.o. rank and file." See Macleod, "The United Farmer Movement," 101; Letter from Alice Webster to W.C. Good, 4 February 1922, Good Papers, na.

106 Letter from W.C. Good to Emma Griesbach, 16 May 1922; Letter from Emma Griesbach to W.C. Good, both Good Papers, na.

107 Sister, "A Page for Women," 6; *Weekly Sun*, 20 February 1918, 6. Prior to the advent of the "Home Page," articles and advertisements of direct interest to women were infrequent. In 1901, for example, the newspaper (then called *The Sun*) published recipes in the January 30th issue only, and a lone article entitled "The Upward Movement of Women" in the February 13th issue. See "For the Housewife," *Sun*, 30 January 1901, 7, and "The Upward Movement of Women," *Sun*, 13 February 1901, 8.

108 *Weekly Sun*, 20 February 1918, 6. Terry Crowley points out that in letters to the women's pages in the agricultural press "the voices are middle-class and largely British or Irish Canadian." Moreover, the letters, though often laden with gender references, "do not regularly reflect conscious or unconscious minority currents in relation to race, religion, or even socio-economic class. ..." See Crowley, "Experience and Representation," 242.

109 *Weekly Sun*, 16 October 1918, 6.

110 "A Page for Women," *Weekly Sun*, 9 January 1918, 1.

111 *Weekly Sun*, 16 October 1918, 6. In the late summer of 1919, the title of Griesbach's column changed from "The Corner" to the more democratic "Our Corner."

112 Diana boasted in January of 1919 that "we have now upwards of a hundred bona fide Sun Sisters, and by that I mean those who have sent in at least one letter to this page." See letter from Sister Lou to Diana [Diana's

response], *Weekly Sun*, 29 January 1919, 6. Regular correspondents included Spunk, Sister Evelyn, Sunflower, and Muuver.

113 Brodie, " 'Three Points,' " 6. The superintendent of the wi was an agent of the provincial Department of Agriculture. Partly because the position originated with the establishment of the male Farmers' Institute, until 1934 only men held the job: they were John I. Hodson, oac professor George Creelman, and George A. Putnam. Putnam assumed the post in 1904 and supervised the wi for the next thirty years. His role was largely administrative, and though he wielded considerable influence, wi women seem to have viewed him as something of a benevolent figurehead. See Ontario Department of Agriculture, *Report of the Women's Institutes*, 1918, 120, qu; Walker et al., *Fifty Years of Achievement*, 99, qu.

114 Annette K. Baxter contends that with suffrage, "the official recognition of equality," the emphasis by club women on female specificity and difference "would cease to be politically respectable." See Baxter, "Preface," xiv.

115 Mrs J.A. Wallace [Simcoe], "How Shall we further organization" [address]; Directors' Meeting, 26 March 1920, 11; Directors' Meeting, 26 March 1920, 12; all ugl, Harman Collection, Minutes ufwo.

116 Sister Diana, "The Passing of Wash Day," 6. Similarly, when bachelor wrote to Diana, acknowledging that she did "not often publish letters from 'mere men,' " Diana replied that she did "not view favourably the practice of men herding themselves together in discussion, and somewhere else women herding themselves together doing the same thing." See letter from bachelor [Lambton County] to Diana, "Here's a Man With Questions," *Farmers' Sun*, 29 (7 May 1919): 6. It could legitimately be argued, however, that the Sun Sisters' page was an expression of female separatism by the ufwo.

117 Diana, "Now Let's See, Where Are We?" 6.

118 "Ideals of the Farm Women," *Weekly Sun*, 25 December 1918, 6.

119 Laws, "Important Notice," 6.

120 ugl, Harman Collection, Minutes ufwo, Executive Meeting, 17 June 1924, 99.

121 "What the u.f.w.o. Means," *Farmers' Sun*, 19 May 1920, 6; "Principles Not Men," *Farmers' Sun*, 24 July 1920, 1; Laws, "Hints for Meetings," 6.

122 Miss Griesbach, *Weekly Sun*, 28 (23 October 1918): 6. Griesbach's use of the term "Shylocks" could indicate anti-Semitism, although racism is not generally evident in Griesbach's writings.

123 "Ideals of the Farm Women," *Weekly Sun*, 25 December 1918, 6.

124 Staples, *The Challenge of Agriculture*, 124.

125 Kechnie, "The United Farm Women," 274.

126 Rankin, "Beyond the Kitchen and the Cornfield," 25.

127 Miss Griesbach, "A Talk on 'Form,' " 6.
128 Secretary Union, u.f.w.o., "A Progressive Club," *Farmers' Sun*, 27 March 1920, 6.
129 Letter from Miss Emma Griesbach to Diana, "Epistolary," *Weekly Sun*, 21 August 1918, 6.
130 Revealingly, in December of 1919, the subtitle of the *Farmers' Sun* – "Published In The Interest Of The Farmer, And His Family" – changed to the more communal but less female-oriented "Published In The Interest Of The Farmer And His Neighbor." In August of 1924, the subtitle changed back to the original version. See *Farmers' Sun*, 17 December 1919, 1, and the *Farmers' Sun*, 14 August 1924, 1.
131 Emma Griesbach, *Farmers' Sun*, 25 February 1920, 6.
132 Staples, *The Challenge of Agriculture*, 119.
133 Griesbach, "Progress of United Farm Women," 23.
134 Kechnie, "The United Farm Women," 274.
135 Letter from Mrs B to Miss Griesbach, "And Here are More Kindred Spirits," *Farmers' Sun*, 11 June 1919, 6.
136 Memoirs of J.J. Morrison (na) 60, in Rankin, "The Politicization of Ontario Farm Women," 314. As discussed in chapter 1, Naomi Black argues that "reformist or revolutionary socialist movements" that considered the " 'woman question' " proved disinterested in women's concerns "mainly because of the difficulty of conceptualizing women as a class or classlike group that could have class consciousness." See Black, *Social Feminism*, 39, Rankin, "The Politicization of Ontario Farm Women," 315, and Kechnie, "The United Farm Women," 274.
137 Letter from Mrs B to Miss Griesbach, "And Here are More Kindred Spirits," *Farmers' Sun*, 11 June 1919, 6.
138 Letter from Mrs A to Miss Griesbach, "Men Not all Alike," *Farmers' Sun*, 11 June 1919, 6.
139 Naomi Black contends that "class analysis … has only two choices in analyzing the specificity of women's situation: to deny it exists or to see any emphasis on it as producing an incompatibility between the sexes analogous to that between economic classes." See Black, *Social Feminism*, 350. The ufwo approach, particularly that of Emma Griesbach, generally conforms to the second "choice." With little regard for her own contradictions, Griesbach's Diana, however, also defended farm men (specifically those of the ufo) when Sun Sisters attacked them in their letters. In response to Sister Flo's condemnation, Diana writes "oh, come, Sister Flo, are you not a little hard on our men?" See letter from Sister Flo to Diana [Diana's response], "Hard on the Men," *Farmers' Sun*, 1 October 1919, 6. See also Griesbach, "Glen Lily's View," 6.
140 Letter from Mrs B to Miss Griesbach [Griesbach's response], "And Here are More Kindred Spirits," *Farmers' Sun*, 11 June 1919, 6.

141 Letter from Mrs A to Miss Griesbach [Griesbach's response], "Men Not all Alike," *Farmers' Sun*, 11 June 1919, 6.

142 Griesbach, "The Corner," 16 October 1918, 6.

143 Griesbach, "Will You Vote for Freedom," 6.

144 Diana, "The Work and Waste of Women," 5 March 1919, 6. Griesbach borrowed the title of this piece from an article of the same name by socialist feminist Charlotte Perkins Gilman, whom she greatly admired. See Diana, "The Work and Waste of Women," 12 March 1919, 6.

145 Sister Diana, "Lords and Commons," 6.

146 *Farmers' Sun*, 15 October 1919, 6.

147 Letter from Andrea Thryne to Diana, "Housewives Vocation," *Farmers' Sun*, 28 August 1920, 6. Thryne wrote that she had known "in the neighborhood of two hundred Ontario farmers, about fifty of whom quite intimately enough to discover their inward workings." Letter from Belinda Bell to Diana, "Defends the Men," *Farmers' Sun*, 18 September 1920, 6.

148 "Farm Women Report Progress; President Pleads for Children," *Farmers' Sun*, 15 December 1920, 1.

149 "Political Success Is Not Only Goal for u.f.o.," *Farmers' Sun*, 18 December 1920, 4. Actually, a male reader did read Griesbach's article about men on their "high-horse." He wrote Diana that "frequently the u.f.w.o. Secretary refers to the men who do not fall in line with women organizing, in terms of bitterness and scorn. As a man I ask is this the wisest policy? … best results are attained when you flatter and coddle the beasts; deliberately criticize them and you get their backs up; 's true! … I do not think that either sarcasm or vituperation may be classed as remedies." See letter from T.S.A. [York County] to Diana, "Down on the Men?" *Farmers' Sun*, 2 July 1919, 6.

150 "Political Success is Not Only Goal for u.f.o.," *Farmers' Sun*, 18 December 1920, 4.

151 Griesbach, "The Views of Our Delegates," 6.

152 Letter from Dorothy Wells to Diana [Diana's response], "Too Busy," *Farmers' Sun*, 12 June 1920, 6. In contrast, a sympathetic Staples excused the absence of men from meetings by maintaining that "it was not so much that they were not interested as, after a hard day's work, it was a real privation to leave a cosy fire and family at home, and go off alone to an uncomfortable schoolhouse or hall for a meeting that was anything but attractive." See Staples, *The Challenge of Agriculture*, 117–18.

153 Letter from Dorothy Wells to Sister Diana, "What is There In it for Charley?" *Farmers' Sun*, 29 (3 December 1919): 6.

154 Griesbach, "A Challenge Accepted," 6.

155 Rankin, "The Politicization of Ontario Farm Women," 317.

156 Letter from Andrea Thryne to Diana [Diana's response], "Housewives Vocation," *Farmers' Sun*, 28 August 1920, 6; Diana, "Ruts," 6; Diana, "The Community Idea," 6.

157 Letter from Andrea Thryne to Diana, "Housewives Vocation," *Farmers' Sun*, 28 August 1920, 6.

158 Diana, "Community or Cooperative Utilities," 6.

159 Letter from Betty Brown to Diana, "Are Women Awake?" *Farmers' Sun*, 21 May 1919, 6; Letter from A.W. to Diana, "Housekeeping Helps and a Bit of Thought," *Weekly Sun*, 27 November 1918, 6.

160 Diana, "Short Lengths," 6.

161 "What Kind of a Woman Are You?" *Young Journal*, in the *Farmers' Sun*, 5 June 1920, 6.

162 Griesbach, "The Farm Woman of To-day," 59. Pauline Rankin contends that "Griesbach's perspective as an unmarried working woman may well have rendered her unsympathetic to the pride farm women took in their domestic chores." See Rankin, "The Politicization of Ontario Farm Women," 318. This assertion erroneously assumes that unmarried women do not perform household labour, and that it could not be as gratifying for them as it might be for their married sisters. Furthermore, Griesbach apparently lived on a farm, and though she had no husband or children, she would have had to perform at least some of the same chores as farm wives.

163 See Macleod, "The United Farmer Movement," 205.

164 Diana, "Short Lengths," 6. The idea of co-operative household labour, despite its promise to relieve the overwork of farm wives, and to provide a modern, sanitary work environment, never captured the interest of most rural women. See, for example, letter from Sunflower to Diana, "Why Not be Content?" *Farmers' Sun*, 9 April 1919, 6; and letter from Alice Webster to Diana, "Obstacles in the Way," *Farmers' Sun*, 31 January 1920, 6. This might be attributable to the farm woman's individualistic pride, to the control that she desired over her own kitchen and laundry, to the possible distance (especially with no car) between her farm and the facility, to the necessity to perform simultaneous (including non-domestic) tasks, and to what she saw as the idea's excessively socialist overtones.

165 Letter from Kentorian to Diana, "Women's Interests," *Farmers' Sun*, 11 December 1920, 6. Of course, WI groups were indeed addressing issues of hydro and temperance.

166 Letter from Fidelis to Diana, "W.I. Versus U.F.W.O.," *Farmers' Sun*, 12 November 1919, 6.

167 Carbert, *Agrarian Feminism*, 13.

168 Joint meeting, 2, 3 January 1924, Smith Falls Minute Book, UGL.

169 Minutes for 1927–8, Smith Falls Minute Book, UGL.

170 See, for example, letter from Matilda [Grey County] to Diana, "Recipe for Potato Soup," *Weekly Sun*, 1 May 1918, 6.

171 Letter from J.C. Ross to Emma Griesbach, 8 February 1922, Good Papers, NA. There was some dispute in UFO circles as to whether Emma Griesbach resigned or was fired from the *Farmers' Sun*. After receiving a letter from the editor which informed her that her columns would be subjected to greatly reduced space, and displaced from the Saturday to the Tuesday edition, a proud and hurt Griesbach perceived, perhaps rightly, that she was being squeezed out of the paper, and angrily refused to resume her post. Griesbach always insisted that she never tendered her resignation, despite a letter to *Sun* director J.J. Morrison in which she bid him farewell, and asked him to sell her co-operative stocks. See letter from J.C. Ross to Emma Griesbach, 26 January 1922; Letter from Emma Griesbach to J.J. Morrison, 1922, Good Papers, NA. Griesbach died of heart attack in Collingwood in 1934. Copy of letter from Simcoe County Archives to Kerry Badgley, 13 July 1999.

172 Letter from J.C. Ross to W.C. Good, 9 March 1922, Good Papers, NA.

173 Letter from Alice Webster to W.C. Good, 20 March 1922, Good Papers, NA.

174 Mrs J.S.A., in Griesbach, "The Corner," 7 May 1919, 6; "Sewing Class Continues," *Farmers' Sun*, 28 July 1920, 6; Shearer, "September Meeting of the Listowel U.F.W.O.," 6.

175 See, for example, letter from Member U.F.W.O. [a teacher from Peterboro County] to Diana, "The Unclean School," *Farmers' Sun*, 7 May 1919, 6; Letter from Molly [Woodstock] to Diana, "Our School Lunch Equipment," *Farmers' Sun*, 3 April 1920, 20; Letter from Mrs M. Sauter [North Bay] to Emma Griesbach, "Now What about Libraries?" *Farmers' Sun*, 11 June 1919, 6; Griesbach, "Letters from Farm Women," 6; Shearer, "Listowel U.F.W.O.," 6; Letter from Mrs S.B.J. to Emma Griesbach, "Here are Stirring Women," *Farmers' Sun*, 30 July 1919, 6; "Rest Room for Farmers' Wives," *Farmers' Sun*, 28 April 1920, 10; Letter from Centre Grey Sister to Diana, "Give Us Electricity," *Farmers' Sun*, 28 August 1920, 6.

176 Griesbach, "Letters from Farm Women," 6; "Caradoc Club," *Farmers' Sun*, 14 April 1920, 6; Laws, "Legal Rights of Canadian Women," 6.

177 See, for example, WI Minute Books, Wilton Grove, UWO; Smith Falls Minute Book, UGL; Shearer, "Listowel U.F.W.O.," 6. Much of their historical studies focused on the history of famous women. See 31 August 1930, 17 February 1937, in WI Minute Books, Wilton Grove, UWO; 18 April 1923, in Smith Falls Minute Book, UGL; "News Flashes From the Branches," *Home and Country* 2 (January 1936): 4.

178 Laws, "Another Busy Week," 6. The attention by these groups to women's own cultural and intellectual development cannot be overesti-

mated. A WI member from Leeds County reported in 1936 that "our meetings have broadened our views ... educated us in many ways, given us more self confidence in conversing and discussing topics ... making us less afraid of the sound of our own voices, brought out hidden talent that was previously unknown to exist." Karen Blair rightly argues that the clubwoman's "development of sufficient audacity to strive for self-improvement in an era that defined ladies as selfless agents devoted to the well-being of others" was highly significant. The pursuit for self-betterment by farm women, however, should not be interpreted as their devaluation of the social feminist trait of service to others; these women did not want their organizations to circumscribe either ambition. See "News Flashes From the Branches," *Home and Country* 2 (January 1936): 4; Blair, *The Clubwoman as Feminist*, 58.

179 See, for example, WI Minute Books, Wilton Grove, UWO, and Smith Falls Minute Book, UGL.

180 Annual Report of the U.F.W.O. Club, 23 November 1922, Smith Falls Minute Book, UGL.

181 Baxter, "Preface," xiii.

182 Griesbach, "The Corner," 2 July 1919, 6; Griesbach, "On Organizing," 6.

183 Letter to Diana, "The U.F.W.O.," *Farmers' Sun*, 13 March 1920, 6; Fazier, "A Woman Worker," 6. Some UFWO clubs either chose or were compelled to affiliate themselves with the WI. But, by the same token, some WI branches considered re-identifying as UFWO clubs. Thus, the interchangeability of the two groups was recognized by the local women in them both. See Griesbach, "The Corner," 4 June 1919, 6; 5 February 1918, in WI Minute Books, Wilton Grove, UWO; and Kechnie, "The United Farm Women," 277.

184 Souter, "East Nipissing News," 6.

185 21 November 1934, and 5 July 1942, in WI Minute Books, Wilton Grove, UWO.

186 Mrs G.A., "Convention Retrospection," *Farmers' Sun*, 7 January 1920, 6.

187 Letter to Diana, "The W.I. and the U.F.W.O.," *Farmers' Sun*, 24 January 1920, 6. This Sun Sister was also a WI member.

188 Kechnie, "The United Farm Women," 275; Laws, "Carleton County Organized," 6; and Cowsrough, "Paisley Plock U.F.W.O.," 6.

189 1909–19, in WI Minute Books, Wilton Grove, UWO; "Wilton Grove Monthly," *Farmers' Sun*, 12 March 1924, 2; and Mitchell, "Wilton Grove Club," 4.

190 Connelly, "Miss Agnes McPhail," see also Pringle, "The Only M.P. who Can –," 45. In order that her constituents could more easily write her last name, Macphail altered its original spelling. As such, the spelling of her name differs from time to time.

191 Crowley, *Agnes Macphail*, 79.

192 Agnes Macphail, 5 November 1932, 3, Macphail Papers, NA, Vol. 6, File 5 – Weekly Letters, 1932–33; "Institute Hears Miss A. Macphail," 12 October 1939, Macphail Papers, Vol. 7, File 10 – Clippings, 1938–39; Agnes Macphail, "Woman in the Present World," 2, Macphail Papers, Vol. 10, File 23 – Women -Role in Society (1929–43), Speeches. The Farmers' Institute had disbanded in 1917. See Walker et al., *Fifty Years of Achievement*, 28, QU.

193 "Woman Runs for the Commons To Improve Lot of Farm Women," *Toronto Star*, 21 September 1921, Macphail Papers, NA, Vol. 6, File 4 – Press Clippings, 1930; Crowley, *Agnes Macphail*, 30.

194 See, for example, Agnes MacPhail, MP, "To the United Farm Women of Ontario," 47–8.

195 Crowley, *Agnes Macphail*, 79.

196 Agnes Macphail, "Major Political Parties"; Agnes Macphail, "loos [sic] self in large …," 4, both Macphail Papers, NA, Vol. 10, File 23 – Women -Role in Society (1929–43), Speeches; Maxine Barrus, "Women Need to Be Useful to Be Happy," *Tulsa Tribune*, 9 January 1936, Macphail Papers, Vol. 7, File 8 – Clippings, 1936.

197 Agnes Macphail, 24 March 1934, 3–4, Macphail Papers, NA, Vol. 6, File 6 – Weekly Letters, 1934; Agnes Macphail, "Agriculture Must Choose" [speech], 6, Macphail Papers, Vol. 8, File 1 – Agriculture. This observation is rather ironic given, as noted earlier, that many local UFWO clubs organized without knowing why, or what to do afterwards.

198 Pennington, *Agnes Macphail*, 26.

199 Macphail, "Woman in the Present World," 1, Macphail Papers, NA, and Agnes Macphail, "How Far Can Women Help Solve National Problems?" [CBC radio address], 21 May 1939, 5, Macphail Papers, NA, Vol. 10, File 23 – Women -Role in Society (1929–43).

200 Macphail, "How Far Can Women Help Solve National Problems?," 9, Macphail Papers, NA.

201 Agnes Macphail, "The Power of Women," 5 December 1942, 9, Macphail Papers, NA, Vol. 10, File 23 – Women -Role in Society (1929–43), Speeches.

202 Macphail, "Woman in the Present World," 3, Macphail Papers, NA; Macphail, "How Far Can Women Help Solve National Problems?" [CBC radio address], 21 May 1939, 8, Macphail Papers, NA, Vol. 10, File 23 – Women -Role in Society (1929–43), Speeches.

203 Crowley, *Agnes Macphail*, 31. As mentioned earlier, it was not unknown for the provincial UFWO, and particularly for Griesbach, to offer expressions of social feminism (nor for the WI to offer expressions of equity feminism). Given Agnes Macphail's public avowal in 1927 that " 'I am a feminist,' " and her notable struggle for acceptance and " 'absolute equality' " within the exclusively male-populated and male-defined

world of federal inter-war politics, however, her espousals of social feminism are all that more significant. See the *Farmers' Sun*, 20 January 1927, and Toronto *Mail*, 16 January 1931, in Crowley, *Agnes Macphail*, 91.

204 Black, "Macphail: First Among Equals," 14; Backhouse, "Agnes Macphail and Feminism," 145–6.

205 Connelly, "Miss Agnes Mcphail."

206 Kechnie, "The United Farm Women," 273–4; Macleod, "The United Farmer Movement," 204.

207 Kechnie, "The United Farm Women," 277; Secretaries Report, 1 December 1922, 1, and Secretaries Report, 5 December 1927, 177, UGL, Harman Collection, Minutes UFWO.

208 See UGL, Harman Collection, File 802; Kechnie, "The United Farm Women," 277.

209 Ambrose, *For Home and Country*, 146.

210 Significantly, while the separatist WI won longstanding support from a government who deemed its work "safe," the "equal" and integrated UFWO received almost no support from their UFO "brothers" who possibly deemed its intentions "too feminist." This scenario, in which the men associated with both groups undermined the reform efforts of women, "suggests the threat that women's clubs represented" to the stability of gender relations. See Baxter, "Preface," xii.

CHAPTER SIX

1 Martin, "Guns or Butter," 3.

2 Duke, "Salute to Members," 1.

3 "War Work Report," *Home and Country* 10 (Summer 1944): 1; Rorke, "Thanks for the Jam," 1; "Summary of Women's Institute War Report," *Home and Country* 12 (Spring 1946): 2.

4 Martin, "Guns or Butter," 1.

5 Duke, "Salute to Members," 1.

6 Kelly, "Home Economics Aids in War Time," 3; Kelly, "Home Economics Challenges Women," 2. The article "Salvage Fats for Canada" echoed this sentiment when it noted that because Canada required fats to make explosives, " 'the hand that holds the frying pan will win the war.' " See *Home and Country* 9 (Spring 1943): 2.

7 Duke, "Salute to Members," 1.

8 Carroll, "The Agricultural Battle 1943," 1.

9 Duke, "Salute to Members," 1.

10 Kelly, "Home Economics Challenges Women," 2.

11 Kelly, "Home Economics Aids in War Time," 3; Kelly, "1944 Calling Farm Daughters," 2.

12 Kelly, "1944 Calling Farm Daughters," 2.

13 Eadie, "Juniors Work Faithfully," 3.
14 Kelly, "Home Economics Aids in War Time," 3.
15 Editorial Comment, *Home and Country* 6 (Winter 1940–41): 2.
16 Kelly, "Home Economics Aids in War Time," 3; Keys, "Home Economics for Total Victory," 2. War work was a priority for the Norton/Wilton Grove WI, for example, but the branch continued to hold talks, activities, and socials unrelated to the war effort. Its home economics standing committee gave at least one talk on "the topic of Home Economics." See May 1942 – April 1945, particularly 21 March 1945, in WI Minute Books, Wilton Grove, UWO.
17 Keys, "Home Economics for Total Victory," 2.
18 19 June 1946, in WI Minute Books, Wilton Grove, UWO.
19 Kelly, "Home Economics Challenges Women," 2.
20 Keys, "Home Economics for Total Victory," 2.
21 Eadie, "Juniors Work Faithfully," 3.
22 Duke, "Resolutions Indicate Interests of Members," 4.
23 "Cooperative Program," *Home and Country* 10 (Winter 1944–45): 2.
24 Dr Helen C. Abell, "Future Role of Farm Women," 1961, 1, 3, Abell Collection, UGL, File – Abell Publications.
25 Fuller, "The Development of Farm Life," 21, table 1.5.
26 Ontario, *Special Study*, Report #1, December 1959, 4. None of the 352 homes had electricity exclusively in the barn. Only 1 per cent or three households had no electricity at all.
27 Fuller, "The Development of Farm Life," 20, table 1.4.
28 Ontario, *Special Study*, Report #1, December 1959, 4.
29 The 1951 census defined the farm population as those persons residing on a farm in a rural area, regardless of their occupation. A farm was defined as "a holding on which agricultural operations are carried out," and as claiming three or more acres, or as comprising less than three acres and earning $250 or more annually through agricultural production. See Canada, Dominion Bureau of Statistics, *Census of Canada 1951*, xv.
30 Fuller, "The Development of Farm Life," 15, table 1.1; and Ladell and Ladell, *Inheritance*, 235. As Fuller and Ladell and Ladell indicate, although the Ontario farming population fell between 1951 and 1971, the total rural population actually experienced an increase in those years, partly due to the influx of urbanites to the country. In 1951, the total rural population numbered 1,346,000, and reached 1,412,000 in 1961 before dropping to 1,359,000 in 1971. Yet, between 1951 and 1971 the rural proportion of the total provincial population fell from 29 to 18 per cent; Cebotarev, "From Domesticity to the Public Sphere," 209.
31 Cebotarev, "From Domesticity to the Public Sphere," 207–8.
32 Fuller, "The Development of Farm Life," 17, figure 1.3; Marshall, *Half Century of Farming in Dufferin*, 49; and Dahms, "Ontario's Rural Communities," 331.

33 Reaman, *A History of Agriculture*, 176; Fuller, "The Development of Farm Life," 19.
34 Reaman, *A History of Agriculture*, 176; Fuller, "The Development of Farm Life," 20, table 1.3. By 1981, the number of tractors had reached 178,000. See Fuller, "The Development of Farm Life," 20.
35 Reaman, *The History of Agriculture*, 177.
36 Fuller, "The Development of Farm Life," 21.
37 Reaman, *A History of Agriculture*, 178. The value of farm machinery in Ontario was $579 million. In Canada, it was over $2 billion.
38 Latzer, *Myrtleville*, 299.
39 Fuller, "The Development of Farm Life," 20.
40 "Record Attendance at Second Provincial Conference," *Home and Country* 16 (Spring 1950): 5; "A Study of Farm Homes and Homemakers," *Home and Country* 25 (Summer 1959): 19; Houck, "Snags and Snails," 3. The WI marked these changes with a transformation of its own: in 1952, *Home and Country*'s long-time newspaper format changed to a more stylish magazine. See *Home and Country* 18 (Summer 1952).
41 Elaine Bitz, interview by author.
42 "Gleanings from Convention Area Meetings," *Home and Country* 16, Summary Issue (1950–51): 6.
43 Ontario, *Special Study*, Report #1, December 1959, 3.
44 See, for example, Rosenfeld, *Farm Women*, 23.
45 Garkovich and Bokemeier, "Agricultural Mechanization," 222.
46 Rosenfeld, *Farm Women*, 71. See also Ross, *Harvest of Opportunity*, 6, and Graff, "Industrialization of Agriculture," 10.
47 Garkovich and Bokemeier, "Agricultural Mechanization," 212. See also Cebotarev, "From Domesticity to the Public Sphere," 204. As Carolyn Sachs points out, large equipment often precluded women from farming because it was designed for the strength and height of men. Thus, it was not that women were not made to operate equipment, but that equipment was not made to be operated by women. See Rosenfeld, *Farm Women*, 22–3.
48 Flora, "Public Policy and Women in Agricultural Production," 277–8. Interestingly, farm women's curtailed job of milking cows was nostalgically referenced in a 1955 advertisement for a consumer canned-milk product for babies called "Farmer's Wife." In the ad, the farm woman is supplanted as the authority of milk by "the medical profession." See "Just What the Doctor Ordered!" [advertisement], *Reader's Digest* (October 1955): 231.
49 "Farm Forum Guide," The Farmer Takes a Wife, 10 November 1947, 2, Morrison Papers, NA, Vol. 12, File – Farm Forum – Newsletters, Clippings, 1941–49.
50 Reaman, *A History of Agriculture*, 214. Ethel Chapman (1888–1976) was the editor of *Home and Country* from 1952 to 1967. Chapman, who grew up

near Milton and was a 1912 graduate of Macdonald Institute, was also the women's page editor of *Farmer's Magazine*, and wrote a regular column, "From a Roadside Window," for the *Farmer's Advocate*. By 1969, she had penned five published books. See Chapman, *Humanities in Homespun*, back cover; Lewis, "Editorial," 3; and Kechnie, "Keeping Things Tidy," 152.

51 Graban, "Buying is Your Business," 24; Tryssenaar, "Changing the Subject," 53. According to Graban, the Canadian Association of Consumers (CAC) informed consumers "of what they should know for their protection for wise and economic buying and discusses with Government officials matters relating to appropriate legislation. It also advises manufacturers regarding consumer opinion with respect to their particular product. We try in every manner possible to help consumers save and stretch dollars and to improve the standard and quality of the merchandise they purchase." For more information on the CAC, see Parr, "Shopping for a Good Stove," 75–97.

52 Chapman, "Let's Not Lose Our Human Appeal," 3.

53 "Gleanings from Convention Area Meetings," *Home and Country* 16, Summary Issue (1950–51): 6; Sachs, *The Invisible Farmers*, 29; Rosenblatt and Anderson, "Interaction in Farm Families," 157. Rosenblatt and Anderson also point out that for farmers, modern labour-saving equipment for the farm may likewise "merely increase the amount that is done in the time available and raise the standard of excellence the farmer attempts to meet."

54 Cowan, *More Work for Mother*, 208.

55 Cebotarev, "From Domesticity to the Public Sphere," 210.

56 Mrs Edith Storr, Provincial Secretary of Ontario Farm Radio Forum, in "National Farm Radio Forum Guide," Equality for Women, 15 December 1958, 11, Farm Radio Forum, NA, Vol. 103, File – Study Guides, 1944–65.

57 Ontario, *Special Study*, Report #9, May 1964, 26, 27. Those who earned an income from non-farm work on the farm most often kept boarders.

58 Ibid., 33.

59 Prentice et al., *Canadian Women*, 412. The first time that the word "feminist" appears in the WI's *Home and Country* magazine is in 1955 to describe eighteenth-century feminist Mary Wollstonecraft. See "The Officers' Conference," *Home and Country* 21 (Summer 1955): 15.

60 Pierson, "The Politics of the Domestic Sphere," 2, and Cohen, "The Canadian Women's Movement," 2.

61 Cohen, "The Canadian Women's Movement," 4.

62 "National Farm Radio Forum Guide," Equality for Women, 15 December 1958, 2, Farm Radio Forum, NA, Vol. 103, File – Study Guides, 1944–65.

63 Spender, "Modern Feminist Theorists," 368.

64 Clark, *Almanac of American Women*, 131; Matthaei, *An Economic History of Women in America*, 271.

65 Pierson, "The Politics of the Domestic Sphere," 2. For a compelling class and race analysis of *The Feminine Mystique,* see bell hooks, *Feminist Theory: From Margin to Centre* (Boston: South End Press 1984), 1–15, reprinted in hooks, "Black Women," 33–9.

66 Albeit farm women's non-domestic work was unpaid and not away from the home.

67 Bruners, "The Influence of the Women's Liberation Movement," 18.

68 McBride, "Women in our Society To-day," 4. The term the "woman question" was a popular turn-of-the-century expression which reflected male scepticism about women's role and place in the wake of the first-wave feminist movement.

69 16 May 1945, in WI Minute Books, Wilton Grove, UWO.

70 McBride, "Women in our Society To-day," 4. The psychological stress among farm women and men who are confronted with changing technologies and roles, and with uncertain financial futures, is explored in a variety of studies, including Jensen, "Stress in the Farm Family Unit," 11–12, and Rosenblatt and Anderson, "Interaction in Farm Families."

71 "Pine Grove, Stormont S.," *Home and Country* 15 (Summer 1949): 6; 29 January 1959, in WI Minute Books, Wilton Grove UWO; "Here and There with the Institutes," *Home and Country* 21 (Winter 1955): 35. In a poem entitled "Yesterday and Today," farm woman Gertrude G. Lipsett venerates the farm woman's traditional role and remains unimpressed by the modernization, mechanization, and consumerism that she saw corrupting farm women's work and their sense of humility and charity: "My Mother had a spinning-wheel/And in the afternoon, To spin a hank of stocking yarn,/Paced up and down the room./My Mother had an old box churn/Equipped with rod, and dash,/And then for hours, she'd turn and turn,/Till butter milk would splash./My Mother had a scrubbing-brush/To clean a rough board floor,/Down on her knees she had to rush/From front, to the back door./My Mother had an old wash-tub/And washing-board to match,/And then the clothes she'd rub and rub/And made the soap suds splash./My Mother ran a leach of lye/To make the season's soap,/She also had a pot of dye/To give worn raiment hope./But Mother had a lot of time/To help a little child./To help a neighbour who was ill,/With confidence and smile./She taught a class in Sunday School,/She helped the Ladies' Aid,/And for the children of the poor/Some useful clothing made./She sang the alto in the Church./The golden rule she lived./Her hopeful voice was ever near/To comfort the bereaved./Now, I have not a spinning-wheel,/My yarn is factory made,/If I, by chance, choose then to knit/The articles all fade./I haven't got a churn at all./The cream man at the door/Hands out my butter,/Takes my cream,/To factory make some more./I do not use a scrubbing brush/Upon my hardwood floors./My Electrolux will soon take up/The mud from out of doors./A

leach of lye I never made – /So many new designs/Of soaps, and pow-
ders, do the work/In all the cleaning lines./But I have not a lot of time/To
lessen others' toil,/No time to help my neighbour out/With willing hands
or smile./My garments all must fit just so,/My nose must never shine,/
My lips and nails must both be bright,/My whole appearance fine./But I
am missing lots of fun/My Mother must have had,/In giving all a helping
hand/While looking after Dad." See Lipsett, "Yesterday and Today," 29.

72 19 March 1952, in wi Minute Books, Wilton Grove, uwo.

73 More specifically, Abell's study was sponsored by the Rural Sociology
Unit of the Economics Division of the Canada Department of Agriculture
and by the Home Economics Service and Farm Economics and Statistics
Branch of the Ontario Department of Agriculture. Likewise, the wi, which
previous to 1945 was represented by the Women's Institute Branch (and
before 1921, by the Women's Institute Branch of the Department of Agriculture), was now a part of the Women's Institute Branch and Home Economics Service. In 1966, this arm of the government was renamed the
Home Economics Branch. See Reaman, *A History of Agriculture*, 210.

74 Ontario, *Special Study* (Questionnaire and Interviewer's Manual), Interviewer's Manual, 1; *Special Study*, Report #2, May 1960, 1.

75 Four additional people also conducted interviews. See Ontario, *Special
Study*, Report #1, December 1959, 1; *Special Study* (Questionnaire and Interviewer's Manual, Interviewer's Manual), 2; *Special Study*, Report #1,
December 1959, 1; and *Special Study*, Report #8, July 1962, Preface. All 352
women were "farm homemakers," but not all were wives: seven were
widows and five were unmarried. Half the sample were members of the
wi. See *Special Study*, Report #9, May 1964, 3 n. 1, and *Special Study*, Report
#8, July 1962, Preface.

76 For an account of all of the issues which the study addressed, see Ontario,
Special Study, Progress Reports #1 through 9. Aware that the intrusive and
exhaustive questionnaire could well alienate the farm women under
study, Abell cautioned her interviewers not to offend their subjects. The
first two pages of the questionnaire, Abell told interviewers, were intended not only to gather "sociological data" about the homemaker and
her family, but to "establish rapport between you and the homemaker."
Accommodating the presumed vanity of women which made them reluctant to reveal their age, Abell instructed interviewers to begin the questionnaire by asking for the specific ages of the children and farm owner
first, and the "approximate age" of the homemaker second. "This tech-
nique is important," noted Abell, "never start this questionnaire by asking the homemaker's age!!!!" Despite such precautions, however,
interviewers, while "made very welcome" in many homes, would merely
"be tolerated" in others. See *Special Study* (Questionnaire and Interviewer's Manual), Interviewer's Manual, 3, 2.

77 For an examination of the ideological and activist roots of National Farm Radio Forum, see Crowley, "The New Canada Movement," 311–25. Many of those who helped establish Farm Radio Forum had been supporters of the United Farmer movement.

78 The number of participants in each group was regularly recorded, although only one of the seven broadcasts mentioned in this chapter ("The Farmer Takes a Wife") specified how many of those were women.

79 Fuller, "Appendix Two," 356. The number of Farm Forums peaked in Ontario (and Canada) between 1949 and 1951. By 1950, there were 875 Forums in Ontario (and 1,606 nationwide). By 1963, however, two years before the program disbanded, there were only 140 Forums in Ontario. See "Overview of Farm Forum History," Farm Radio Forum, NA, Vol. 12, File – B14, Statistics (1941–55); "Rise and Fall in Farm Forums," Lambton Farm Courier, October 1963, 1, Farm Radio Forum, NA, Vol. 108, File E – Clippings etc.

80 "The Forums Speak!" Provincial Summary of Forum Findings, Equality for Women, 15 and 16 December 1958, 2, Farm Radio Forum, NA, Vol. 98, Binder. "Equality for Women" was the only broadcast out of the seven with questions specifically designated for women to answer.

81 "National Farm Radio Forum Guide," Equality for Women, 15 December 1958, 9, Farm Radio Forum, NA, Vol. 103, File – Study Guides, 1944–65.

82 "Farm Forum Guide," The Farmer Takes a Wife, 10 November 1947, 3, Sim Papers, NA, Vol. 3, File 3–23 – National Farm Radio Forum (CBC Correspondence 1941–42).

83 See, for example, Maplegrove Forum, Stormont, and Church St. and Kerrs Ridge Forum, Dundas, in "Farm Forum Findings," Farm Women in Public Life, 10 November 1952, Farm Radio Forum, NA, Vol. 70, File – Farm Forum Findings, 19 March-10 November 1952-"Farm Women in Public Life" (1952); Phillipsburg Forum, Waterloo, in ibid.

84 Islay Forum, Victoria, in ibid.

85 Cuboss Alpo Forum, Bruce, in ibid.

86 Providence Forum, Haldemand, in ibid.; Bethany Forum, Wellington, in "Farm Forum Findings," Partners All: Farm Wives as Working Partners, 9 November 1953, Farm Radio Forum, NA, Vol. 72, File – Farm Forum Findings, 2 November-16 November 1953-"Most Farm Wives Working Partners" (1953); Springlake Forum, Grey, in ibid.

87 Denfield Forum, Middlesex; Sunnybrook Forum, Wellington; Crumlin Forum, Middlesex; Cuboss Centre, Bruce; and S.S. No. 6 Elderslie and Sullivan Forum, Bruce, all in "Farm Forum Findings," The Farmer Takes a Wife, 10 November 1947, Farm Radio Forum, NA, Vol. 60, File – Farm Forum Findings, 3 November-24 November 1947-"The Farmer Takes a Wife" (1947).

88 Rosebank Forum, Waterloo, in "Farm Forum Findings," Equality for
Women, 15 December 1958, Farm Radio Forum, NA, Vol. 82, File – Farm
Forum Findings, 1 December-15 December 1958-"Equality for Women"
(1958).

89 Throughout the war, the provincial WI reported a shrinking membership.
In March of 1939, it stood at just over 42,000; by March of 1945, it had
fallen by 25 per cent to 32,000. The number of branches also fell. In March
of 1939, there existed 1,374 clubs; by March of 1945, there were 1,248. This
wartime drop was understood to be temporary, however, as it was attributed in part to rural women's war work, which superseded regular Institute affairs and occupied farm wives who participated more fully in
emergency agricultural labour. One reason for the WI's immense popularity in the immediate post-war years was its introduction at that time of
group health insurance, which preceded the advent of universal health
care in Canada by more than two decades. See Ambrose, *For Home and
Country*, 146, 147–8, 157–8.

90 *Home and Country* 12 (Spring 1946): 1.

91 "Superintendent Visits All Conventions," *Home and Country* 12 (Fall and
Winter 1946–47): 2; "F.W.I.O. Membership Award Result," *Home and
Country* 15 (Fall and Winter 1949–50): 3; "President's Corner," *Home and
Country* 14 (Fall and Winter 1947–48): 2.

92 "Superintendent Visits All Conventions," *Home and Country* 12 (Fall and
Winter 1946–47): 2. The Mount Royal WI in Wentworth County formed a
war bride committee that visited war brides and offered them free membership. See "News Flashes," *Home and Country* 11 (Winter 1945–46): 4.

93 "Over 600 Women Assemble at First F.W.I.O. Officers' Conference," *Home
and Country* 15 (Summer 1949): 1; Carbert, *Agrarian Feminism*, 17; "Over
600 Women Assemble," 1.

94 "President's Corner," *Home and Country* 14 (Fall and Winter 1947–48): 2.
Ontario membership comprised just over half of the total Canadian membership, and made up 1,350 Institute clubs across Ontario. See "Tribute to
Stoney Creek 1897 Institute 1947," *Home and Country* 12, Golden Anniversary Issue (1947): 2; "Report of the Director, Women's Institute Branch,"
Home and Country 13 (Fall and Winter 1947–48): 1; and "F.W.I.O. Membership Award Result," *Home and Country* 15 (Fall and Winter 1949–50): 3.

95 Ambrose, *For Home and Country*, 157; Hodgins, "F.W.I.O. Board Meeting,"
6. The fiftieth anniversary celebrations in June of 1947 took place at the
OAC in Guelph, where 1,200 women converged. Delegates arrived from all
over Ontario and Canada, and from the United States, Great Britain, and
New Zealand. The WI regarded the celebration as "the greatest gathering
of members of any one women's organization ever assembled in the Dominion of Canada." See "Women's Institutes Celebrate 50th Anniversary," *Home and Country* 13 (Summer 1947): 1.

96 Hodgins, "F.W.I.O. Board Meeting," 6. That year the decrease numbered 2,039 members.
97 *Home and Country* 21 (Winter 1955): 42; Leatherdale, "Provincial Board Celebrates Silver Anniversary," 3.
98 Chapman, "Could We Make This a Summer Fallow Year?" 3.
99 Houck, "Snags and Snails," 3.
100 In Abell's 1959 study of 352 farm homemakers, the average age of the 176 WI members was forty-seven years. One-third of these women were between fifty and eighty-one years of age. See Ontario, *Special Study*, Report #2, May 1960, 2.
101 "Here and There With the Women's Institutes," *Home and Country* 17, Overseas Tour Issue (February 1952): 12; "Cayuga, Haldimand," *Home and Country* 14 (Spring and Summer 1947–48): 5; "Here and There With the Women's Institutes," *Home and Country* 14 (Winter 1949): 8.
102 Chapman, "Senior Neighboring," 3.
103 Chapman, "Could We Make This a Summer Fallow Year?" 3.
104 Chapman, "Senior Neighboring," 3; Ethel Chapman, editorial, *Home and Country* 27 (Winter 1961): 3.
105 Chapman, "Could We Make This a Summer Fallow Year?" 3.
106 Chapman, "Senior Neighboring," 3.
107 Ibid.
108 Carbert, *Agrarian Feminism*, 17.
109 "In Memory," *Home and Country* 20 (Winter 1954): 18. Helen MacMurchy had headed the Maternal and Child Welfare Division of the National Department of Health in Ottawa.
110 Chapman, "Senior Neighboring," 3.
111 Chapman, "A Distinctive Organization," 3.
112 Ibid.
113 Carbert, *Agrarian Feminism*, 17.
114 Chapman, "Sixty-Fifth Anniversary," 3; Chapman, "Can't We Study the Family, Too," 3; and Chapman, "Let's Not Lose Our Human Appeal," 3.
115 Ambrose, *For Home and Country*, 149. As mentioned in chapter 5, the WI had encouraged clubs since the 1920s to document their local history.
116 The Federated Women's Institutes of Ontario, *Fiftieth Anniversary Celebration*, 7, QU.
117 Ambrose, *For Home and Country*, 178.
118 The meetings of 24 May 1944, 8 October 1950, in WI Minute Books, Wilton Grove, UWO, provide examples of references at WI meetings to the significance of women in history; "In Memory of Nellie McClung," *Home and Country* 23 (Fall 1957): 17; Pardy, "Adelaide Hoodless Said," 3; the quotation comes from Chapman, "Sixtieth Anniversary," 3. In June of 1957, the Women's Institutes of Grey County "completed one of the finest projects yet undertaken in the interest of Canadian history. They

unveiled the cairn they had erected to the memory of the late Nellie Mc-
Clung." McClung died in Victoria, British Columbia in 1951. See "In
Memory of Nellie McClung," 17.

119 "The Eyes of the Institute would Look in Gratitude to Stoney Creek,"
Home and Country 12, Golden Anniversary Issue (1947): 2; Houck,
"Snags and Snails," 3.

120 Houck, "Snags and Snails," 3.

121 Ibid.; *Home and Country* 21 (Winter 1955): 42.

122 This response is in keeping with the fact that farm women already felt
overburdened by their own responsibilities and work. "The Forums
Speak!" Provincial Summary of Forum Findings, Equality for Women, 15
and 16 December 1958, 2, Farm Radio Forum, NA, Vol. 98, Binder. These
151 groups in Ontario comprised 1,981 farm women and men. In tabulating the answer data, Farm Radio Forum listed a variety of viewpoints it
had collectively extracted from the group response sheets, and then indicated the number of groups that specifically asserted each view. This
means the same group for any given question was likely represented by
more than one opinion, as the statements, rather than being oppositional,
were often compatible and consistent with each other. Because Farm Radio Forum did not specifically indicate by what view and how often a particular group was represented, a solid statistical analysis of the responses
as they appear in the data sheets is impossible. By acknowledging the
"greatest number of groups" that claimed a particular viewpoint, however, we can at least determine the majority viewpoint among groups.

123 Ibid.

124 Brookdale Forum, Hastings, in "Farm Forum Findings," Equality for
Women, 15 December 1958, Farm Radio Forum, NA, Vol. 82, File – Farm
Forum Findings, 1 December–15 December 1958-"Equality for Women"
(1958).

125 The women in at least one group questioned whether they had privileges as women at all. See Harmony Forum, Bruce, in ibid.

126 "The Forums Speak!" Provincial Summary of Forum Findings, Equality
for Women, 15 and 16 December 1958, 1, Farm Radio Forum, NA, Vol. 98,
Binder.

127 Ibid.

128 "The Forums Speak!" Provincial Summary of Forum Findings, Women
in Their Place, 25 November 1968, 1, Farm Radio Forum, NA, Vol. 99,
Binder.

129 Ibid.

130 Ibid., 2. The largest number of groups, forty-two out of eighty-nine, gave
this response.

131 "Provincial Summary of Forum Findings," Farm Women in Public Life,
10 November 1952, 2, Farm Radio Forum, NA, Vol. 98, Binder. This summary report was based on 270 of the 540 groups which participated.

132 "Women's Institutes Celebrate 50th Anniversary," *Home and Country* 13 (Summer 1947): 1; Houck, "Snags and Snails," 3; Chapman, "The Women's Institute and the Family," 2.

133 Chapman, "Sixty-Fifth Anniversary," 3.

134 "Convention Areas Go Forward in Thinking And Working Toward Lasting Peace," *Home and Country* 12 (Fall and Winter 1946–47): 1.

135 As demonstrated in chapter 5, in the case of Emma Griesbach and UFWO followers, the opinions of provincial leaders could dramatically diverge from the views of local group members. Although it is difficult to establish with certainty that the perceptions of Ethel Chapman entirely reflected those of the larger WI membership, WI sources offer no indication that her views conflicted with popular opinion. She had long been an organizational leader, was seemingly moderate in her views, and was entirely sympathetic to the plight of the modern farm woman. Indeed, Chapman was greatly admired in rural Ontario. See Ambrose, *For Home and Country*, 183.

136 Chapman, "Can't We Study the Family, Too," 3; Chapman, "Women's Institutes and Home Economics," 3.

137 McBride, "Women in our Society To-day," 4.

138 Ibid.

139 "Mrs R.G. Purcell Elected Provincial President at Board Meeting," *Home and Country* 16, Summary issue, (1950–51): 1; "Here and There With the Women's Institutes," *Home and Country* 16, Summary Issue (1950–51): 8; "Here and There With the Women's Institutes," *Home and Country* 17, Overseas Tour Issue (February 1952): 12.

140 "Farm Women in Public Life," radio script, 10 November 1952, 4, 6, 7, Farm Radio Forum, NA, Vol. 15, File – C2-Radio Scripts, 1952–53.

141 McBride, "Women in our Society To-day," 4.

142 Ibid.

143 Pardy, "Adelaide Hoodless Said," 3.

144 Chapman, "Women's Institutes and Home Economics," 3; Chapman, "Can't We Study the Family, Too," 3.

145 Carbert, *Agrarian Feminism*, 17.

146 Ibid., 18.

147 Ibid.; Ambrose, *For Home and Country*, 191.

148 In schools, consumer education became part of a home economics curriculum designed "to keep up with our present complex society." See Marie Flanagan, "Boys Flock to Home Economics Course," *Toronto Star*, 19 April 1960, MIR, UGL, Macdonald Institute – History.

149 Chapman, "A Distinctive Organization," 3; Chapman, "The Women's Institute and the Family," 2.

150 Chapman, "The Road Ahead," 1; Graban, "Buying is Your Business," 24.

151 Graban, "Buying is Your Business," 24.

152 Keys, "Home Economics for Home and Country," 3.

153 Chapman, "Sixtieth Anniversary," 3.
154 Chapman, "Creative Homemaking," 3.
155 Ibid. Despite the WI's appreciation for women's traditional homemaking work, the term "creative homemaking" was never used at this time to mean a return to women's wholesale domestic production. "Creative homemaking" referred more to an approach to homemaking (resourceful and self-expressive) than it did to specific domestic assignments.
156 Cowan, *More Work for Mother*, 192. Cowan notes that "at the end of a day of housework, weary women know that, whether what they have been doing all day is called 'consumption' or 'purchasing' or 'maintaining our social status,' it still takes time and energy" (193). Cynthia Wright makes the interesting point that consumption must be defined by more than the purchase. It also includes "window-shopping [and] consumer desire," which also take up time and energy. See Wright, " 'Feminine Trifles of Vast Importance,' " 232.
157 Chapman, "Sixty-Fifth Anniversary," 3.
158 Cowan, *More Work for Mother*, 193.
159 Chapman, "To Learn About Family Living," 3. Perhaps indicative of a declining farm membership, farm women's paid labour was never conceptualized by the WI as "off-farm" employment, but more generically as work outside the home.
160 Chapman, "Can't We Study the Family, Too," 3; "Here and There With the Institutes," *Home and Country* 2 (Fall 1956): 27.
161 Chapman, "Can't We Study the Family, Too," 3; Chapman, "To Learn About Family Living," 3.
162 Leatherdale, "Provincial Board Holds Annual Meeting," 2; MacPhatter, "The President's Corner," 5.
163 Chapman, "A Thought for the Family," 3.
164 Pardy, "Adelaide Hoodless Said," 3.
165 Ibid.
166 Ibid.
167 Chapman, "To Learn About Family Living," 3.
168 FWIO, *Board Minutes*, May 1951, in Ambrose, *For Home and Country*, 160. The WI was lobbying for the Ontario Female Employees Fair Remuneration Act, which, when passed in 1951, became the first law in Canada to address equal pay for equal work. See Dranoff, *Women in Canadian Law*, 73. Of course, a system of equal pay for equal (same) work hardly proved advantageous to women who, because of a sexually segregated job market, seldom performed the identical work of men; McBride, "Women in our Society To-day," 4. Shared household labour, argued the Bluevale WI in Huron County, ultimately disadvantaged women, given that "women can do men's work better than men can do women's work." In light of this viewpoint, it should not be surprising that the

Fisherville wɪ in Haldimand-Norfolk gladly shared ideas about " 'what I leave my husband to eat when I am away for the day.' " See "Here and There With the Women's Institutes," *Home and Country* 24 (Summer 1958): 30, and *Home and Country* 22 (Summer 1956): 29.

169 Mrs T.D. Cowan, "Citizenship," *Home and Country* 8 (Spring 1942): 2.

170 See n. 148 above.

171 Chapman, "Programmes for Men, Too," 3.

172 "News Flashes," *Home and Country* 13 (Spring 1947): 2.

173 McBride, "Women in our Society To-day," 4.

174 Chapman, "Programmes for Men, Too," 3. Despite discussion of men joining the wɪ, the organization has essentially maintained its exclusively female membership.

175 Tryssenaar, "Changing the Subject," 56; Chapman, "Can't We Study the Family, Too," 3.

176 Tryssenaar, 53, 54, 132, 62, 110. Some of the home economics curricula persisted, as evidenced by the kitchens and sewing machines in many family studies classrooms. See 112.

177 Chapman, "A Distinctive Organization," 3.

178 Chapman, "Sixty-Fifth Anniversary," 3.

179 Chapman, "To Learn About Family Living," 3.

180 Ibid.

181 Chapman, "Sixtieth Anniversary," 3.

182 Chapman, "Can't We Study the Family, Too," 3, and Chapman, "To Learn About Family Living," 3; Chapman, "Sixty-Fifth Anniversary," 3.

183 "Extension Services for Homemakers," *Home and Country* 21 (Summer 1955): 20.

184 Chapman, "Programmes for Men, Too," 3.

185 *Home and Country* 22 (Fall 1956): 20.

186 Chapman, "Programmes for Men, Too," 3. The mention of boys here is in keeping with Chapman's consideration of co-education and home economics, but Chapman did not speak to the possibility of their housekeeping training.

187 Chapman, "A Distinctive Organization," 3.

188 Lewis, "Sincerely and Affectionately Yours," 2. McDermand was the superintendent from 1934 to 1939. She graduated from Macdonald Institute with a B.Sc., and attended Teachers' College at Columbia University. See Edith Collins, "Our Superintendents Throughout the Years," *Home and Country* 12, Golden Anniversary Issue (1947): 7; Sumners, "Our Tribute," 2; and Collins, "Our Superintendents Throughout the Years," 7. Mary A. Clarke was superintendent from 1939 to 1945; Collins, "Our Superintendents Throughout the Years," 7. Anna Lewis was superintendent from 1945 to 1955; "Our New Director," *Home and Country* 22 (Winter 1956): 4. Helen McKercher was director (of the Home Economics

Service of the Extension Branch of the Department of Agriculture) from 1956 to 1976. Many Canadian home economists did graduate degrees in the United States because Canadian universities, with the exception of the University of Toronto, did not offer graduate programs in home economics until the 1960s. The University of Toronto offered a Master's Degree beginning in 1914 and a PhD beginning in 1950. See Saidak, "The Inception of the Home Economics Movement," 156.

189 A booklet published by Macdonald Institute itself admitted in 1953 that there are people "who consider the study of home economics a 'frill' and perhaps even a waste of time." See *A Fiftieth Anniversary Sketch of the Development of Macdonald Institute, Ontario Agricultural College*, 1953, MIR, UGL, Macdonald Institute – History. Perhaps Chapman was herself the exception to the underappreciated home economist: for her contributions to Ontario rural life as a home economist, WI leader, journalist, and author, Chapman was awarded an honourary LLD from the University of Guelph in 1966. See Chapman, *Humanities in Homespun*, back cover, and Lewis, "Editorial," 3.

190 Chapman, "Women's Institutes and Home Economics," 3.

191 Tryssenaar, "Changing the Subject," 113.

192 Chapman, "Women's Institutes and Home Economics," 3.

193 Chapman, "New Trends and Old Traditions," 3.

194 "Here and There With the Institutes," *Home and Country* 22 (Summer 1956): 29.

195 Chapman, "Sixty-Fifth Anniversary," 3; "Record Attendance at Second Provincial Conference," *Home and Country* 16 (Spring 1950): 5; MacPhatter, "A Word From the President," 7.

196 Chapman, "New Trends and Old Traditions," 3.

197 "Programmes with a Broader Vision," *Home and Country* 18 (Summer 1952): 9.

198 Chapman, "New Trends and Old Traditions," 3.

199 MacPhatter, "A Word From the President," 7; "Superintendent Visits All Conventions," *Home and Country* 12 (Fall and Winter 1946–47): 2.

200 Chapman, "New Trends and Old Traditions," 3; Hodgins, "F.W.I.O. Board Meeting," 9; Chapman, "Sixty-Fifth Anniversary," 3. A member's address at a Wilton Grove WI meeting in 1951 reflected this new global outlook, and a new sensitivity to race relations. The talk, entitled "Racial Prejudice," condemned just that, and was the first of its kind at the club. See 17 May 1951, in WI Minute Books, Wilton Grove, UWO. In 1968, against the backdrop of the American civil rights movement, the Wilton Grove club again expressed a sensitivity to issues of race, although its efforts would be considered somewhat offensive and politically naive today. Discussions included "The Many Phases of Human Rights," "An Indian I Have Known or Read About," and "The Status of Indians in

Canada." At the final November meeting, members joined together to sing the civil rights anthem "We Shall Overcome," a supportive gesture, but one which seemed highly inappropriate for the virtually all white members. See 18 September and 20 November 1968, in WI Minute Books, Wilton Grove.

201 "We Face the Future," *Home and Country* 31 (Summer 1947): 2.

CHAPTER SEVEN

1 Cebotarev and Beattie, "Women Strengthening the Farm Community," 258.

2 Rankin, "The Politicization of Ontario Farm Women," 313.

3 Zwarun, "Farm Wives 10 Years After Irene Murdoch," 178. Property law was made more equitable for Ontario women in 1978 with the passage of the Family Law Reform Act, and again in 1986 with the act's revision. Since 1986, property acquired during marriage is to be divided equally between the spouses, as is their net worth, which includes income derived from property owned by a spouse before marriage (in the case of farming, more often the farm husband due to the patrilinear tradition of farm inheritance), and that property's increase in value. The matrimonial home is also to be divided equally, regardless of ownership, or when and how it was acquired. See Boivin, "Farm Women," 63–4, 67; Keet, "Matrimonial Property Legislation," 177. In 1976, the Alberta Supreme Court ruled in favour of a $65,000 divorce settlement for Murdoch, an amount worth only 25 per cent of the ranch's value. See Zwarun, "Farm Wives 10 Years After Irene Murdoch," 176.

4 Ibid., 59. The Murdoch case inspired other farm wives to claim property rights. Rosa Becker, for example, was an Ontario farm woman who in 1972 petitioned her abusive common-law husband of seventeen years for joint property rights after he ordered her off their honey farm. Although, unlike Murdoch, she had made a direct financial contribution to the farm, the case dragged on for years. It was 1980 before Becker finally won a settlement of $150,000 plus interest. Her former partner, however, balked at the order, and when the court went to confiscate his assets, he drained them by killing off the bees. Becker recouped $68,000 from a farm sale of what remained, but the full amount went straight to legal fees. In 1986, the year that the Family Law Reform Act was amended, a hopeless and penniless Becker committed suicide as an act of protest. See Smith, "Murdoch's, Becker's and Sorochan's Challenge," 158. The Canadian Advisory Council on the Status of Women dedicated its publication *Growing Strong: Women in Agriculture* to the memory of Rosa Becker.

5 Rankin, "The Politicization of Ontario Farm Women," 320, 322. The WSA (Dundas County), CFW (Bruce County), and OFWN were founded in 1975, 1981, and 1989 respectively.

6 Cebotarev and Beattie, "Women Strengthening the Farm Community," 259. These new farm women's organizations, however, sought government funding, protesting like the UFWO in the 1920s that which had long been exclusively allocated to the WI. See Ambrose, *For Home and Country*, 198–9.

7 Ontario, *Women in Rural Life*, 4. In conducting the study, the Ministry held forty-eight public hearings in twenty-four regions, and entertained 129 submissions from both individuals and groups. The report made thirty-three recommendations for the betterment of farm women's status and lives. See 4, 57–65. Louise Carbert asserts that "this report was for Ontario farm women the equivalent of the report of the Royal Commission of the Status of Women (1970) for all Canadian women." See Carbert, "Agrarian Feminism," 83.

8 Ambrose, *For Home and Country*, 194; Ontario, *Women in Rural Life*, 4.

9 See, for example, Carbert, "Agrarian Feminism"; Carbert, *Agrarian Feminism*; and Brandt and Black, " 'Il en faut un peu,' " 73–96.

10 Carbert, *Agrarian Feminism*, 27.

11 Carbert, "Agrarian Feminism," 108–9; Haley, "Getting Our Act Together," 172.

12 For a full explanation of this division, see Carbert, "Agrarian Feminism," 83.

13 Bongers, "Torn Between Tradition and Transition," 4.

14 Rankin, "The Politicization of Ontario Farm Women," 324.

15 Why the UFWO was not as successful as the new farm women's movement in crippling the social feminist influence of the WI may be attributed to a variety of reasons. The new movement was comprised of a network of autonomous groups to whom government funding was ultimately available; the UFWO stood alone as a "rival" to the WI, and was financially dependent on the unreceptive and politically doomed UFO. Moreover, farm women in the 1970s had a half-century longer to reflect on the limitations of social feminism, and, unlike farm women of the 1910s, were supported by a popular equity feminist women's movement that was defined not by a one-issue fight for equal rights (that is, suffrage), but by a number of equal rights concerns. The language of equal rights was far more prevalent in the 1970s than in the 1910s with the activism of other civil rights movements in Canada and the United States. Against this backdrop of equal rights battles, especially the Murdoch case, social feminism seemed dangerous. For many farm women, female domesticity came to mean female vulnerability, female specificity came to mean female discrimination, and female separatism came to mean female exclusion.

16 Rankin, "The Politicization of Ontario Farm Women," 324; Carbert, "Agrarian Feminism," 106.

17 Brigid Pyke, in Rankin, "The Politicization of Ontario Farm Women," 313.
18 Ontario, *Women in Rural Life*, 24.
19 Ibid.
20 Ibid., 47. Farm women found little use for these courses partly because information of this kind was easily accessible in newspapers and magazines.
21 Ibid., 38. Their resistance to traditional same-sex groups, in particular, is partly attributable to "women's time pressures, their interest in single-purpose issues, and their desire to pursue hobbies in depth," none of which were accommodated by traditional organizations, like the wi, "with their all-encompassing objectives and programs" (39).
22 Rankin, "The Politicization of Ontario Farm Women," 322.
23 Ibid.
24 Ibid. Like the ufwo over a half-century before, cfw, particularly in Bruce and Grey Counties, despite its "initial subordination of women's issues and its commitment to working co-operatively with existing agricultural interest groups," faced "overt hostility from male farmers." Eventually, this treatment "forced cfw to confront the pervasiveness of gender bias within the rural community," and compelled the group to address "women's issues" along with critical economic concerns (323).
25 Ibid., 325, 326.
26 Cebotarev, "From Domesticity to the Public Sphere," 214; Cebotarev and Beattie, "Women Strengthening the Farm Community," 260.
27 Carbert, "Agrarian Feminism," 233.
28 Ibid.
29 Ambrose, *For Home and Country*, 198.
30 Moreover, given the decreasing number and declining political influence of rural Ontarians over the century, the government saw little political benefit in continuing to sponsor the wi. See ibid. Almost certainly, Molly McGhee's study *Women in Rural Life* was commissioned, in part, to confirm for the government that the wi no longer warranted provincial support.

Bibliography

ARCHIVAL SOURCES

HAMILTON PUBLIC LIBRARY SPECIAL COLLECTIONS (HPL)
Hoodless, Adelaide Hunter. Scrapbook (1894–   )

KITCHENER PUBLIC LIBRARY: GRACE SCHMIDT ROOM
OF LOCAL HISTORY (KPL)
Oral History Tapes, Rural Women (OHT)
– Lucinda Allendorf, interview by Joanne Venton, 18 April 1982
– Selina Horst, interview by Frances Hoffman, 28 March 1990
– Roxie Hostetler, interview by Ryan Taylor, 27 July 1992
– Louise Ritz, interview by Joanne Venton, 26 March 1987
– Abigail Shearer, interview by Frances Hoffman, 19 September 1989
– Beatrice Snyder, interview by Joanne Venton, 2 June 1982

MARKHAM DISTRICT HISTORICAL MUSEUM (MDHM)
Anna Burkholder Diaries, 1899–1903; prior to 1911

NATIONAL ARCHIVES OF CANADA (NA)
W.C. Good Papers
– Volume 5, File – Correspondence, 1922
Agnes Macphail Papers
Neil Morrison Papers
National Farm Radio Forum. Section II – Ontario Farm Radio Forum
Robert Alexander Sim Papers

Women's Institute at Stoney Creek
– Minute Book, Woman's Institute of Saltfleet

QUEEN'S UNIVERSITY: THE EDITH AND LORNE PIERCE
COLLECTION OF CANADIANA, JOSEPH S. STAUFFER
LIBRARY (QU)
Federated Women's Institutes of Canada. Pamphlet. October 1977
The Federated Women's Institutes of Ontario. *Fiftieth Anniversary Celebration.*
Souvenir program. 18 June 1947
Ontario Department of Agriculture. *Report of the Women's Institutes of the Prov-
ince of Ontario*, 1909, part 1. Toronto: 1910
– *Report of the Women's Institutes of the Province of Ontario, 1916,* part 1.
Toronto: 1917
– *Report of the Women's Institutes of the Province of Ontario, 1917,* part 1.
Toronto: 1918
– *Report of the Women's Institutes of the Province of Ontario, 1918,* part 1.
Toronto: 1919
– *Report of the Women's Institutes of the Province of Ontario, 1922.* Toronto: 1923
Nash, Mrs. Chester. *The First Women's Institute in the World was Founded in
Stoney Creek.* Pamphlet. 1966
Rand, Elizabeth. *Federated Women's Institutes of Canada.* Pamphlet. 1961
South Waterloo District Women's Institute and Its 15 Branches, 1903–1953. Pam-
phlet. 1953
Walker, Annie, et al. *Fifty Years of Achievement.* n.p.: Federated Women's Insti-
tutes of Ontario 1948

SIMCOE COUNTY ARCHIVES, MINESING, ONTARIO (SCA)
Collingwood Enterprise-Messenger
Death Register for Johanna Griesbach, 1913

UNIVERSITY OF GUELPH LIBRARY ARCHIVAL
COLLECTIONS (UGL)
Helen C. Abell Collection
Lillian A. Beattie Papers 1911–c.1950
– "Working for Skirts" (unpublished memoir)
The Canadian Countryman (Box 3309)
– Black, J.R. "A Plea for Farmers' Daughters." Vol. 3 (24 October 1916): 11
– Brown, Edna I. "What Girls Need Most in a Rural Community." Vol. 15
(15 May 1926): 14, 20–21
– Corkery, Mary. "What Girls Need Most in a Rural Community." Vol. 15
(15 May 1926): 14, 20–21
– Ladd, Mariella. "The Farmer's Wife as a Partner[:] How to Cash in on
the Woman's Intuition, Common Sense and Power of Argument!" Vol. 3
(15 August 1914): 6

– McIntosh, J.E. "Lo! The Poor Farmer's Wife." Vol. 16 (10 September 1927): 2, 35
– Pringle, Jennie A. "What Girls Need Most in a Rural Community." Vol. 15 (15 May 1926): 14, 20–21
Leonard Harman/United Cooperatives of Ontario Collection. The United Farm Women of Ontario
– Minutes of Meetings of United Farm Women, 1918–1948
Hoodless Family Papers (HFP)
Huron County Oral History Project Collection (1980–81, 1991) (OHP)
– Anne Henry, interview by Catherine A. Wilson and Gordon H. Hak
– Emma Johnston, interview by Catherine A. Wilson and Gordon H. Hak
– Janet McPherson, interview by Catherine A. Wilson and Gordon H. Hak
Macdonald Institute Records 1903–64 (MIR)
– Associate Director, Dorothy M. Lindsley (1947–49), Correspondence
– Macdonald Institute – History. Development of Home Economics in Canada
Ontario Farm Movements Collection
Smith Falls, Town of. Minute Book of the Smith Falls UFWO

UNIVERSITY OF WATERLOO SPECIAL COLLECTIONS (UW)
Elizabeth Smith Shortt Collection. Correspondence
Elizabeth Smith Shortt and Muriel Clarke

THE UNIVERSITY OF WESTERN ONTARIO: THE J.J. TALMAN
REGIONAL COLLECTION (UWO)
Women's Institute. Minute Books. Wilton Grove and Norton Branch, East Middlesex County, Ontario 1909–87

OTHER PRIMARY SOURCES

Elaine Bitz. Interview by author, 15 April 1993, London, Ontario
Ethel Hillier (MacDonald) Diaries, 1904–27
"This is My Story," by Jean Lozier. Unpublished Memoir, 1993
Vera May Hood. Interview by Melanie Clare, 11, 15, 18 March 1994, Frankford, Ontario
Women's Institute, Newspaper Clippings

PRINTED SOURCES

Aitken, Kate. Never a Day So Bright. Toronto: Longmans, Green 1956
Ambrose, Linda. "Problems in Doing Rural Women's History: The Case of the Ontario Women's Institutes." (Paper presented at the Annual Meeting of the Canadian Historical Association, Calgary, AB 1994)
– " 'The University for Rural Women': The Role of the Women's Institutes of Ontario as a Solution to Rural Isolation, 1897–1920." (Paper presented at

"Women Overcoming Obstacles," The Ontario Women's History Network, University of Guelph October 1993)

Ambrose, Linda M. *For Home and Country: The Centennial History of the Women's Institutes in Ontario*. Erin, ON: Boston Mills Press 1996

– "'What Are the Good of Those Meetings Anyway?'": Early Popularity of the Ontario Women's Institutes." *Ontario History* 87 (Spring 1995): 1–19

Ambrose, Linda M., and Margaret Kechnie. "Social Control or Social Feminism: Two Views of the Ontario Women's Institutes," *Agricultural History* 73 (Spring 1999): 222–37

Amey, Edward. *Farm Life As It Should Be and Farm Labourers' and Servant Girls' Grievances*. Toronto: Ellis and Moore 1885[?]

Anderson, Allan. *Remembering the Farm: Memories of Farming, Ranching and Rural Life in Canada, Past and Present*. Toronto: Macmillan 1977

Atkeson, Mary Meek. "Women in Farm Life and Rural Economy." *The Annals of The American Academy of Political and Social Science* 143 (May 1929): 188–94

Babb, Nettie. "A Young Woman's Accomplishments." *Home and Country* 1 (March and April 1934): 7–8

Bacchi, Carol. "Divided Allegiances: The Response of Farm and Labour Women to Suffrage." In *A Not Unreasonable Claim: Women and Reform in Canada, 1880s-1920s*, edited by Linda Kealey, 89–107. Toronto: Women's Press 1979

– *Liberation Deferred? The Ideas of the English-Canadian Suffragists, 1877–1918*. Toronto: University of Toronto Press 1983; reprinted 1989

Backhouse, Constance B. "Agnes Macphail and Feminism." Review of *Agnes Macphail and the Politics of Equality* by Terry Crowley. *Canadian Journal of Law and Society* 7 (1992): 143–52

Barber, Marilyn. "Help for Farm Homes: The Campaign to End Housework Drudgery in Rural Saskatchewan in the 1920's." *Scientia Canadensis* 9 (June 1985): 3–26

Bass, T.H. "The Woman on the Farm." *O.A.C. Review* 24 (July 1912): 560–2

Bassett, Isabel. *The Parlour Rebellion: Profiles in the Struggle for Women's Rights*. Toronto: McClelland and Stewart 1974

Baxter, Annette K. "Preface" to *The Clubwoman as Feminist: True Womanhood Redefined, 1868–1914*, by Karen Blair. New York: Holmes and Meier Publishers 1980

Beattie, Jessie. *Along the Road*. Toronto: Ryerson Press 1954

– *A Season Past: Reminiscences of a Rural Canadian Childhood*. Toronto: McClelland and Stewart 1968

– *A Walk Through Yesterday: Memoirs of Jessie L. Beattie*. Toronto: McClelland and Stewart 1976

Bercuson, David J., and J.L. Granatstein. *The Collins Dictionary of Canadian History, 1867 to the Present*. Don Mills, ON: Collins Publishers 1988

Bettmann, Otto L. *The Good Old Days – They Were Terrible!* New York: Random House 1974

Black, Naomi. "Macphail: First Among Equals." Review of *Agnes Macphail and the Politics of Equality* by Terry Crowley. *Globe and Mail*, 23 February 1991, section c, 14

– *Social Feminism.* Ithaca: Cornell University Press 1989

Black, Naomi, and Gail Cuthbert Brandt. *Feminist Politics on the Farm: Rural Catholic Women in Southern Quebec and Southwestern France.* Montreal and Kingston: McGill-Queen's University Press 1999

Blair, Karen. *The Clubwoman as Feminist: True Womanhood Redefined, 1868–1914.* New York: Holmes and Meier Publishers 1980

Bloomfield, Elizabeth, et al. *Guelph and Wellington County: A Bibliography of Settlement and Development Since 1800.* Guelph: Guelph Regional Project, University of Guelph 1988

– *Inventory of Primary and Archival Sources: Guelph and Wellington County.* Guelph: Guelph Regional Project, University of Guelph 1989

Boivin, Michelle. "Farm Women: Obtaining Legal and Economic Recognition of Their Work." In *Growing Strong: Women in Agriculture*, 49–90. Ottawa: Canadian Advisory Council on the Status of Women 1987

Bongers, Agnes. "Torn Between Tradition and Transition, Women's Institute." *Ontario Farm Women* 1 (17 March 1985): 4–5, 9

Bovy, Barbara. "Feminist Research: Implications for Home Economics Education." In *Knowledge Technology, and Family Change*, edited by Patricia J. Thompson, 293–316. Bloomington, IL: Bennett and McKnight 1984

Brandt, Gail Cuthbert, and Naomi Black. "'Il en faut un peu': Farm Women and Feminism in Quebec and France Since 1945." *Journal of the Canadian Historical Association* 1 (1990): 73–96

Breault, Erin. "Educating Women About the Law: Violence Against Wives in Ontario, 1850–1920." M.A. thesis, University of Toronto 1986

Breese, M. "The Woman Upon the Farm." *o.a.c. Review* 24 (June 1912): 494–6

Brodie, Mrs George A. "'Three Points' of the United Farm Women." *Farmers' Sun*, 13 August 1919, 6

Brookes, A.A., et al. "Religion and the Rural Community, 1890–1930: Some Oral Testimony From North Huron." Fifth Annual Agricultural History of Ontario Seminar, 52–66. University of Guelph 1980

Brookes, Alan A., and Catharine A. Wilson. "'Working Away' From the Farm: The Young Women of North Huron, 1910–1930." *Ontario History* 77 (December 1985): 281–300

Brown, Robert Craig, and Ramsay Cook. *Canada 1896–1921: A Nation Transformed.* Toronto: McClelland and Stewart 1974; reprinted 1988

Bruère, Martha, and Robert Bruère. "The Revolt of the Farmer's Wife!" *Harper's Bazaar* (November-April 1912–13): "War on Drudgery," 539; "Waylaying Education," 601–2; "The Social Significance of the Bumper

Crop," 15–16; "The Campaign Against Sickness," 67–8; "The Waste of Old Women," 115–16; "After the Revolt," 166

Bruners, Daina. "The Influence of the Women's Liberation Movement on the Lives of Canadian Farm Women." *Resources for Feminist Research* 14 (1985): 18–19

Buchanan, W. "The Woman on the Farm." *o. a. c. Review* 24 (May 1912): 448–50

Campbell, Helen Richards. *From Chalk Dust to Hayseed.* Belleville, on: Mika Publishing Company 1975

Canada. Dominion Bureau of Statistics. *Seventh Census of Canada, 1931*
– Dominion Bureau of Statistics. *Census of Canada* 1951
– Minister of Supply and Services. *Women's Archives Guide: Manuscript Sources for the History of Women*, by Joanna Dean and David Fraser 1991

Carbert, Louise I. "Agrarian Feminism: The Politicization of Ontario Farm Women." Ph.D. diss., York University 1991
– *Agrarian Feminism: The Politics of Ontario Farm Women.* Toronto: University of Toronto Press 1995

Carroll, J.A. "The Agricultural Battle 1943." *Home and Country* 9 (Spring 1943): 1–2

Cebotarev, E.A. (Nora). "From Domesticity to the Public Sphere: Farm Women, 1945–86." In *A Diversity of Women: Ontario, 1945–1980*, edited by Joy Parr, 200–31. Toronto: University of Toronto Press 1995

Cebotarev, Nora, and Kathleen Beattie. "Women Strengthening the Farm Community: The Case of the 'Concerned Farm Women' Group in Ontario." In *Farming and the Rural Community in Ontario: An Introduction*, edited by Anthony M. Fuller, 255–328. Toronto: Foundation for Rural Living 1985

Chambers, Lori. *Married Women and Property Law in Victorian Ontario.* Toronto: Osgoode Society for Canadian Legal History 1997

Chapman, Ethel. "Can't We Study the Family, Too?" *Home and Country* 30 (Fall 1964): 3
– "Could We Make This a Summer Fallow Year?" *Home and Country* 22 (Winter 1956): 3
– "Creative Homemaking." *Home and Country* 24 (Winter 1958): 3
– "A Distinctive Organization." *Home and Country* 32 (Fall 1966): 3
– Editorial. *Home and Country* 27 (Winter 1961): 3
– "How the Women's Institutes can Cooperate with Fair Boards." *Ontario Farmer* (20 February 1926): 18
– *Humanities in Homespun.* Toronto: Ryerson Press 1969
– "Let's Not Lose Our Human Appeal." *Home and Country* 29 (Fall 1963): 3
– "Machinery For Women – Why it Pays." *Farmer's Magazine* (1 December 1918): 54
– "Mrs. Adelaide Hoodless," 14–20. In *Pioneers in Adult Education*, 14–20. Toronto: Thomas Nelson and Sons 1953

- "New Trends and Old Traditions." *Home and Country* 28 (Fall 1962): 3
- "Programmes for Men, Too." *Home and Country* 22 (Fall 1956): 3
- "The Road Ahead." *Home and Country* 12 (Fall 1945): 1
- "Senior Neighboring." *Home and Country* 30 (Winter 1964): 3
- "Sixtieth Anniversary." *Home and Country* 23 (Winter 1957): 3
- "Sixty-Fifth Anniversary." *Home and Country* 28 (Winter 1962): 3
- "A Thought for the Family." *Home and Country* 20 (Summer 1954): 3
- "To Learn About Family Living." *Home and Country* 32 (Winter 1966): 3
- "Women's Institutes and Home Economics." *Home and Country* 33 (Winter 1967): 3
- "The Women's Institute and the Family." *Home and Country* 35 (Winter 1969): 27–9

Clare, Melanie. "Sacrifice, Reward and Equality: Women on Rural Ontario Farms." Undergraduate history essay, Queen's University 1994

Clark, Judith Freeman. *Almanac of American Women in the 20th Century*. New York: Prentice Hall 1987

Cleverdon, Catherine. *The Women's Suffrage Movement in Canada*. Toronto: University of Toronto Press 1950; reprinted 1975

Cohen, Marjorie Griffin. "The Canadian Women's Movement." In *Canadian Women's Issues: Twenty-Five Years of Women's Activism in English Canada*, vol. 1: *Strong Voices*, edited by Ruth Roach Pierson et al., 1–31. Toronto: James Lorimer & Company 1993

- "The Decline of Women in Canadian Dairying." In *The Neglected Majority: Essays in Canadian Women's History*, vol. 2, edited by Alison Prentice and Susan Mann Trofimenkoff, 61–83. Toronto: McClelland and Stewart 1985

- *Women's Work, Markets, and Economic Development in Nineteenth-Century Ontario*. Toronto: University of Toronto Press 1988

Collins, Edith. "Our Superintendents Through the Years." *Home and Country* 12 (Golden Anniversary Issue, 1947): 7

Connelly, Kate I. "Miss Agnes McPhail M.P. Friend of Farm Women." *London Advertiser*, 5 April 1926, 4

Conroy, Mary. *300 Years of Canadian Quilts*. Toronto: Griffin House 1976

Cook, Elizabeth Adell. "Measuring Feminist Consciousness." *Women & Politics* 9 (1989): 71–88

Costantakos, Chrysie M. "The Home Economics Idea: An Etymological Odyssey." In *Knowledge, Technology, and Family Change*, edited by Patricia J. Thompson, 176–94. Bloomington, IL: Bennett and McKnight 1984

Cott, Nancy F. *The Grounding of Modern Feminism*. New Haven: Yale University Press 1987

- "What's in a Name? The Limits of 'Social Feminism'; or, Expanding the Vocabulary of Women's History." *Journal of American History* 76 (December 1989): 809–29

Cowan, Ruth Schwartz. *More Work for Mother: The Ironies of Household Technology from the Open Hearth to the Microwave.* New York: Basic Books 1983
Cowan, T.D. "Citizenship." *Home and Country* 8 (Spring 1942): 2
Coward, Raymond T., and William M. Smith, Jr. "Introduction" to *The Family in Rural Society,* edited by Raymond T. Coward and William M. Smith, Jr. Boulder: Westview Press 1981
Cowsrough, J. "Paisley Plock U.F.W.O." *Farmers' Sun,* 22 December 1920, 6
Cragg, Kenneth C. *Father on the Farm.* Toronto: Longmans, Green 1947
Crowley, Terry. "Adelaide Hoodless' Vision." (Paper presented at "Women Overcoming Obstacles," The Ontario Women's History Network, University of Guelph October 1993)
– *Agnes Macphail and the Politics of Equality.* Toronto: James Lorimer & Company 1990
– "Experience and Representation: Southern Ontario Farm Women and Agricultural Change, 1870–1914." *Agricultural History* 73 (Spring 1999): 238–51
– "J.J. Morrison and the Transition in Canadian Farm Movements During the Early Twentieth Century." *Agricultural History* 71 (Summer 1997): 330–56
– "Madonnas Before Magdalenes: Adelaide Hoodless and the Making of the Canadian Gibson Girl." *Canadian Historical Review* 67 (1986): 520–47
– "The New Canada Movement: Agrarian Youth Protest in the 1930s." *Ontario History* 80 (September 1988): 311–26
– "The Origins of Continuing Education for Women: The Ontario Women's Institutes." *Canadian Woman Studies* 7 (Fall 1986): 78–81
Dahms, Fred A. "Ontario's Rural Communities: Changing Not Dying." In *Farming and the Rural Community in Ontario: An Introduction,* edited by Anthony M. Fuller, 329–49. Toronto: Foundation for Rural Living 1985
Davies, Stephen James. "Ontario and the Automobile, 1900–1930: Aspects of Technological Integration." Ph.D. diss., McMaster University 1987
Dawson, M.C. "Politics, Woman and the Boon She Will Crave." *Farmer's Advocate* 54 (11 December 1919): 2233–4
– "The Woman on the Farm." *O.A.C. Review* 24 (May 1912): 405–7
Densmore, David. *Seasons of Change: Sketches of Life on the Farm.* Toronto: Summerhill Press/Etue and Company 1987
Diana [Emma Griesbach]. "The Community Idea." *Farmers' Sun,* 13 August 1919, 6
– "Community or Cooperative Utilities." *Farmers' Sun,* 31 January 1920, 6
– "Now Let's See, Where Are We?" *Weekly Sun,* 3 July 1918, 6
– "A Peep at My Letters." *Weekly Sun,* 5 March 1919, 6
– "Ruts." *Farmers' Sun,* 15 October 1919, 6
– "Short Lengths." *Weekly Sun,* 12 February 1919, 6
– "The Work and Waste of Women." *Weekly Sun,* 5 March 1919, 6
– "The Work and Waste of Women." *Weekly Sun,* 12 March 1919, 6

Dranoff, Linda Silver. *Women in Canadian Law.* Toronto: Fitzhenry & Whiteside 1977

Dubinsky, Karen. *Improper Advances: Rape and Heterosexual Conflict in Ontario, 1880–1929.* Chicago: University of Chicago Press 1993

Duke, Emma M. "Resolutions Indicate Interests of Members." *Home and Country* 10 (Winter 1944–45): 4

– "Salute to Members." *Home and Country* 8 (Winter 1942–43): 1, 4

Durnin, F. "Family Relationships Important." *Home and Country* 1 (January 1935): 3

Dutchak, Phyllis E. *College With a Purpose: A History of the Kemptville College of Agricultural Technology 1916–1973.* Belleville, Ontario: Mika Publishing Company 1976

Dymond, Allan M. *The Laws of Ontario Relating to Women and Children.* Toronto: Clarkson W. James 1923

Eadie, F.P. "Juniors Work Faithfully." *Home and Country* 9 (Summer 1943): 3

Edwards, O.C. "Compilation." In *Women of Canada: Their Life and Work,* 63–90. Compiled by the National Council of Women of Canada, 1900; reprinted National Council of Women of Canada 1975

Elbert, Sarah. "The Challenge of Research on Farm Women." *Rural Sociologist* 1 (November 1981): 383–6

– "The Farmer Takes a Wife: Women in America's Farming Families." In *Women, Households, and the Economy,* edited by Lourdes Beneria and Catharine R. Stimpson, 173–97. New Brunswick: Rutgers University Press 1987

Fazier, F.H. "A Woman Worker." *Farmers' Sun,* 22 December 1920, 6

Ferguson, Alice A. "Should Daughters Be Compensated for Their Labor?" *Farm and Dairy* (8 October 1914): 6

– "What Education Should Farmers' Daughters Receive." *Farm and Dairy* (8 January 1914): 17

Ferguson, J.J. "Giving the Girls a Chance." *Farmer's Advocate* 35 (15 January 1900): 35, 36

Fink, Deborah. *Agrarian Women: Wives and Mothers in Rural Nebraska, 1880–1940.* Chapel Hill: University of North Carolina Press 1992

– "Sidelines and Moral Capital: Women on Nebraska Farms in the 1930s." In *Women and Farming: Changing Roles, Changing Structures,* edited by Wava G. Haney and Jane B. Knowles, 55–70. Boulder: Westview Press 1988

Flora, Cornelia Butler. "Public Policy and Women in Agricultural Production: A Comparative and Historical Analysis." In *Women and Farming: Changing Roles, Changing Structures,* edited by Wava G. Haney and Jane B. Knowles, 265–80. Boulder: Westview Press 1988

Freedman, Estelle. "Separatism as Strategy: Female Institution Building and American Feminism, 1870–1930." In *Women and Power in American History: A Reader,* vol. 2, edited by Kathryn Kish Sklar and Thomas Dublin, 10–24. Englewood Cliffs, NJ: Prentice Hall 1991

Friedan, Betty. *The Feminine Mystique*. New York: Dell Publishing 1963; reprinted 1974

Fuller, Anthony M. "Appendix Two: National Farm Radio Forum." In *Farming and the Rural Community in Ontario: An Introduction*, edited by Anthony M. Fuller. Toronto: Foundation for Rural Living 1985

Fuller, Tony. "The Development of Farm Life and Farming in Ontario." In *Farming and the Rural Community in Ontario: An Introduction*, edited by Anthony M. Fuller, 1–46. Toronto: Foundation for Rural Living 1985

Garkovich, Lorraine, and Janet Bokemeier. "Agricultural Mechanization and American Farm Women's Economic Roles." In *Women and Farming: Changing Roles, Changing Structures*, edited by Wava G. Haney and Jane B. Knowles, 211–28. Boulder: Westview Press 1988

Good, William Charles. *Farmer Citizen: My Fifty Years in the Canadian Farmers' Movement*. Toronto: Ryerson Press 1958

Graban, Florence S. "Buying is Your Business." *Home and Country* 22 (Summer 1956): 24–5

Graff, Linda L. "Industrialization of Agriculture: Implications for the Position of Farm Women." *Resources for Feminist Research* 11 (March 1982): 10–11

Graham, Elizabeth. "Schoolmarms and Early Teaching in Ontario." In *Women at Work, 1850–1930*, edited by Janice Acton et al., 165–209. Toronto: Canadian Women's Educational Press 1974

Graham and Hemming (Misses). "Women in Agriculture." *O.A.C. Review* 32 (1920): 468–9

Grayson, Linda, and Michael Bliss, editors. *The Wretched of Canada: Letters to R.B. Bennett, 1930–1935*. Toronto: University of Toronto Press 1971

Griesbach, Emma. "A Challenge Accepted." *Weekly Sun*, 19 March 1919, 6

– "The Corner" [regular column]. *Weekly Sun*, 16 October 1918, 6

– "The Corner." *Farmers' Sun*, 4 June 1919, 6

– "The Corner." *Farmers' Sun*, 2 July 1919, 6

– "The Farm Woman of To-day." *O.A.C. Review* 32 (1919): 57–9

– "Glen Lily's View." *Weekly Sun*, 15 January 1919, 6

– "Letters from Farm Women." *Farmers' Sun*, 25 June 1919, 6

– "On Organizing." *Farmers' Sun*, 22 October 1919, 6

– "Progress of United Farm Women Reported by the Secretary." *Farmers' Sun*, 24 December 1919, 23

– "A Talk on 'Form.'" *Farmers' Sun*, 9 July 1919, 6

– "The Views of Our Delegates." *Weekly Sun*, 18 December 1919, 6

– "Will You Vote for Freedom." *Farmers' Sun*, 8 October 1919, 6

Growing Strong: Women in Agriculture. Ottawa: Canadian Advisory Council on the Status of Women 1987

Haley, Ella. "Getting Our Act Together: The Ontario Farm Women's Movement." In *Women and Social Change: Feminist Activism in Canada*, edited by

Jeri Dawn Wine and Janice L. Ristock, 169–83. Toronto: James Lorimer & Company 1991

Halpern, Monda. "Beyond the Dell: Farm Women and Feminism in Early Twentieth-Century Ontario." *Matrix* (July/August 1992): 7–10

– "Beyond the Dell: Farm Women and Feminism in Early Twentieth-Century Ontario." In *(SA)FIRE WORKS: More Works in Progress by Students of Feminism(s)*, 36–40. Published as Centre for Women's Studies and Feminist Research, Working Paper No. 10, vol. 2, March 1994. SAFIRE Conference: (SA)FIRE WORKS, University of Western Ontario April/May 1992

– " 'Practically Part of the Government': The Women's Institutes of Ontario, 1897–1919." Graduate history essay, Queen's University 1989

Halpern, Monda M. " 'Our Mother Earth Has Called Us': A Study of the Woman's Land Army of America, World War I." M.A. thesis, The University of Western Ontario 1988

Haney, Wava G., and Jane B. Knowles. "Introduction: Making 'The Invisible Farmer' Visible." In *Women and Farming: Changing Roles, Changing Structures*, edited by Wava G. Haney and Jane B. Knowles. Boulder: Westview Press 1988

Hayden, Dolores. *The Grand Domestic Revolution: A History of Feminist Designs for American Homes, Neighborhoods, and Cities*. Cambridge: MIT Press 1981

Hodgins, Ina. "F.W.I.O. Board Meeting." *Home and Country* 22 (Winter 1956): 5–7

Holt, Marilyn Irvin. *Linoleum, Better Babies, and The Modern Farm Woman, 1890–1930*. Albuquerque: University of New Mexico Press 1995

hooks, bell. "Black Women: Shaping Feminist Theory." In *Issues in Feminism: An Introduction to Women's Studies*, edited by Sheila Ruth, 33–9. Mountain View, CA: Mayfield Publishing 1990

Hopkins, Maria V. "The Trend of the Women's Institutes in Ontario." *Farmer's Advocate* 63 (16 February 1928): 251

Houck, J.E. "Snags and Snails in Women's Institute Work." *Home and Country* 15 (Summer 1949): 3

Houlton, Emilia. "Gardening as a Profession for Women." *Farm and Dairy* Third Annual Special Magazine Household Number (5 October 1911): 4

Hovius, Berend, and Timothy G. Youdan. *The Law of Family Property*. Scarborough: Carswell 1991

Hughs, John Starrett. "The Madness of Separate Spheres: Insanity and Masculinity in Victorian Alabama." In *Meanings for Manhood: Constructions of Masculinity in Victorian America*, edited by Mark C. Carnes and Clyde Griffen, 53–66. Chicago: University of Chicago Press 1990

Hundertmark, Susan. "Rural Feminism." *Healthsharing* (Winter 1985): 14–17

Hunter, Georgina. "Compilation." In *Women of Canada: Their Life and Work*, 112–49. Compiled by the National Council of Women of Canada 1900; reprinted National Council of Women of Canada 1975

Jensen, Joan M. *With These Hands: Women Working on the Land*. Old Westbury, NY: The Feminist Press 1981

Jensen, Leda. "Stress in the Farm Family Unit." *Resources for Feminist Research* 11 (March 1982): 11–12

Johnston, Charles M. " 'A Motley Crowd': Diversity in the Ontario Countryside in the Early Twentieth-Century," In *Canadian Papers in Rural History*, vol. 7, edited by Donald H. Akenson, 237–56. Gananoque, ON: Langdale Press 1990

Johnston, William Victor. *Before the Age of Miracles: Memoirs of a Country Doctor*. Toronto: Fitzhenry and Whiteside 1972

Jones, David C. " 'From Babies to Buttonholes': Women's Work at Agricultural Fairs." *Alberta History* 29 (1981): 26–32

Jull, W.M. "Ready Money Representing Real Profit Made by a Woman." *Farm and Dairy* Third Annual Special Magazine Household Number (5 October 1911): 3

Kaledin, Eugenia. *Mothers and More: American Women in the 1950s*. Boston: Twayne Publishers 1984

Kechnie, Margaret. "Keeping Things Tidy for Home and Country: The Early Years of the Ontario Women's Institutes." Ph.D. diss., Ontario Institute for Studies in Education 1995

– "The United Farm Women of Ontario: Developing a Political Consciousness." *Ontario History* 77 (December 1985): 267–80

– "The Women's Institutes in Northern Ontario, 1905–1930: Imitators or Innovators?" In *Changing Lives: Women in Northern Ontario*, edited by Margaret Kechnie and Marge Reitsma-Street, 263–74. Toronto: Dundurn Press 1996

Keet, Jean E. "Matrimonial Property Legislation: Are Farm Women Equal Partners?" In *The Political Economy of Agriculture in Western Canada*, edited by G.S. Basran and D.A. Hay, 175–84. Toronto: Garamond Press 1988

Kelly, J.K. "Home Economics Aids in War Time." *Home and Country* 6 (Winter 1939–40): 3

– "Home Economics Challenges Women." *Home and Country* 7 (Fall 1941): 2

– "1944 Calling Farm Daughters." *Home and Country* 9 (Winter 1944): 2

Keys, G.W. "Home Economics for Total Victory." *Home and Country* 11 (Spring 1945): 2

Keys, Mrs Wilmer. "Home Economics for Home and Country." *Home and Country* 10 (Spring 1944): 3

Kinnear, Mary. " 'Do You Want Your Daughter to Marry a Farmer?': Women's Work on the Farm, 1922." In *Canadian Papers in Rural History*, vol. 6, edited by Donald H. Akenson, 137–53. Gananoque, ON: Langdale Press 1988

Knowles, Jane B. " 'It's Our Turn Now': Rural American Women Speak Out, 1900–1920." In *Women and Farming: Changing Roles, Changing Structures*, edited by Wava G. Haney and Jane B. Knowles, 303–18. Boulder: Westview Press 1988

Kohl, Seena B. "Image and Behaviour: Women's Participation in North American Family Agricultural Enterprises." In *Women and Farming: Changing Roles, Changing Structures*, edited by Wava G. Haney and Jane B. Knowles, 89–108. Boulder: Westview Press 1988

– "The Making of a Community: The Role of Women in the Agricultural Setting." In *Kin and Communities: Families in America*, edited by Allan J. Lichtman and Joan R. Challinor, 175–86. Washington, D.C.: Smithsonian International Symposium Series 1979

Koven, Seth, and Sonya Michel, editors. *Mothers of a New World: Maternalist Politics and the Origins of Welfare States*. New York: Routledge 1993

Kraditor, Aileen S. *The Ideas of the Woman Suffrage Movement, 1890–1920*. New York: Columbia University Press 1965; reprinted New York: W.W. Norton & Company 1981

Ladell, John, and Monica Ladell. *A Farm in the Family: The Many Faces of Ontario Agriculture Over the Centuries*. Toronto: Dundurn Press 1985

– *Inheritance: Ontario's Century Farms Past and Present*. Toronto: Macmillan of Canada 1979

Langford, Nanci, and Norah Keating. "Social Isolation and Alberta Farm Women." In *Women: Isolation and Bonding*, edited by Kathleen Storrie, 47–58. Toronto: Methuen 1987

Latzer, Beth Good. *Myrtleville: A Canadian Farm and Family, 1837–1967*. Carbondale and Edwardsville, IL: Southern Illinois University Press 1976

Lawr, D. A. "The Development of Ontario Farming, 1870–1914: Pattern of Growth and Change." *Ontario History* 64 (December 1972): 239–51

Laws, H.L. "Another Busy Week." *Farmers' Sun*, 5 June 1920, 6

– "Hints for Meetings." *Farmers' Sun*, 28 January 1920, 6

– "Important Notice." *Farmers' Sun*, 8 December 1920, 6

– "Legal Rights of Canadian Women." *Farmers' Sun*, 18 August 1920, 6

Laws, Meta Schooley. "Carleton County Organized." *Farmers' Sun*, 3 November 1920, 6

Leatherdale, W.B. "Provincial Board Celebrates Silver Anniversary."*Home and Country* 10 (Winter 1944–45): 3

– "Provincial Board Holds Annual Meeting." *Home and Country* 8 (Winter 1942–43): 2–3

Leckie, Gloria J. "Female Farm Operators, Gender Relations and the Restructuring Canadian Agricultural System." Ph.D. diss., University of Western Ontario 1991

Lemons, J. Stanley. *The Woman Citizen: Social Feminism in the 1920s*. Urbana: University of Illinois Press 1973; reprinted Charlottesville: University Press of Virginia 1990

Leslie, Genevieve. "Domestic Service in Canada, 1880–1920." In *Women at Work, 1850–1930*. Edited by Janice Acton et al., 71–125. Toronto: Canadian Women's Educational Press 1974

Lewis, Anna P. "Editorial." *Home and Country* 18 (Summer 1952): 3
– "Sincerely and Affectionately Yours." *Home and Country* 14 (Winter 1949): 2
Lipsett, Gertrude G. "Yesterday and Today." *Home and Country* 22 (Fall 1956): 29
MacDonald, Cheryl. *Adelaide Hoodless: Domestic Crusader.* Toronto: Dundurn Press 1986
MacDougall, John. *Rural Life in Canada: Its Trends and Tasks.* Toronto: Westminster Company 1913
Macleod, Jean. "The United Farmer Movement in Ontario, 1914–1943." M.A. thesis, Queen's University 1958
MacMillan, J.D. "Training Future Housekeepers." *Home and Country* 1 (August 1934): 6
MacMurchy, Marjorie. *The Woman – Bless Her.* Toronto: George H. Doran Company 1916
MacPhail, Agnes. "To the United Farm Women of Ontario." *Farmer's Advocate* 59 (10 January 1924): 47–8
MacPhatter, Mrs Gordon. "The President's Corner." *Home and Country* 21 (Summer 1955): 5
– "A Word From the President." *Home and Country* 20 (Winter 1954): 7
Macpherson, Marion J. In Joan. "In Answer to Pollyanna." *Farmers' Sun,* 3 January 1929, 11
Maddock, Blanche. "Why Women's Institutes Should be Organized." *Farmer's Advocate* 35 (2 July 1900): 380–1
Marsh, Margaret. "Suburban Men and Masculine Domesticity, 1870–1915." In *Meanings for Manhood: Constructions of Masculinity in Victorian America,* edited by Mark C. Carnes and Clyde Griffen, 111–27. Chicago: University of Chicago Press 1990
Marshall, John Ewing. *Half Century of Farming in Dufferin.* n.p. 1978
Martin, A.H. "Guns or Butter." *Home and Country* 7 (Spring 1941): 1, 3
Matthaei, Julie A. *An Economic History of Women in America: Women's Work, the Sexual Division of Labor, and the Development of Capitalism.* New York: Schocken Books 1982
McBride, Irene H. "Women in our Society To-day." *Home and Country* 14 (Fall 1948): 4, 8
McCall, Cicely. *Women's Institutes.* London: William Collins of London 1943
McCannell, Kathryn F., and Barbara M. Herringer. "Changing Terms of Endearment: Women and Families." In *Living the Changes,* edited by Joan Turner, 57–67. Winnipeg: University of Manitoba Press 1990
McCutcheon, Elizabeth. "The Single Woman in the Country[:] Can the Spinster Remain on the Farm and be Independent?" *Farm and Dairy* (8 October 1914): 5
McDiarmid, Allan. "Should Farm Women Go On Strike?" *Farmer's Advocate* 55 (17 June 1920): 1136

McDowell, Helen. "Greetings From the Provincial President." *Home and Country*, 2 (January 1936): 2

Merrell, Rose H., et al. "Home Economics, Feminism and the Family." In *Knowledge, Technology, and Family Change*, edited by Patricia J. Thompson, 265–91. Bloomington, IL: Bennett and McKnight 1984

Mika, Nick and Helma. *Places in Ontario: Their Name Origins and History*, Parts 1, 2, 3. Belleville, ON: Mika Publishing Company 1977, 1981, 1983, respectively

Mills, Margery. "The U.F.W.O." *Weekly Sun*, 18 September 1918, 6

Mitchell, I.M. "Wilton Grove Club." *Farmers' Sun*, 29 March 1924: 4

Mitchinson, Wendy. "Early Women's Organizations and Social Reform: Prelude to the Welfare State." In *The Benevolent State: The Growth of Welfare in Canada*, edited by Allan Moscovitch and Jim Albert, 77–92. Toronto: Garamond Press 1987

Neth, Mary. "Building the Base: Farm Women, the Rural Community, and Farm Organizations in the Midwest, 1900–1940." In *Women and Farming: Changing Roles, Changing Structures*, edited by Wava G. Haney and Jane B. Knowles, 339–56. Boulder: Westview Press 1988

– *Preserving the Family Farm: Women, Community, and the Foundations of Agribusiness in the Midwest, 1900–1940*. Baltimore: Johns Hopkins University Press 1995

Norell, Donna. " 'The most humane institution in all the village': The Women's Rest Room in Rural Manitoba." *Manitoba History* 11 (Spring 1986): 38–50

O'Neill, William L. *Everyone was Brave: The Rise and Fall of Feminism in America*. Chicago: Quadrangle Books 1969

Ontario. Department of Agriculture, Home Economics Service and Farm Economics and Statistics Branch. *Special Study of Ontario Farm Homes and Homemakers* (Progress Reports #1–9), by Dr Helen C. Abell 1959–64

– *Special Study of Ontario Farm Homes and Homemakers* (Questionnaire and Interviewer's Manual), by Dr Helen C. Abell June-July 1959

Ontario. Lieutenant-Governor. *Report of the Commission of Inquiry as to the Ontario Agricultural College and Experimental Farm, 1893*. Toronto: Warwick and Sons 1893

Ontario. Ministry of Agriculture and Food. *Women in Rural Life – The Changing Scene* by Molly McGhee. Toronto: 1984

Ontario. Ministry of Agriculture and Food, Rural Organizations and Services Branch. *Home and Country*. Toronto: 1933–69

Oppenheimer, Jo. "Childbirth in Ontario: The Transition from Home to Hospital in the Early Twentieth Century." *Ontario History* 75 (March 1983): 36–60

Osterud, Nancy G. "Land, Identity and Agency in the Oral Autobiographies of Farm Women." In *Women and Farming: Changing Roles, Changing Structures*, edited by Wava G. Haney and Jane B. Knowles. 73–87. Boulder: Westview Press 1988

Osterud, Nancy Grey. *Bonds of Community: The Lives of Farm Women in Nine-teenth-Century New York*. New York: Cornell University Press 1991

Pardy, Maryn. "Adelaide Hoodless Said." *Home and Country* 33 (Winter 1968): 3

Parr, Joy. "Hired Men: Ontario Agricultural Wage Labour in Historical Per-spective." *Labour/Le Travail* 15 (Spring 1985): 91–103

– *Labouring Children: British Immigrant Apprentices to Canada, 1869–1924*. Lon-don: Croom Helm 1980

– "Shopping for a Good Stove: A Parable about Gender, Design, and the Market." In *A Diversity of Women: Ontario, 1945–1980*, edited by Joy Parr, 75–97. Toronto: University of Toronto Press 1995

Pedersen, Diana. " 'The Scientific Training of Mothers': The Campaign for Domestic Science in Ontario Schools, 1890–1913." In *Critical Issues in the History of Canadian Science, Technology and Medicine*, edited by Richard A. Jarrell and Arnold E. Roos, 178–94. Thornhill and Ottawa: HSTC Publica-tions 1983

Pennington, Doris. *Agnes Macphail: Reformer*. Toronto: Simon and Pierre 1989

Phillips, Susan D. Review of *Social Feminism* by Naomi Black. *Canadian Jour-nal of Political Science* 23 (March 1990): 157–8

Pierson, Ruth Roach. "The Politics of the Domestic Sphere." In *Canadian Women's Issues: Twenty-Five Years of Women's Activism in English Canada*, vol. 2: *Bold Visions*, edited by Ruth Roach Pierson and Marjorie Griffin Cohen, 1–33. Toronto: James Lorimer & Company 1995

Powell, M. Viola. "Out of the Past – Courage, Unity, Service."*Home and Coun-try* 11 (Winter 1945–46): 1

Powell, Sheila. "The Opposition to Woman Suffrage in Ontario, 1872–1917." M.A. thesis, Carleton University 1987

Prentice, Alison, et al. *Canadian Women: A History*, 2nd edition. Toronto: Har-court Brace & Company 1996

Pringle, Gertrude. "The Only M.P. who Can – ." *Macleans*, 15 January 1922, 45–7

Rankin, L. Pauline. "Beyond the Kitchen and the Cornfield: The Political Activism of Ontario Farm Women." M.A. thesis, Carleton University 1987

Rankin, Pauline. "The Politicization of Ontario Farm Women." In *Beyond the Vote: Canadian Women and Politics*, edited by Linda Kealey and Joan Sang-ster, 309–32. Toronto: University of Toronto Press 1989

Rasmussen, Linda, et al. *A Harvest Yet to Reap: A History of Prairie Women*. To-ronto: Women's Press 1976

Reaman, G. Elmore. *A History of Agriculture in Ontario*, vol. 2. Toronto: Saun-ders 1970

Riordon, Michael. *Out Our Way: Gay and Lesbian Life in the Country*. Toronto: Between the Lines 1996

Roberts, Barbara. " 'A Work of Empire': Canadian Reformers and British Female Immigration." In *A Not Unreasonable Claim: Women and Reform in Canada, 1880s-1920s*, edited by Linda Kealey, 185–202. Toronto: Women's Educational Press 1979

Roberts, Wayne. " 'Rocking the Cradle for the World': The New Woman and Maternal Feminism, Toronto, 1877–1914." In *A Not Unreasonable Claim: Women and Reform in Canada, 1880s–1920s*, edited by Linda Kealey, 15–46. Toronto: Women's Press 1979

Rorke, Ruth B. "Thanks for the Jam." *Home and Country* 10 (Summer 1944): 1

Rosenblatt, Paul C., and Roxanne M. Anderson. "Interaction in Farm Families: Tension and Stress." In *The Family in Rural Society*, edited by Raymond T. Coward and William M. Smith, Jr., 147–66. Boulder: Westview Press 1981

Rosenfeld, Rachel Anne. *Farm Women: Work, Farm and Family in the United States*. Chapel Hill: University of North Carolina Press 1985

Ross, Alexander M. *The College on the Hill: A History of the Ontario Agricultural College, 1874–1974*. Toronto: Copp Clark 1974

Ross, Jean. "Legislation." *Home and Country* 1 (September 1934): 4–5

Ross, Lois L. *Harvest of Opportunity: New Horizons for Farm Women*. Saskatoon: Western Producer Prairie Books 1990

Row, L.A. "Saving Labour in the Home." *Home and Country* 1 (August 1934): 3

Rutherford, Laurena. "What the Institute Has Meant to Me." *Home and Country* 3 (September 1933): 6

Sachs, Carolyn. *Gendered Fields: Rural Women, Agriculture, and Environment*. Boulder: Westview Press 1996

– *The Invisible Farmers: Women in Agricultural Production*. Totawa, NJ: Rowman and Allanheld 1983

Saidak, Patricia. "The Inception of the Home Economics Movement in English Canada, 1890–1910: In Defence of the Cultural Importance of the Home." M.A. thesis, Carleton University 1987

Schull, Joseph. *Ontario Since 1867*. Toronto: McClelland and Stewart 1978

Scott, Jean Thomson. *The Conditions of Female Labour in Ontario*. Toronto: Warwick and Sons 1892

Shearer, Mrs Ed. "Listowel U.F.W.O." *Farmers' Sun*, 11 August 1920, 6

– "September Meeting of the Listowel U.F.W.O." *Farmers' Sun*, 22 September 1920, 6

Sheehan, Nancy. " 'Teasippers or Crusaders?' The I.O.D.E. as a Women's Organization, 1900–1925." Paper no. 62, Canadian Historical Association, University of Guelph June 1984

Siltanen, Janet, and Michelle Stanworth. "The Politics of Private Woman and Public Man." *Theory and Society* 13 (1984): 91–118

Sister [Emma Griesbach]. "A Page for Women." *Weekly Sun*, 17 November 1917, 1

– "A Page for Women." *Weekly Sun,* 20 February 1918, 6
Sister Diana [Emma Griesbach]. "Lords and Commons." *Weekly Sun,* 6 February 1918, 6
– "The Passing of Wash Day." *Weekly Sun,* 19 June 1918, 6
Skocpol, Theda. *Protecting Soldiers and Mothers: The Political Origins of Social Policy in the United States.* Cambridge, MA: Belknap Press of Harvard University Press 1992
Smith, Pamela. "Murdoch's, Becker's and Sorochan's Challenge: Thinking Again About the Roles of Women in Primary Agriculture." In *The Political Economy of Agriculture in Western Canada,* edited by G.S. Basran and D.A. Hays, 157–74. Toronto: Garamond Press 1988
Souter, M. "East Nipissing News." *Farmers' Sun,* 21 July 1920, 6
Spender, Dale. "Modern Feminist Theorists: Reinventing Rebellion." In *Feminist Theorists: Three Centuries of Key Women Thinkers,* edited by Dale Spender, 366–80. New York: Pantheon Books 1983
Stamp, R.M. "Adelaide Hoodless, Champion of Women's Rights." In *Profiles of Canadian Educators,* edited by Robert S. Patterson et al., 215–32. n.p.: D.C. Heath Canada n.d.
Stamp, Robert M. "Teaching Girls their 'God Given Place in Life.'" *Atlantis* 2 (Spring 1977): 18–34
Staples, Melville H. *The Challenge of Agriculture: The Story of the United Farmers of Ontario.* Toronto: G.N. Morang 1921
Stephen, Laura Rose. "Appeal to the Reader." *Canadian Farm* (19 March 1915): 21
Stoddart, Jennifer, and Veronica Strong-Boag. "'… And Things Were Going Wrong at Home.'" *Atlantis* 1 (Fall 1975): 38–44
Strong-Boag, Veronica. "Discovering the Home: The Last 150 Years of Domestic Work in Canada." In *Women's Paid and Unpaid Work: Historical and Contemporary Perspectives,* edited by Paula Bourne, 35–60. Toronto: New Hogtown Press 1985
– "'Ever a Crusader': Nellie McClung, First-Wave Feminist." In *Rethinking Canada: The Promise of Women's History,* 2nd edition, edited by Veronica Strong-Boag and Anita Clair Fellman, 308–21. Toronto: Copp Clark Pitman 1991
– "Pulling in Double Harness or Hauling a Double Load: Women, Work and Feminism on the Canadian Prairie." *Journal of Canadian Studies* 21 (Fall 1986): 32–52
Sumners, Mildred. "Our Tribute." *Home and Country* 11 (1945): 2
Talman, J.J. "Reading Habits of the 1917 Ontario Farmer." 2nd Annual Agricultural History of Ontario Seminar, University of Guelph October 1977
Tebbutt, Melanie. *Women's Talk? A Social History of 'Gossip' in Working-class Neighbourhoods, 1880–1960.* Aldershot, England: Scolar Press 1995

Thompson, Patricia J. "Home Economics: A Knowledge System – Not a Gender System." In *Knowledge, Technology, and Family Change*, edited by Patricia J. Thompson, 317–41. Bloomington, IL: Bennett and McKnight 1984

Thryne, Andrea. "Housewives Vocation." *Farmers' Sun*, 28 August 1920, 6

Todd, W. "The Work of Women's Institutes in Canada." *Social Welfare* (1 October 1922): 15

Tryssenaar, Laura. "Changing the Subject: From Home Economics to Family Studies." M.A. thesis, The University of Western Ontario 1993

Vanek, Joann. "Work, Leisure, and Family Roles: Farm Households in the United States, 1920–1955." *Journal of Family History* 5 (Winter 1980): 422–31

Vickers, Jill McCalla. "Feminist Approaches to Women in Politics." In *Beyond the Vote: Canadian Women and Politics*, edited by Linda Kealey and Joan Sangster, 16–36. Toronto: University of Toronto Press 1989

Von Baeyer, Edwinna. *Ontario Rural Society, 1867–1930: A Thematic Index of Selected Ontario Agricultural Periodicals*. Ottawa 1985

Watson, Mary Urie. "The New Venture." *Farmer's Advocate* 50 (23 December 1915): 2052

Woltz, W.A. "Neighbourliness and Good Cheer." *Home and Country* 1 (September 1934): 6

Wright, Cynthia. " 'Feminine Trifles of Vast Importance': Writing Gender into the History of Consumption." In *Gender Conflicts: New Essays in Women's History*, edited by Franca Iacovetta and Mariana Valverde, 229–60. Toronto: University of Toronto Press 1992

Yates (Miss). "Agriculture for Women." *O.A.C. Review* 21 (December 1908): 183–5

Young, W. R. "The Countryside on the Defensive: Agricultural Ontario's View of Rural Depopulation, 1900–1914." M.A. thesis, University of British Columbia 1971

Zwarun, Suzanne. "Farm Wives 10 Years After Irene Murdoch." *Chatelaine* (March 1983): 59, 176–82

Index